Blink of an Eye

Blink of an Eye

The
Journey of a Refugee

Written by

Karl J. Landesz

Copyright © 2010 by Karl J. Landesz.

Library of Congress Control Number:		2010900591
ISBN:	Hardcover	978-1-4500-2716-8
	Softcover	978-1-4500-2715-1
	E-book	978-1-4500-2717-5

All rights reserved. No part of this book may be reproduced or transmitted in any form or by any means, electronic or mechanical, including photocopying, recording, or by any information storage and retrieval system, without permission in writing from the copyright owner.

This book was printed in the United States of America.

If you want to read a story that is written
in proper English,
then this is not for you.

To order additional copies of this book, contact:
Xlibris Corporation
1-888-795-4274
www.Xlibris.com
Orders@Xlibris.com

CONTENTS

I.   Preface 13

II.   About My Parents 15

III.   The Early Years 20

IV.   Growing up in Hungary......................................39

V.   Hungarian Uprising and the Escape....................63

VI.   Beginning a New Life in the USA 86

VII. The Turbulent '60s 101

VIII. The Decade of the '70s 149

IX.   The '80s...186

X.   The '90s through June of 2000 229

XI.   The "Pasture" Years 251

XII. Observation 274

XIII. The Conclusion 296

To my parents

and

to all the people who helped me throughout my life's journey.

A refugee writes his *journey*.

This writing is his voice.

Special thanks to
my *family*—Jeanette, Randy, Corey, Ashleigh, and
Owen and the Horan Family—for being there
and for being a part of my life.

I

Preface

The East Coast architect office of Harry Weese & Associates where I worked for over twenty-two years closed its doors on June 30, 2000, in Arlington, Virginia. I decided not to look for other employment, and I retired.

First, at home I was very restless; it was very strange for me to be home all day. In the past forty-three years, every morning I got up and went to work, and now I don't have to do that. I never imagined that some day like this would come. I always believed I would work in an office till I die. I am the type of person that cannot be idle, I have to be busy, I have to do something.

In a few days, I came up with a list of things to-do around the house, which was neglected in the past. Then another to-do list, which included tasks like organizing my stamp and coin collections or the items I collected on projects I worked on, like the Union Station in Washington DC, the Grand Central Terminal in New York City, and the Baltimore, Miami, Washington Metro projects—just to name some of the projects I managed or worked on—then to research and organize my family tree, do some travel, and so on. In time, the list got so long with the to-do things that if I live another twenty-five years, I would not have sufficient time to complete everything.

One of the items at the bottom of the to-do list was to write about my past—my life before, during, and after World War II; in the Middle East

13

where I was born; Europe where I grew up in the '40s and '50s—my new life and experiences in this country, which I call my home for the past forty-six years, and how a six-year-old boy begged on the streets for food to support his family during World War II ended up in this country; and with hard work, he and his company received two presidential awards for Outstanding Achievement in Design Excellence.

The problem is, as you will see, I don't know how to write; and it is the least favorite of activities for me. Several of my family members and friends in this country and in Hungary find my stories of my life experiences interesting, and they convinced me to collect my thoughts and put it on paper. They think I had an interesting life and I should share it with everyone. This also will give me an opportunity to thank all the people who helped me throughout my journey, even if some of them are not with us anymore.

Here I go!

II

About My Parents

My parents are Károly Landesz and Mária Soós. They met when my Father was visiting my future grandmother in her home in Nagytétény to deliver a gift from one of her daughters who lives in Tehran. My Father was home for a vacation from Tehran, Persia, now Iran, where he was employed by the *Consortium Kampsax de Government Imperial de Iran* as a design engineer for the *trans Arabian railroad* projects. My Mother was living with her mother, and she was working as a dentist's assistant in Budapest, Hungary.

After three months of courtship, they were married on July 10, 1937, in my Mother's hometown of Nagytétény, a suburb of Budapest.

Upon return from their honeymoon in the town of Balatonalmádi by Lake Balaton in Hungary, they returned and settled in Tehran, Iran.

My Father (a Catholic) was born on November 23, 1894, in Budapest, Hungary. He was the fourth child of ten children, seven of which grew up to be adults, five boys and two girls. His mother died of cancer on January 22, 1923, in Budapest. His father was a farm manager, an overseer of several flour and lumber mills and, later, hail-damage assessor for an insurance company. He wrote an illustrated book different diseases on agricultural in 1927 and updated it in 1932.[1] This book was a required reading for the students in the agricultural university in Budapest till the late 1970s.

---

[1] I have a copy of his book with the 1932 updates.

When the children were growing up, they all had to help around the house, clean the apartment, wash dishes, take out the garbage, and help with the cooking. All the boys had to study at least two languages; after taking language lessons, they then traveled to the country to live and work there for the summer. Their father only paid for a one-way ticket to the particular country; the boys had to work there and pay for their living and their return-trip expenses. They had to be fluent in that language after three months when they return home. All this had to be accomplished before turning twenty. My Father learned to speak six languages. He was wounded in World War I in Italy and lived and worked first in Hungary, then in Turkey and in Iran—the last two countries—for ten years each. All the boys had to finish college, and the girls had to learn a profession. My Father died of cancer at his home on October 18, 1967, in Dunakeszi, Hungary, at the age of seventy-two.

One of his brothers became a civil engineer, later a contractor; and two of his younger brothers were merchant marine captains. Two died in Argentina, South America, and one in Seattle, Washington, USA. The oldest brother and the two sisters settled and died in Hungary.

My Mother (a Reformer) was born on April 8, 1904, in Nagyszalonta, Hungary. She was the seventh child of ten children; seven grew up to be adults—one boy, the youngest, and six girls. At the end of World War I, the family was deported from Nagyszalonta when it became part of Romania after World War I.

They were settled early 1918 in Nagytétény, Hungary. Shortly after, on October 23 of the same year, her father passed away at the age of fifty-one. He was a master carpenter and a contractor. Her mother raised the remaining seven children; the youngest was nine years old. The children started working at an early age, but all had to complete high school and had to learn a profession; it was uncommon at the time. During these years, the older girls gave what income they earned to their mother for the support of the rest of the family. When my Mother was a young adult, she was a good tennis player.

After my Father's passing, she visited me three times (1968, 1970, and 1977), before she died of cancer at her home on November 19, 1982, in Dunakeszi, Hungary, at the age of seventy-eight.

All her siblings lived and died in Hungary, with the exception of one; she lived in Iran then in Israel for several years, and after her husband passed away in Israel, she returned to Hungary.

Both of my parents are buried in the Farkasréti (wolf meadow) Cemetery in Budapest, Hungary.

My Mother's family (Soós).
Nagytétény, Hungary, July 1937.

1. Mr. Nándor Tessely
   (*Uncle Nandor*)
3. Ms. Emmi Moskovics
5. **Ms. Mária Soós**
   (*My Mother*)
7. Mr. Kovács Sándor
   (*Aunt Margit's husband*)
9. Master Sándor Kovács
   (*cousin Öcsi*)
11. Mrs. Ferenc Soós
    (*Grandmother*)
13. Mrs. Ferenc Soós
    (*wife of Ferenc*)
15. Mr. József Tilly

2. Mrs. Nándor Tessely
   (Zsuzsanna Soós, *Aunt Zsuzsa*)
4. Mrs. Lászlo Bordás
   (Juliana Soós, *Aunt*)
6. **Mr. Károly Landesz**
   (*My Father*)
8. Mrs. Sándor Kovács
   (Margit Soós, *Aunt Margit*)
10. Ms. Zsuzsanna Kovacs
    (*cousin Zsuzsa*)
12. Mr. Ferenc Soós
    (*Uncle*)
14. Ms. Zsuzsanna Soós
    (*cousin*)
16. Mrs. József Tilly
    (Erzsebet Soós *Aunt*)

My Father's family (Landesz).

Budapest, Hungary, 1912.

Left to right: Lajós, József Sr. *(Grandfather, Landesz Jzsef)*, Károly *(my Father)*, Béla, Izabella, József Jr., Erzsébet, Gyula, and Erzsébet *(Grandmother, Jantsky Erzsébet)*.

III

The Early Years

(1938 through summer of 1946)

World War II was expanding in the world, reaching into Iran. In early 1942, the British, French, and Soviet military forces occupied the capital city, Tehran, as well as the rest of Iran. All foreign citizens had to leave the occupied Iran, no exceptions. We were in the British sector; all the families in this sector were to return to their country of origin. We were lucky. In the Soviet sector, the male family members between sixteen and sixty were sent to Siberia to labor camps. Some of my father's friends and their children ended up there; one of those children is my godson's father. He was barely sixteen at the time, and he survived the labor camp and now lives in Florida.

Up to this time, my parents had an uneventful, comfortable life in Tehran. I was born Károly Landesz Jr. on June 5, 1938, and my sister, Mária, on March 28, 1941—both occurring in Tehran. It appears that my Mother had some difficulty in the end of her pregnancy with me. She wrote a note to my Father, saying that if anything happens to her, not surviving the childbirth, not to tell me when I grow up that the reason she died was because of my birth. Also, my Mother asked him to continue to support her mother as they agreed on before their wedding and thanked him for the happiness and love he has given to her.[2] My Mother survived my arrival in

---

[2]   I have my Mother's note, dated May 3, 1938.

good health. According to my parents, we lived in a nice house, had a nice yard, with a small pool with goldfishes.

The garden had lots of plants and flowers, my Father liked to garden. My Mother had a nanny for us children and a person to clean the house. My parents also had a car. The family vacationed in the summer in Basra, Iraq, and by the Caspian Sea or by the Persian Gulf. The first languages I learned were Hungarian from my parents and Parsi, an Iranian dialect, from the nanny. From Parsi, I don't remember one word. My parents told me Tehran in the summer is very hot. The temperature in the daytime can be as high as 110 to 120 degrees Fahrenheit. To cool off the air for the night, in the bedroom, my Father "invented the early air-conditioning system." It consisted of a rope attached at the opposite walls of the room, close to the ceiling. Draped over it was a wet bedsheet. At one corner of the hanging sheet was where he attached a string; one of them pulled the string back and forth to cool the air in the room till they fall asleep.

These past years of my parents' life were the last peaceful and worry-free years, in they life before the beginning of the "storm" in Europe and in their life.

According to my parents, the British military assembled several of the families in to a passenger car caravan, with small pickup trucks to carry their belongings. We left Tehran in late February of 1942, with the British military escort to our return trip to Hungary. We did not know that time that the trip will be so long; it took us over two months to complete our trip. The military escort was to protect us from the local hostile tribes in the mountains and to provide security during our trip. Leaving Tehran by car caravan, we drove over the mountains on a winding single-lane road with hairpin turns, drove at night to see the oncoming car lights in the distance, and waited for the incoming cars in the bypass. In the past, not too long ago, only camel caravans had used this narrow mountain road. We slept and ate in the car, cooked on a portable stove. This took us several weeks to get to the British military camp in south Iraq, to the area where the Tigris and Euphrates rivers meet. We lived in tents, and we were well cared for, sleeping in hammocks covered with cheesecloth against mosquitoes and other flying insects. In the morning, everybody had to check their clothing and shoes for scorpions before dressing. The reason for using a hammock for our "bed," which is supported from pools with "bug guards" attached to it is to prevent small animals from crawling in to our "bed" and be our bedmates. We stayed there for several weeks. My sister was one year old in the camp; I was four years old. Then with car caravan, we continued our trip to Baghdad, Iraq, where we spent several days there before we departed by train to Budapest, Hungary.

Our British guards during our travel were the Kurdish unit. According to my parents, the Kurdish guard's only weapon was a big knife, like a bayonet. The rule was when they remove the knife from the housing, they have to use it, and only then can it be returned with blood on it. They also had exceptionally good hearing and smell to detect the intruders or the enemies. The British government paid for our trip to Hungary.

Upon arrival at Hungary in the end of April 1942, we were staying with my maternal grandmother and my Mother's sister Margaret's home in Nagytétény. Father had no problem finding employment. He started working in Györ, the city located northwest of Hungary, for a railroad car manufacturing company that also manufactured the Messerschmitt military airplanes for the German military. Hungary and Germany were allies by this time. Next to the factory was a large field used as an airport for test flights. To camouflage the airfield, it was set up as a sheep farm. The sheep maintained the grounds; grazing sheep kept the grass short and even. He was responsible for the buildings and grounds. We lived in Györ till early 1943 when we were to move to Budapest, the capital of Hungary.

The fighting of the war was getting close, and the airplane factory in Györ had to be dismantled and reassembled in Budapest in the mountain caves, which were used for wine cellars. The reinstallation of the factory machinery and the equipment could not be completed; the Soviet army's closing in on Budapest. The German military collected and transported the machinery and the equipment to Germany.

In spring of 1943 in Hungary, the German authorities directed that families with surnames similar to Jewish surnames must prove, with church records back to three generations, that they have not changed their name from a Jewish to a Christian surname. The Landesz surname is not derived from Landesman, which is a Jewish name in Hungary; therefore, our ancestors cannot be Jews. The first Landeszes who settled in Hungary in the mid-seventeen hundreds were Roman Catholic.

The German SS gave us only a short time to exonerate ourselves, but we were in luck. My grandfather completed assembling this information in 1933 in the process when he was researching the Landesz family tree. He had copies of all the birth, marriage, and death certificates of our ancestors from the Catholic Church, dating back one hundred and ten years to 1833. I have a copy of these documents.

Until the German authorities reviewed and accepted our documents, we had to wear the same yellow star that the Jewish people had to wear every time they went out in public. During this time, my family was humiliated. I never will forget this time of my life. How can a human being behave like that to other human beings? It took me years before I had enough courage to see the movie *Schindler's List* because the street scene in the early part of the film and the train ride that I both experienced created bad memories for me. To this date, I have not seen the Holocaust Memorial Museum in Washington DC. Later, I found out from my parents that they were aware of the existence of the gas chambers and what happened to the Jewish population in Hungary at the time. What a frame of mind, what emotional pressure my parents experienced this time in their life. Now I recall why we visited family friends and relatives, saying good-bye to them. Thanks to my grandfather and his collection of the birth and marriage certificates, he saved his family from extinction. The time allowed by the German SS was not sufficient to secure all the necessary documents if we had to do the research and to collect the documents from the beginning.

In the spring of 1944, we moved from Budapest to Nyúlfalú to a small farming town, fifteen kilometers (nine miles) south of Györ. My parents rented part of a farmhouse; they felt that it was safer for us if we moved out of the city. The Allied forces were bombing all major cities and, to prevent the German army from retreating, bombing the bridges over the rivers. The owner of the farmhouse was a middle-aged couple with grown children. Their names are Mr. and Mrs. István Pintér. Shortly after we moved in, my aunt Margit and her two children, Zsuzsa (Mrs. Oliver Mátay) and Öcsi[3]—his nickname—(Dr. Sándor Kovács), moved in with us. My uncle, they father was supposed to follow them in a few days. Later, we found out that he was killed in one of the bombings in the city of Budapest.

When we children played outside, we watched the airplanes fly over us, and if they let go of their bombs above us, we continued to play. The bombs came in an angle that did not affect us, landing several miles away from us. When they released the bombs in front of us, then we ran and crawled in to a thirty-inch diameter concrete storm pipe under a road, in front of the house where we lived, and waited. After the explosions, we came out and continued to play; or if the explosions were close by, then

---

[3]   Öcsi is my cousin. We are keeping in touch, and when I visit Hungary, I stay with them. His daughter is Cicka (Hajnalka Kovács). In 1991, on my trips to Hungary, Öcsi, his wife, and I visited Nyúlfalú and looked up the old house where we lived and the concrete storm pipe where we hid.

we looked for wounded people or animals in the farm. Then, six-year-olds were more sophisticated, knew where to hide and what to look for after a bomb attack.

On December 25, 1944, Christmas day, we were ready to sit down to dinner when there was a knock on the door; the German SS troopers came for us with a truck to take us away. Lucky for us, my Father spoke German and offered our dinner to them. In turn, they gave us one hour to collect what we could carry; in the meantime, the Germans ate our dinner.

Our parents dressed us warmly, putting on in layers all the warm clothes they can find for us. The rest of our belongings stayed behind in the house. We got on the truck; some people were already on it. It was very cold, and lots of snow were on the ground.

We did not know what was happening, where they were taking us. We were scared. After several hours, stopping several times and picking up more people, we ended up in the railroad yard in Györ. After standing outside in the cold and on the snow-covered ground for a long time, we were put on railroad cars, the kind that is used to transport livestock. Inside were bunk beds built of rough lumber with straw in them. The bunks were spaced twenty-four inches apart from the ceiling and thirty inches between bunks. In the middle of the car was a stove for heating and some firewood adjacent to it. After the SS filled up each railroad car with two people per bunk, they shut and locked the doors. Everyone was scared and asking why we were there. Children and some adults were crying.

One lady tried to commit suicide by cutting herself. The rest of the people restrained her. You don't forget these kinds of things, even when you are only six and a half years old. We did not start moving until the next morning. One time, they opened the doors to let us out to relieve ourselves and gave us a bucket for future use. Later, I found out that the German military personnel had told Father that the people on this train were those who had worked for different companies all having to do with military production. They were being transported to Germany to help with the war effort.

We were living on the train for over six weeks before we arrived at a town that will be our final destination, the town called Niederumelsdorf, close to Munich in Germany. Most of the time, our train was parked on the sidetracks. The main track was used for military trains, some to deliver supplies and equipment to the front, where the fighting was. But majority of the time, the trains were actually returning as Red Cross hospital trains with wounded military personnel. To occupy my time to kill boredom, I whittle.[4] It helped me to pass time and not to think of what was happening. At times, the train stops suddenly. On one such occasion, the knife slipped, and I cut my left pointing finger by the nail. It was a deep cut. My parents bandaged the cut together. I still have the scar.

After weeks on the train, we are arrived in Germany. The guards now allowed us to leave the train and get outside, only to the adjacent of the train. We could now wash ourselves in the snow as well as eat some snow—it was refreshing. The guards told us that if anyone tried to escape, "when they were captured, they will be shot." No one tried to escape. The food during our train ride was scarce; sometimes we received only a small amount of water, frozen potatoes, and stale dry bread. Many times, we children did not eat or drink for days. For the adults, it was so much worse. This was why eating snow was so great. Now some winters, when it snows where I live, I go outside to my yard and have some snow; it is just as refreshing as it was almost sixty years ago and helps me appreciate the finer things of life. Sometimes, the stove was used for cooking, if we had something to cook.

---

[4]   I have the knife and keep it on the shelf in one of the bedrooms.

The children between six and fourteen years of age were allowed to leave the train to collect firewood in the nearby woods and farms.

We children in that age were eager, daring, and fearless; and our parents were very concerned and worried for us. It was not easy to do anything outside; it was very cold and hard to walk on deep snow. We were put into groups, four to six children in each. Our group broke into an abandoned-looking building nearby. We were looking for firewood, sometimes we found food—an overwhelming amount of dry goods, potatoes, smoked meat, ham, and bacon. It was a great addition to our "nonexistent food "reserve."

This was where some of the local farmers had been hiding their extra food from the German authorities. Escorted by guards, some of the adults emptied the building, including removal of windows, doors, and their frames for firewood. As our reward, we who found the "golden egg" could eat as much as we could that day. After the military's take, the rest was divided between the train's people. We the children were responsible for a train full of people livelihood, for food to eat, and firewood to keep warm. Every time the train stopped, we were looking for food; sometimes we stole live chickens or other animals and firewood from the nearby farms. I found out later that this experience would be very useful for me in the future. We the children had to grow up fast. In later years, I realized now how big a responsibility it was for us, but then it was great to be outside and active.

The floor space between bunks was not sufficient for everyone to be up in the same time. Many people stayed in bed and, in time, became weak. During the train ride, we had some casualties from lack of proper food for the infants and the young and lack of food and the cold temperature for the weak and the old. When the train stopped, the adults dug a shallow grave in the frozen ground by the railroad track, and they were buried there. We had no access to medical personnel or medicine—only medicine that each family brought with them for their own use. For hygiene, we wash ourselves in the snow when it was possible, but we wore the same clothes. The guards replaced the straw periodically, and at the same time, they sprayed us naked outside in the open with a white powder as a disinfectant and to kill the fleas, lice, and bedbugs. It was very embarrassing and degrading, particularly to the females in the group; we had no female guards. They also sprayed the inside and outside of our clothes and everything inside the railroad cars. When you breathed in the powder, you'd feel that you are suffocating.

Finally, we arrived at our destination, Niederumelsdorf. The German SS guards transported us several kilometers to a refugee camp. It was an abandoned old building, which used to be the local movie theater; the seating was removed and replaced with wooden bunk beds, big burlap bags filled with straw to sleep on for each bed, and two blankets per bed. About one hundred to one hundred twenty families were housed in this camp. We had one sink and one toilet in the building; only the sick could use it. For the rest of us, we were to use the outside toilets; the big leaves from the trees became very handy. The dormitories were very crowded. Our area was the space between two bunk beds, about three feet. We had two double-deck bunk beds for four of us—two beds per bunk, for my parents and for my sister and me; these accommodations were much better than two people per bed when we were on the train. The town's population was made up of females, children up to age fourteen years (man over the age of fourteen years was in the military), and men over sixty-five and disabled young men without leg or arm. The police chief was a fourteen-year-old boy; the rest of his staff were of the same age or younger. The barbershop staff was also very young; to cut your hair, they used a bowl on your head as a guide to see where to cut the hair. I learned the German language fast while playing with German children. The food was scarce; everything was rationed. A family of four receives a one-kilo (2 lb.) bread and a stick of margarine for a week; parents with infants, an additional one-liter milk. Adults and children begged in the street corners. The trees lost their barks; people ate it. People lay in bed weak from the lack of food, and many of them died. The town had no doctor or pharmacy. Later, the camp provided a room in a house on the second floor for the gravely ill and their families.

The first family moved in where the husband had a bleeding ulcer, and the bleeding would not stop. The past difficult and stormy circumstances had its toll on my Father; his ulcer started bleeding and would not stop. He was so weak he could not get out of bed; any movement would increase the bleeding. He could not eat and was losing weight. Someone suggested for him to drink raw egg whites on an empty stomach to line the wall of the stomach, and then maybe he could eat some light food. The problem was there were no eggs anywhere, except the farmers with chickens, but they were not selling it or trading it.

Meantime, the person in the house with the bleeding ulcer died; the rest of his family had to move out and be back to the refugee camp. The place was assigned to my family; we moved in. This time, I started going house-to-house and begging for eggs for my Father. I had some success, and he started drinking the raw egg white, which lined his stomach, and the bleeding slowly stopped. He started eating and stopped losing weight.

In the winter, it snowed a lot; and every day, I played in the snow or went sledding in a nearby hill with some German children. These times were responsible and worry-free times for me. This was the time when I felt my age. I was seven years old.

One spring day, it was time to start with my schooling. These times, there were no schools in Germany; the teachers were my parents. Five days a week, we had four hours of "school" and two hours of homework. My parents got the lessons from a fourth-year student from a teacher's university living in the refugee camp. At the end of the school year, I received a certificate that I successfully completed the first grade.[5]

On Mother's Day in 1945, in front of the house where we were living were several beautiful white flowering fruit trees. I broke off a small flowering branch, approximately six inches long, for my Mother as a Mother's Day gift. She was very happy and complimented me for remembering Mother's Day, but at the same time, she scolded me for removing the branch without the owner's permission. She explained that the flowers bore fruit and I deprived the owner from fruit; therefore, I stole from them. I had to explain what I did and apologized to the owner. I learned a big lesson, which I will never forget as long I live.

Many times when my parents had a discussion about the family's affairs, they wanted me to be involved in these discussions. According to my Father, this is part of my education and growing up. First, they have a discussion about the issue; and before they make a decision, they ask for my comment and opinion. I tried to comply with their request, even many times it was over my head, and then they make the decision.

They asked me to watch and see how the decision would turn out; I could learn from it. My Father told me, "*It is never too early to learn, particularly the time we live in, never know when you have to make your own decisions.*" It was in the later years when I truly appreciated what he was trying to do.

It was early summer by now; the farmers started collecting some of the early harvests. One day, I followed horse-drawn wagons to the field. I found a lot of wheat grains discarded on the ground. With permission, I

---

[5]   I have this certificate and every report card throughout my school years, including some of the second- and third-grade school and homework books.

collected the grains, grain by grain; for this occasion, I removed my stockings and used it for a bag to carry home my collection. At home, the grains were cooked, and we ate it. And some other time, I collected whole or pieces of animal beets. The farmers used the beets to feed the animals; the animal beets have some sugar contents. We ground it up, cooked it to a molasses, and we used it as a sugar substitute. I did this "collecting" every day week after week throughout the summer and fall, looking for different things, like potatoes, onions, different wild berries—everything that is edible. Some days, after a good long rain, we went to pick mushrooms in the woods with some adults from the refugee camp or with my Mother; it was a good two hours' walk. We were not familiar with the different types of mushrooms and which were poisonous, but we picked them anyway. We took it home, separated them by the different types, and cooked it with a silver spoon; someone suggested that if the spoon tarnished during cooking, the mushroom is poisonous. We are lucky we survived. Other source of food were the country roads aligned with fruit trees. Every family received two trees to maintain it for the fruit; our trees were apple. We traded the apple for other fruits. These things kept us alive and having some food to eat. My Father was too weak to provide for us; my Mother had to stay home with him and with my sister It was my responsibility to provide for the family.

The room where we were living had no stove to cook or any way to heat the room. My Mother used portable—wood, charcoal fired—hot plate to cook on, and we had to make the charcoal in the backyard. My Father decided to build a stove with brick and mortar and use a steel plate on the top as a cooking surface.

We collected the brick and the steel plate from bombed-out and collapsed buildings. He started building. When he had to break a brick, he held the brick in his hand, supported by his lap, and hit the brick with the hammer on the location where he wanted to break it. Each time when he did this, the movement weakened his stomach's wall; and eventually, he started bleeding. He had to stop and rest until the stomach's bleeding stopped. Sometimes, it took several weeks; then he started working again, and the bleeding started all over again. This happened many times, and each time, it took longer and longer to recuperate. He was determined to build it; it was painful, and the construction lasted through the summer up to the fall. During the time of construction, my Father was taken to the hospital; his ulcer was bleeding a lot for a long time. He needed more attention than my Mother could provide. About this time, when my Father was in the hospital, my Mother had an accident. She fell down and broke her leg, and she also ended up in the hospital. This was the first time we are all alone. I was seven; my sister was four years old. I had to help her dress and comb her hair and take care of her all day and, in the evening, put her to bed. This was the first time for me to cook. The first day I prepared scrambled eggs; it was very strange-looking. It was very dry, not the way I remembered my Mother's scrambled eggs looked and tasted, but we ate it. I found out later that I did not use any grease on the pan. That was the result of my first cooking experience. For the rest of the time, I did not make any more eggs; we survived. We were home alone for seven days and six nights; everything went fine.

Both of my parents returned home. Now I had to help more around the house till my Mother's cast was removed. My Father completed the construction of the stove before the start of the cold weather.

During this time, Budapest was under siege that lasted for forty-six days. During this time, no food was available. If you were lucky, you had meat from starved-to-death horses from the street. Most of the buildings in the city were collapsed. There were piles of stone and brick debris; all the bridges were in ruins.

In the meantime, the Second World War was coming to the end. We were in the American occupation zone; life was getting better now, and the city's giving away some food, like sugar, flour, salt, and some canned goods. The closest city was Munich. My Mother and I decided to try it; we heard the lines started between three and four in the morning. We had a good two hours' walk in front of us. After we arrived in Munich and after the sunrise, every building as far as the eye could see—it was in ruins, a pile of rubble. I don't recall seeing a standing building anywhere. Anyone who survived lived in a bomb shelter underground, below the ruins of the buildings. The roads were wide enough for one lane; the rest were debris. The city parks, the apartment building courtyards, and the yards in front of the buildings were filled with graves where the casualties were buried. When we found the place where they gave away the food, we heard only one family member from each family will receive food. We decided to stand in two separate lines; we did not talk to or see each other for the rest of the day. In the end, after ten hours standing in line, each of us received one kilogram (2 lb.) of flour, one kilogram (2 lb.) of sugar, ten dekagram (1/4 lb.) of salt, and a can of milk. The walk home was nothing because we were so excited and very happy, but very hungry and very tired.

The mail service slowly started up; my parents corresponded with some of the relatives in Hungary. They informed my parents that they read it in the newspaper that the Soviet military court, in absentia, sentenced my Father to death for treason and anybody anywhere can execute the sentence. My parents did not know what to do and did not know why! They had many discussions and sleepless nights because of the news.

From the refugee camp, in one day, several men showed up in the place where we lived and asked my Father if he would be interested to translate for them. The catch was that where the translation was needed was several miles away in an American army officers club where they found work. But none of them could speak English. My Father was too weak to walk; they decided that they will carry him in a homemade stretcher every day. He only had to translate for them; they will do all the work and split the pay in five ways. He brought home plenty of food, chocolates, chewing gum, cigarettes, and several pairs of nylon stockings; they traded the cigarettes and the stockings with the local people. The most important thing was he saw a doctor and received some medication; this was worth more than anything else he could bring home to us. The doctors recommended surgery, but it was very risky based on the circumstances. With a doctor's help, medication, and some proper food, he gained some of his strength back, and he could walk again the first time after a long time.

My Father befriended a military officer, and with his connection, they offered him a job in the States. The whole family was excited; but in the end, the decision was he did not want to settle in a new country because if he would not survive the stomach surgery, then my Mother, with two small children, would be all alone in the strange country. In the end, they exchanged addresses; and after my Father's successful operation, hopefully in Hungary, then he would get in touch with them.

During all this time, my Father tried to locate the disassembled factory machinery and the equipment from his company, which the German army moved to Germany. Some of it he located next to the railroad tracks throughout southwest Germany. He sent it back to Hungary; for this effort, he received commendation from the Hungarian government and which saved his life later in a new trial.

The International Red Cross organized trains to repatriate displaced people to their homeland. After a long consideration because of my Father's death sentence, in the end, my parents decided to return to Hungary and see what the future would bring. We left Niederumelsdorf, Germany, by passenger train in the late summer of 1946 to return to Hungary. By now, I was eight years old.

Closing this chapter on my life and looking back, it appears that I went through a lot in my young life in such a short time. Yes, I did, but so did many of my generation in Europe because of the circumstances at the time. I feel very lucky that I am alive. I thank God for that because so many of my generation were not that lucky, and they did not make it!

With my parents.
Tehran, Iran, September 8, 1938. I am three months old.
I have the dress my Mother is wearing.

The family car. Tehran, Iran, October 1940.

With my sister, Maria, shortly before we left Tehran. Tehran, Iran, January 1942.

In front of the farmhouse with my sister, where we lived by the 13 km. marker. Nyúlfalú, Hungary, Spring 1944.

With my parents and sister. I'm six years old. Budapest, Hungary, July 1944.

The following drawings are by Stephen Zador
from the book *Budapest 1945*.

In front of the Royal Palace.

Budapest 1945

Entrance of the tunnel from the Christiania District.

Budapest 1945

IV

Growing up in Hungary

(Late summer of 1946 to autumn of 1956)

The return train ride to Hungary was faster, and it was more comfortable; it could not be compared to the train ride nineteen months ago. The train cars were passenger cars, with toilets. We could walk around, and the train stopped for meals three times a day. We only had to spend four nights on the train. The International Red Cross informed the Hungarian government ahead of time of the returning refugees. We crossed the border from Austria in the summer of 1946 and arrived in Györ, Hungary. The Hungarian police was waiting for us; they did not arrest my Father. His bleeding ulcer was acting up; he was too ill and weak. The police did not want to take responsibility for his health, but he had to provide them with an address where he would be staying. Then he found out that he was accused of the dismantling and shipping the factory equipment to Germany for the company he worked for. The Soviet military court considered this act as treason. Actually, the German military ordered the dismantling, and they did the shipping.

At the end of the Second World War, because of all the bombings in the cities, the housings were very scarce. We moved to Nagytétény, ten miles south of Budapest, to my Mother's old home—where my Mother and her siblings lived before they got married—and now where my grandmother

39

and my aunt Margit (Mrs. Sándor Kovács) and her two children, Zsuzsa and Öcsi, call their home.

This house was part of a one-story duplex. This unit had four medium size rooms, a kitchen, indoor washroom with a tub, and an outside toilet. When we moved in, already living there were my grandmother; my Mother's sisters, Margit with her two children, Aunt Zsuzsa with her husband, Nándi (Mr. and Mrs. Nándor Tessely); and my Mother's brother, Ferkó, with his wife (Mr. and Mrs. Ferenc Soós). In this place with us now lived five families—a total of twelve people, eight adults and four children.[6] We helped one another any way we could, and everyone helped around the house with the chores. In time, my aunts and/or uncles found employment and places to live, then they moved out. We lived here till the fall of 1947.

In August of 1946, I took an equivalency test in the school for first grade. My parents' teaching in Germany paid off; I passed it, and in September, I started my schooling in the second grade. After this test, I was still one year behind in my schooling.

Meantime, my parents found a doctor for my Father who could help him with his bleeding ulcer, a hospital that was relatively in a working condition, with sufficient staff and with some medical supplies, and a doctor who was willing to do the surgery. Before the surgery, two things had to happen according to the doctor. My Father had to be strong enough to survive the operation and to clear himself in the court. They didn't operate on people who may end up in jail or executed later, because of the limited resources.

---

[6] I bought this unit from the Hungarian government in 2000 and gave it to my goddaughter, Zsuzsanna "Kati" Mátay, who now lives there (she is my cousin Zsuzsa Kovács Mátay's daughter).

March of 1947, my Father had his new trial in Györ in front of a Hungarian judge. With no jury, the trial lasted for one day, and he was acquitted from all charges. The previous witnesses against my Father could not be located. The letter of commendation from the Hungarian government for his work in Germany for locating and returning the factory machinery and equipment was a big help to prove his innocence.

After this big burden was off my parents' shoulders, he was now ready to go and have his lifesaving surgery. The operation for my Father's stomach ulcer took place in Budapest; the doctor removed 65 percent of his stomach.

All the necessary medication during and after the surgery was the patient's responsibility to provide. My parents bought the medication on the black market, only what was available. To cover the doctor's expense, medicine, and our living expenses, my parents sold some of the Persian rugs they have brought with them from Tehran. During the war, it was buried in Nyúlfalú in the farm where we lived in 1944. The surgery was a success. After the surgery, the maximum he could eat each time was a teaspoonful of liquid, like tea with lots of sugar. The hospital, being short of nurses, requested that a family member stay with a patient during his stay in the hospital. So my Mother moved in and provided twenty-four-hour nursing care to my Father. During his stay in the hospital, he got pneumonia with a very high fever; the doctors gave up on him. His sister went to a close-by Catholic church and got a priest to give my Father the "last rite." My Father's oldest brother, trying to be helpful and at the same time not thinking before he checked with someone in the family, sent to the hospital room where my Father was staying a coffin for his remains. When the coffin arrived, my Mother was not in the room; and when she returned, she saw the coffin and my Father was not in his bed. She got very emotional and upset, according to my aunt who was with her at the time. My Father was taken to the emergency room; that was the reason he was not in his bed. After two months in the hospital, he returned home to Nagytétény. All of us were happy that he was alive and healthy. It took several more months for him to regain his strength and be in a condition where he could walk and stay up for any length of time.

With help from a friend of my parents' (they knew them from Tehran and were living in a small town called Alag, ten miles north of Budapest) they bought a large house—in Hungarian standard—in 1943 for four kilos of rock salt (approximately nine pounds). Then the salt was worth more than gold because the farmers used the salt to preserve the meat for food for them after they killed the livestock. We moved in and shared the house with them in early fall of 1947. They have two daughters and one son. We had two rooms and a small makeshift kitchen with hot plate. There were separate entrances to our living area.

My Father wrote to the American military officer whom he had befriended and offered him employment in the United States and exchanged addresses with in Germany. The correspondence between the United States and Hungary took time. In the end, the offer of employment was confirmed in writing. With this letter, my parents applied for a passport. Meantime, because everything took a long time, my Father looked for a job and found employment in a design engineering office in Budapest.

He took a train from Alag to Budapest; the train ride took, in normal circumstances, forty-five minutes. No passenger train cars were available for the public; the "cattle" cars, the closed-in freight cars, were used, some with rough wood benches nailed to the floor deck. It took about ninety minutes' walk each way, rain or shine each day to get to the train station from where we lived. This walk every day, particularly in the snowy or in the rainy days, was very hard on him and on his health. He was not a big man, but he was lean and strong. He was about 5' 4" and weighed less than 100 lb.

After good several months of waiting, we received our passport; we could leave Hungary and could travel to the New World. We were excited again; my parents bought the train tickets to the closest seaport, and from there, we would take an ocean liner to New York. To finance the trip, they sold some Oriental rugs. They planned out everything to the last detail. They started saying good-bye to some friends and relatives.

About ten days before we were scheduled to leave, in one late evening, the secret police, AVO, came and confiscated our passport, saying, *"It was a mistake. If Father is good for the Americans, then he is good for Hungary."* This was very hard on my parents. They knew now they had to live the rest of their lives in a "prison" under difficult circumstances and with hardship. They had to start thinking of our future and our life in Hungary.

For a start, they had an opportunity to buy an "illegal" pig weighing over 330 lb. from a farmer. Let me explain what *illegal* meant: the farmer's livestock, what they raise, had to be turned over to the government; the farmers could not keep anything for themselves or for sale. The penalty was automatic imprisonment for an indefinite time.

This farmer reared this pig in his basement in his house, and the government did not know about it. He killed it in his place and brought the carcass to our home. In normal circumstances, the pig's "hair" is to be burned off, but that smoke has a distinctive smell to it, and it would be recognized. What we had to do was to boil water and pour it on the pig to soften up the hair and then try to shave it off. It took six of us, four adults and two children, all night. Two persons brought in the water from the outside well and kept the fire going and poured the boiling water on the pig; two shaved it; and the other two continually sharpened the razor blades. The razor blade we were using was what, not too long ago, men shaved with. The next night, the pig was butchered, and the non-eatable parts were buried. The pig was split between the two families. This family, in 1956, left Hungary and settled in Australia.

My parents requested from the local government for a new place to live, with a doctor's certificate for medical reason because of my Father's health, to be closer to the railroad station for his commute to his workplace. After a relatively short time, we moved to the neighboring town, into two rooms, at Bem Street in Dunakeszi from fifteen minutes' walk to the railroad station. We shared a small house with another family. We haven't lived here too long when my parents got acquainted with a town official, and after a bribe, we moved to a small house all by ourselves.

It was a two-room house with a foyer, kitchen with a small pantry, and a bathroom, and had a small yard. The total area of the house was less than six hundred square foot. To take a bath, we had to carry in water from the outside well to fill up the tub. The tub was attached with two pipes to a wood-burning stove. The stove had pipes inside, the flames warmed up the water in the pipe, the water circulated through the pipe and heated up the water in the tub. This process took over two hours. We children were first, then the parents, using the same water, skimming the top after each use. We only took a bath once a week. For emergency, we also had an outhouse to use. The house was located in the same town on Malinovszki Street. not far from the railroad station. In this home, we were independent; we didn't have to share our place with anyone. The year was 1948, and now I was in the third grade. Because of the war, almost everyone in the school was one year behind based on their age.

In the fall of this year, for my Father's fifty-second birthday, we gave him a crucifix. It hung on the wall by his bed till he passed away, and now I have it in my bedroom by my bed. This was the place where I left from and where my parents died in and where my sister is still residing.

This home is about twenty-five minutes' walk to my school. The town had one school up to eight grades, the mandatory schooling in Hungary. The school building was two stories high; each floor had four classrooms. One classroom was for each grade. In the winter, the rooms were heated with a wood-burning stove located in one corner of the room. When I started in this school in 1948, the school was a parochial school, part of the Catholic Church. The teachers were nuns, and they lived next door to the school in a convent. By midyear, the government confiscated from the church the school and the building where the nuns were living. They were at the mercy of the townspeople. The government assigned new teachers, and the nuns were jobless and homeless.

It became very dangerous to attend Sunday church service; members of the secret police (AVO) stood outside the church entrance and took note of all the people who attended the service. Now only the very old attend religious services. My sister and I received our religious education at home from my Mother, but we were not talking about it to anyone because if it became public that you had a religious education, then you and your family could get into big trouble, like disappear for the rest of your life; it happened to some people I know.

To find out what was happening in the world, my Father listened to the radio broadcast of Radio Free Europe, Voice of America, the Radio Vatican, or the BBC (British Broadcasting Corporation), depending on which one was not jammed that particular night. At the same time, we also had to listen to the Hungarian news broadcast to be informed and accidentally not to say something that we heard from the "free" broadcasts. We were under constant surveillance by the secret police—what you do or what you say, the adults at work, and the children in school.

The school's schedule in Hungary, including my school, was six days a week from eight in the morning to four forty-five in the afternoon. Each hour was fifty minutes in the classroom and ten minutes' break. Lunchtime was forty-five minutes; you brought your own food if you had something to eat. Some of my schoolmates did not have lunch. During the break between classes or during the lunch break, some individuals walked through the area where the students were congregating and whistled the beginning of Beethoven's Fifth Symphony. Then they would see how the children reacted to it. If any of them recognized it, we didn't see them in the school anymore. They disappeared with their families. The Beethoven Fifth was the call music before the Free Europe news broadcast. To recognize what it meant that the parents were listening to the broadcast, which was not allowed, and it was against the "law"; it was illegal to listen to Western broadcast.

My parents, in this insane world, tried to rear us to give us guidance and to understand life in general and what is considered a normal behavior. My Father's income was so meager that we hardly had enough money for food for us. But once every year, at one of the holidays, a homeless person or a couple was invited to share our holiday dinner with us. My parents tried to show us that there were less fortunate people out there than us. By seeing them and hearing what they had to say, we children can appreciate more what we had. Meeting our guests and having dinner with them and listening to what they had to say meant more than my parents saying a thousand words on this subject. At the same time, it taught us children to share even if we don't have much to share.

When we were growing up as children, we were told by my Father that we have to respect everybody, but on top of the list was God, then our Mother, and our country, in that order; and we should never forget that! Our country will not be this way forever; everything someday will come to an end, and we can be proud of it again. We as a family had to share the responsibilities and work together as one to survive each day. My Father explained it this way, "*When the horses are hitched on* *to the front of a wagon, they all pull the same direction.*" We as a family had to put our strength together, and we had to pull our "wagon" the same direction to survive and to go forward. If not everyone pulled that wagon as a team, we won't survive. If only one or two persons pulled the wagon, then the one who pulled it won't survive under the heavy weight, which they had to carry. Then the whole team will perish. We needed everyone in the team, in the family, for us to survive. The family that works together survives together. All of us had a special task assigned to pull that "wagon." My Father was a "breadwinner"; he went to work every day. He woke up about five in the morning, read one hour, then he got up to get ready to have a cup of tea with toast. He took the six forty-five train to Budapest and be in his office by eight in the morning. He worked till five, was home by six-thirty, had dinner, listened to the Western news broadcast, and then he was in bed by 10:00 p.m., read some more before he fell asleep. The workweek was six days, forty-eight hours a week. On certain days, he did some shopping in Budapest for items that were not available in our town, and he took a later train home. On his payday, he brought us a quarter pound of cold cuts or two pieces of candy, on some big occasions, a bar of "chocolate" smaller than the "Snickers fun-size bar." But this bar was not made of cocoa beans but from regular beans with added flavor. The cocoa bean had to be imported since it was not available in Hungary. My Mother got different small items. My Father felt once a month we should have some small joy in our life; his joy was the giving. My Mother was doing the shopping, cooking, washing and ironing, and the sewing. Each of us had one pair of shoes. For me, the size was one to one and half sizes bigger than what I need in the beginning. When I outgrew it, my sister inherited it, if it could still be worn. My parents had to make do with the clothing they bought before they were married. We children had two sets of clothing, one to wear when the other one was washed. My Mother did all the sewing and mending for our clothing. When the man's shirt collar was worn-out and it could not be mended anymore, she turned around the collar, and the shirt was "new" again. She mended our pants, socks, shirts, and coat sleeves when it was too worn. My Mother used to say this, *"The clothes are old and worn but clean and mended, and don't be ashamed to wear it."* For washing, she had to heat the water on the woodstove, wash it by hand in a wood tub, and hang it outside. In the winter, it took a long time to dry and had to be careful; when it was frozen, we didn't try to fold it because the clothes would break. The iron for ironing was made of cast iron heated over the stove or with hot wood charcoal placed inside. I have my sister's small working cast-iron iron.

The shopping was not as simple as we have in this country. Every category of items was sold in separate stores. She had to visit every store every day to see what was available that day and stand in line for it. She leaves home at eight thirty in the morning and gets home at four to four thirty in the afternoon, without eating lunch. Many times, she had nothing to show. She stood in line for hours for a particular item, then in the end, it was no longer available when she got there. Some days, she walked five to eight miles a day before she got back home. The cooking was for what we happened to have; we never knew what she found in the store or from the farmers, what they allowed to sell. Food was rationed, and we only could buy a limited amount each time. It was barely enough for a meal for the four of us, and we were small eaters.

After school, I had to check some stores on my way home. To relieve some burden from my Mother, I got a used bicycle; and in this way, particularly in the summer, I can cover a larger area faster for quest of food. The bicycle was a female type; this way, my sister could also use it. I learned early about marketing. For example, sometimes, to buy a kilo of bread (2 lb.), we had to buy the same amount of mushy, smelly, rotten potato, which you dump outside in a container as soon you leave the store, even the animals would not eat it. Or when the government wanted to increase prices on certain items, then those items disappeared from the market for weeks or months. Then they reappeared and had a higher price. We had one kind of bread; it was called white, then it got darker and darker, reaching the good dark fertile soil color. Then the government, with big fanfare, blamed someone for the deteriorating bread color and came out with a new white bread with a higher price. For shoes, we had one design for all ages and sexes, in two colors, black and brown. For raincoats or for any other clouding, it was the same one color and one style for all. The government figured out and established what size the population was; and according to that information, they manufactured limited amount in pre established sizes. The government was regulating every minute of your life, your welfare; you ended up without a "mind" to think with. We didn't have a life; we just bred and tried to survive.

In the autumn, the non farming population had to "volunteer" one week of their vacation time and goes to the fields and helps collect that year's harvest. We had no income tax in Hungary, but you agreed and "volunteered" and "donated" with a "happy face" 15 to 20 percent of your income to the government; the amount was established for you. If you object in any way, watch out! Maybe for you, there is no tomorrow!

But some people were so fanatic about Communism and about Joseph Stalin, the Soviet dictator, that one of my teachers induced her labor for her child to be born on Stalin's birthday.

In the summer of 1950, after I completed the fifth grade, I had the opportunity to attend summer school for the sixth grade and, then at the end of the summer, take a test; and if I passed it, then in September, I will be in the seventh grade. The summer school was a success; I gained a year, and I was now in the seventh grade.

In the last two years in this school, like any other school when you are thirteen to fourteen years old, you do some pranks. Our art teacher was an older gentleman; in his late sixties, he was preoccupied majority of the time. We decided on one occasion for this class that we tie a thin wire to all chalks and to the chalk eraser and some items on the teacher's desk and route the wires up to the ceiling or on the floor to different students. When he reached for the item, it slowly started moving. He acted like nothing happened; because of that, we had to hold back our excitement and laughter. In the end of it, nothing happened.

Starting with the fifth grade, for each subject, we had different teachers. On the teacher's desk in the classroom was a log where they kept all the grades and comments on each student in the class throughout the year. The log was carried into the classroom in the morning by the first teacher, and at the end of the day, the last teacher returned it to the office. During the day, it stayed in the classroom. On one fall day before they started to prepare the midyear report cards, we decided to burn the book. It created a big uproar in the school. When it was asked who did it, everyone in the class stood up. The authority could not suspend the whole class; it would be a bad reflection on the school and the school administration. Therefore, we got away with it. After this, we behaved very well for the rest of the school year. The midyear grades were estimated, and no one failed.

The winter of 1950 was very cold; after a rainy autumn, we had early freeze, then snow. The majority of the roads in this town were dirt roads; only two main roads were paved. After the rain on the wet dirt road, the horse-pulled wagons leave their marks in the mud, and it froze, then it snows; walking on this surface is difficult and treacherous. One morning, my Mother, while shopping, fell and broke her ankle; it was an open break. The bone penetrated through her skin. She had to stay in pain till the mid afternoon before the ambulance arrived. In the hospital, they set her leg and, around midnight, brought her home. We did not know till then what happened to her. We were worried and exasperated by then. The police and the townspeople would not say anything because the police directed them not to tell us what happened to her. In the following weeks, she complained of itching and pain in her broken ankle, and she had a fever. Finally, she convinced the local doctor to send her back to the hospital and to remove the cast from her leg and see what was happening. After the removal of the cast, they found the open wound was infected and small worms were curling in it. The x-ray showed the ankle was not set properly; they re broke her ankle and reset it with new cast. (All these happenings are according to my Mother.) It appears that the first medical team did not clean the wound properly. Because of this setback, it took her a good several months to get well. Then we had to massage her leg—there was no therapy available—for her leg to get back its proper circulation.

In early 1951, my Father was asked to draw illustrations for a technical book, which was to be published later that year. My parents decided to use this money for a summer vacation. We ended up in the town of Fonyódliget by Lake Balaton. The government assigned the town, the place, and the rooms for your vacation. This was our first and my only vacation with my parents. They rented two rooms in a house; one room had two double-bunk beds, and the other room was used as living room / dining kitchen. My Father stayed with us in the weekends; we stayed for two weeks. We had lots of fresh fruit and stayed almost all day in the water. In the weekends, we visited the neighboring towns by train. We as a family played together for the first time; it appeared for a moment my parents forgot the time we were living in.

At the beginning or end of each summer, I spent one week in Nagytétény with my aunt Margit, with my grandmother, and my cousins Zsuzsa and Öcsi. And with their friends, we played and spent all the time together during my visit. One summer, they taught me how to swim in the Duna River. We visited a peach orchard; I ate a green fruit, and I went home with jaundice. According to the doctor, eating green fruit was the cause of my illness. When I was fourteen years old, my parents let me bicycle by myself to Nagytétény through Budapest; it is about twenty-five miles each way. In 1956, during my visit, we listened to the Olympics radio broadcast together; we had no television then.

In June of 1952, I graduated from the eighth grade with honors.[7] That summer, after my fourteenth birthday, I had my first job, which I got paid for. Before, my friend and I painted rooms or did minor repairs around homes of friends and relatives. We had no problem finding work by helping people. My new job was about three kilometers (two miles) from my home; it was in a lumberyard where dismantled building materials were deposited and sorted for reuse. I took my bicycle to work. My assignment was to remove all nails, including rusty ones, straighten them out, sort them by size, and also to clean used bricks and stack them for reuse. My hourly rate, using the exchange rate at the time, was one-tenth of one cent (for ten hours' work, I received one cent). With my parents' help, I used the money I earned to by my own clothes.

I bought a jacket, pants, and two shirts that I needed for the next school year. From then on, I worked every summer; and from that time on, I provided for my own clothing. In the future Christmases, my parents provided the food, and I had a small gift for everyone under the tree. I liked to give, but it was difficult for me to receive gifts.

In September, I started to commute by train on the "cattle" cars to my new school in Budapest. The "cattle" cars refer to train cars used for transporting livestock. Sometimes the train was so crowded we had to stand between cars on the bumpers. In the wintertime, it was very cold when

---

[7]   I have the certificate.

it rained or snowed. I left home by 7:00 a.m. for the 7:20 train; the class started at 8:30 a.m. and lasted till 4:30 p.m., with forty-five minutes for lunch in the school cafeteria. I got home by 6:00 p.m., had dinner, did my homework till 9:30-10:00 p.m., was in bed by 11:00 p.m., and was up in the morning by 6:15 a.m.

To save money for my parents, during lunchtime, I helped out in the school kitchen; for the work, I received a free lunch. The government directive stated that the children of white-collar workers were not allowed to attend any university, except if their parents were good Communist Party members. The government assigned the school and your future occupation for you. Because I graduated with honors, I could select my own occupation and school. I tried to select a school that would give me a good education and foundation for my future without attending college. I selected a similar occupation as my Father—to be closest as possible to be an engineer. I was accepted in the Kvassay Jenö Közlekedés Epitöipari Technikum it was a civil engineering technical school in Budapest, major in steel and reinforced concrete bridges and water-dam design and construction. This was a four-year school; we had fourteen subjects each year; some were the same subjects, but in a different level. Classes were six days a week and lab class all day Saturday. For the summers, the school assigned us to different construction projects for a duration of six weeks to practice what we learned in the previous school year. This way, the government got free labor. We were graded; if we failed the summer work assignment, then we had to repeat the preceding school year even if we graduated with all As. The summer work assignment at the end of the first school year was to lay cobblestones on the streets of Budapest. The following summer, as a good gesture from the Hungarian government, we were sent to Czechoslovakia, to the city of Komárno (Komárom), to build a bridge over the Duna River. We prepared reinforced steel cages for future use in the concrete, hauled one-hundred-pound cement bags on our shoulder, hand-mixed and placed concrete in the form. I was sixteen years old. It was a hot, humid summer, and the cement dust got into our wet hair; and from the perspiration, it hardened. By the end of the day, you'd feel like you have a helmet on your head. In the evening, you have to cut pieces out of your hair; you could not wash out the hardened cement. It was interesting to see the female classmates' hair each morning. Even when you cover your head, it did not help. The last summer, the assignment was similar, but with a managerial training added to our assignment. The accommodations were the local school classrooms where bunk beds were set up in dormitory style. The three meals provided by the company/government were the same as for the other workers, and we worked ten hours a day and one hour for lunch. It was a good disciplinary experience; I learned a lot, which helped me to be a disciplined and accommodating person later in life. For the rest of the summer, I had a summer job, and I worked for money.

On the first year in the technical school, we started with two classes, a total of seventy students. At the end of the fourth year, we had one class with thirty students. The rest either quit because it was too hard or failed. If you failed one or two subjects at end of the school year, then before the school starts next September, you had the opportunity to take a makeup test; if you passed both subjects, you can continue your education. If you only passed one of the subjects or you failed three or more of the subjects at end of the school year in June, then you were out from this school or any other schools in Hungary. There was no makeup test and no appeal. By the end of the fourth year, if you passed all the subjects, then you had to take written and oral tests on six subjects; it covered what you studied the last four years. If you passed, then you will receive your diploma.

To take the written test, the procedure was as follows: you walk into the classroom where the test is given; one student at a time up to ten students were taking the test each day. We pick a piece of paper from a desk in front of the five judges; the paper is facedown, and the assignment written on it is the subject you have to write about. The time allocated for each subject is six hours. We are provided with the pen and paper. The written test is in six consecutive days, with a different subject each day. The oral test is similar; you pick the assignment the same way. Two students are in the room. At any time, one gives the oral response; in the meantime, the other student can collect it thought's and make notes of it. You have to talk, minimum of one hour, on that subject in front of the five judges; you can run over five to ten minutes but not more and cannot be less than an hour. Each judge grades you separately, and the average is your grade. If during the test you have to leave the room for whatever reason, you automatically fail that subject, and there's no makeup test. Thirty of us finished the four years, but only twenty of us passed the final test for the diploma; the other ten had no second chance.

I graduated on June 21, 1956. During the ceremony when we received our diploma, we also received a walking stick (approximately twenty-eight inches long); attached to it on one end was a small cloth sack, which contained a small bottle of wine (timbale size), a small loaf of bread (thumb size), and a hand-rolled small cigarette.[8] This bread and wine is a symbol that you don't leave empty-handed into the world when you start your life's journey.

Looking back in the past four years, it occurred to me we did the same pranks in this school. For example, one nice spring day, we had a spring fever. We wanted to be outside, but we could not skip class. Each classroom had a lock, and the key was in the teacher's desk drawer. We decided that when we leave the classroom for a break, we will lock the door behind us and drop the key into the storm sewer in the street. At

---

[8]   I have the walking stick with the small cloth sack, the bottle, and the hand-rolled cigarette in it; I keep it in a bookcase in the family room.

the end of our break, we were waiting outside the classroom door in the corridor when the teacher showed up. The school had no duplicate key. We spent the rest of the day receiving instructions outside in the close-by park. In another occasion, we were scheduled to have a Russian language test. No one liked this subject. I had to take eight years of Russian language courses, but I don't know one word. The instructor was a young lady in her late twenties, and she didn't like any type of animals, and some of them she was scared of. The classroom was setup where, in order to come into the room, you had to walk through the room to reach the teacher's desk, which was on a six-inch-high platform. The students' desks were set up at the perimeter walls, and in the middle of the room was a passage. That particular day, we brought in several frogs and released them in the passageway. When she saw it, she jumped onto the top of her desk and screamed, and we broke out in a big laugh. Some people heard it outside and came in to see what was happening. The school got into a big investigation; when they asked who brought the frogs in and who released it, the entire class stood up. The school administration could not eliminate a whole class. We were reprimanded; letters were sent home to the parents. That day, we didn't have a test.

During those years, because of food shortage, the government allowed people who were living in towns and in the countryside—and if they had a yard where they lived—to have their own vegetable garden and raise animals for their own consumption. It meant a lot; the life was getting better. We could have a vegetable garden now, and we raised pigeons first, then chickens, ducks, and a pig. For a vegetable garden, we grew beans, peas, carrots, tomatoes, green pepper, cucumbers, dill, and all kinds of other vegetables. We harvested vegetables from early spring until fall. We had two walnut and two peach trees in our yard, and we didn't have to turn in to the government the yearly harvest from those threes. In the past, if you ate a fruit from your tree and someone saw it and reported it, you or your parents got into big trouble. You could be sent away for several months or even a year to labor camp.

Sometimes, I climbed up on one of the trees, which was in the front yard of our home, and I spent a lot of time there, daydream a lot, wishing things to be different, to live in a different world or not live at all. Our life was better now that we had meat, eggs, and vegetables to eat from the garden; and we didn't have to stand in line for hours for it. My Mother's time was concentrated more in the vegetable garden and with the animals. We had thirty-plus chickens, bought them when they were a day old. Some of the chickens were the type that lays two small eggs a day. We also had half a dozen or so ducks, force-fed them with corn by stuffing kernels down their throat with our finger, gave them a limited space to walk around in; this way, they gained weight fast. We also bought the ducklings when they were only a few days old. To feed the animals, we bought some grain, collected weed and stinging nettle from the roadside and with the kitchen trash, dry bread, and contaminated flour or meal. The dishwater was for the pig to mix his food with. Soap was not used in the dishwater. The pig was about six weeks old when we bought it; it grew into a four-hundred pound hog by late fall when it was slaughtered by a butcher and prepared the meat for us. The following year, we had smoked meat, ham, sausage, bacon, and lard to cook with. We only had to supplement with a small amount of items from the store. Later, it was allowed to raise two pigs, one for personal consumption and the other to sell; that covered the expenses for both of the pigs. Beside the vegetable garden, we also grew items for the animals. We also had my Father's beautiful flower garden—his pride and joy. To water the garden, it was my job to hand-pump about 120 buckets of water each time from the well. The well was located in our yard. Watering the garden took several hours. Generally on the weekend, when my Father was home, he liked to do the watering.

For the vegetables during the winter, we stored it in the basement where we had ventilation and even temperature, with sandy dirt floor. We put the vegetables in the loose sand; for some reason, it helped the vegetables stay fresh throughout the winter till the next spring.

In the late spring of 1954, my Father let us know that his hip on the left side was bothering him for a long time. He requested a permission paper from the government to see a doctor. After a thorough and detailed examination and x-ray, the conclusion was that the density of the upper bone in his leg, which is connected to the hip, was diminished to a dangerously low level; and it became very fragile. The doctor directed him to stay in bed till his bone got better and to eat lots of food with calcium in it; no medication was given because it was not available. For my Father to stay in bed for a longer time meant he would get pneumonia with high fever, and there was no medication for it. To lower his temperature, my Mother covered him with cold, wet towels. He had pneumonia thirty-eight times in his life. After three months of his condition not improving, his outlook on life was diminishing. One day, he asked my Mother and me to go to the cemetery, where his parents were buried, and find out what was the procedure if he wants to be buried there. The news was not good from the cemetery's office; they told us first he had to be dead before they were ready to talk with us; second, he lived outside the cemetery's district, and he could not be buried there. When we left the cemetery's office with this news, we decided we would not tell my Father what they told us; it would disappoint him. But we would tell him we got the runaround and required more visits. It had some truth to it because, generally, the officials never gave you straight answers.

As long as we were in the cemetery, we decided to visit my grandparents' grave. When we were walking, my Mother told me that I have a sister and her name is Gisela—her nickname is Babsy—from my Father's first marriage;

and she lives somewhere in Middle East. I was very surprised; I never recalled overhearing any conversation or reference about her. She continued telling me that she has an aunt and uncle living in Budapest. She only knows their last name is Zsille and the name of the street and the general area where they live. She asked me not to let my Father know that she gave me this information. According to Mother, my Father's last time to be in touch with her daughter was about eighteen years ago.

Since then they had no contact. Then she was married to an architect from Switzerland; his name is Otto Oesch. He worked with my Father in the same office in Tehran. They have one son, Roland. He is twenty days younger than I am.

With this information, on one Saturday when the classes ended early, I went to search for my sister's relatives. I found the street, and then I went apartment building to apartment building down the street till I found my newfound sister's aunt and uncle's name on the apartment building's registry. My research bore fruit. When I knocked on the door, my heart was beating in my throat. When they opened the door, I introduced myself. They were surprised to see me and of my visit. I explained to them why I was there, what I knew, and when I found out, and that I wanted to know more about my sister. They were very helpful with information; I found out that she lives in Beirut, Lebanon. She got divorced from her first husband, remarried, and had three sons. Her husband is an American she met in Iran, and he works for an American oil company; his name is Alexander Campbell. Her mother, Oma, is living with them; she separated or divorced from her second husband. They also told me she knew of my existence. They gave me her address. I returned several times after this visit, and I found out more about her and her family and about her mother.

I found out later from my Mother that my sister gave birth to her oldest son, Roland, in the same place and in the same bed where I was born.

After some consideration, seeing my Father's lack of interest in his future, I decided to write to my half sister and tell her my Father's condition. If she wanted to write to him, it was up to her, but I didn't let him know I wrote this letter. Her letter had to appear to be from her—that it was she who initiated to get in touch with her father. After about six weeks, he received a letter from his daughter; he was very happy, and in time, they started corresponding. Meantime, my Father found out from his doctor that a medicine was available in the West, which could help him. Reluctantly, he relayed this information to her; with Express Mail, she sent the medicine. In a relatively short time, he was up; and according to the doctor, if he was cautious, then he could go back to work.

My sister Gisela visited her father in 1963 in Hungary. The last time they saw each other was twenty-five years ego in Tehran, Iran.

With my parents' permission in June of 1956, after my eighteenth birthday—this is the age in Hungary that you are considered to be an adult—I applied to the Hungarian government for passport and requested immigration to Iran. Then the plan was not to settle there, but with my half sister Gisela's help, to move to some other country from there. This time, the Iranian government acknowledged and accepted as a citizen individuals who were born and lived there in the first five years of their life. I was born there, and we left Tehran when I was four months shy of my fifth birthday. I had to try it even if it had consequences later; it was a better life out there in the world than in here under Communism. If I didn't try it, nothing would happen; maybe I would be lucky!

On July of 1956, I started working for the Hungarian State Surveying and Cartographic Office in Budapest as an assistant civil engineer, crew chief for a surveying team, surveying and triangulating the Hungarian countryside.

These were some of the happenings in our life under Communism. This kind of life I don't wish on anyone, but sometimes, I see people spoiled too much in this country and demanding things that are unreasonable. Those people should have my life experience and hardship to appreciate life more and appreciate what they have.

It helped me appreciate life's small rewards and deal with everyday problems in my life. Under these circumstances, you have to see everything in a positive way and live your life in the same way. Don't complain, roll with the "punches." Otherwise, you don't survive. The glass is half-full but never, never half-empty!

The family passport photo.

I am nine years old, June 1947.

The tree I daydreamed on, in our front yard.

Dunakeszi, Hungary Spring 1955

V

Hungarian Uprising and the Escape

(Autumn of 1956 through spring of 1957)

Here is a timeline before and just after October 23, 1956, when the Hungarian uprising took place:

- *February 24:* Nikita Khrushchev, the Soviet politburo member, gives a speech in Moscow to the Soviet Twentieth Congress of the Communist Party, where in his address he denounces Joseph Stalin, the Soviet dictator who died in Moscow on March 5, 1953. The Soviet dictator committed atrocious acts of mass murder in creating and sustaining his powerful reign of terror.
- *October 25:* Thousands of young Poles demonstrate in Poland against the Soviet domination of their country. The Communist government, with a Soviet military's help, crushes the demonstration.
- *October 29:* British, French, and Israeli forces attack Egypt. It is a follow-up to the Egyptian president Nasser's announcement on July 26 of the nationalization of the Anglo-French-controlled Suez Canal, a vital conduit for oil supplies to the West.

The living condition in Hungary deteriorated to the point that in public, no more than three persons could assemble, walk on the street, or stop to visit. That meant that if a family of four, like my family, went out in public together and walked together, we would be arrested. You were in constant fear. When you go shopping and you needed to buy bread, sugar, or flour—the basic essentials, you had to buy items you didn't need. Without

63

it, you were not getting the essential items you came for. The income was meager, hardly enough for the basic minimum for food; anything else was a luxury, including clothing.

With the unbearable fear, poverty in Hungary, and other happenings in the world, a group of Hungarian students and workers marched to the House of Parliament, the radio station, and to the offices of the leading government newspaper on a Tuesday, October 23. They presented a list of grievances, including demands for educational and political reforms.

What was started as a peaceful demonstration became a revolution against the Communist government when the secret police, the AVO, fired on the students. Elements of the Hungarian Army sided with the demonstrators; the secret police were routed, and the Hungarian people won a short-lived victory in a few days.

During this time, I was on my work assignment, for a week of the time Monday through Friday, from the Hungarian State Surveying and Cartographic Office in Budapest where I was employed. I was working in the countryside as a cure chief, surveying the farmland and triangulating the western part of Hungary. We had limited access to the radio, and when we did have access, not much information were provided (the radio stations were government-owned). The only news we had of the happenings in Budapest was from travelers coming from there. The telephone call from the coworkers from the home office alerted us to be careful in our return travels. The group decided that on Thursday midmorning, we would leave and go home.

We boarded the train to Budapest, which was to arrive at the Eastern Railroad Station; and from there, I took a streetcar to Western Railroad Station and took a second train to my home in Dunakeszi, which is ten miles north of Budapest. This trip from my assignment to home normally took me between two and a half to three hours. That Thursday, the trip was much longer and very dangerous. The train stopped more than two miles outside the Eastern Railroad Station, where it was scheduled to arrive. We had to walk the rest of the way to our destination. I walked to Budapest, and from there, through the city to the other railroad station; no public transportation was available.

I saw people in the street burning a portrait of Stalin, the Soviet Communist dictator, and other propaganda documents. My walk took me by the way of the Heroes' Square, where Stalin's twenty-foot-high bronze statue was located and where we had to parade and march in front of it on different Communist holidays.

But this time, the statue was lying on its side, with a rope around his neck. The rope was used to pull it down, and lots of people were around it, hammering it to pieces—maybe for a souvenir or to relieve their anger and frustration. Maybe it was the first time they had a chance to let go of their fear. With what I saw now, I realized what indeed was happening. The people were not afraid anymore. I don't recall ever seeing people so happy and carefree. Up to this point in our life, we could not even imagine that something like this could happen; we were so scared and brainwashed we had no imagination left in our brain. From one railroad station to the other station, my walk took me about six-plus hours, sometimes dodging bullets from the street fights.

During my walk, I observed that several store windows were broken, but the public was not stealing. I could see a basket, bucket, or cardboard box inside or outside or in front of the stores with money in it. Whatever the people were taking, they were paying for it. No one was stealing the merchandise or the money, and no one was looting. I also could see fresh graves in the parks, the front yards of building, or in the courtyards. On the streets were some dead horses; part of their extremities were missing. I found out later that the poor people with no money took it for food rather than steal from the stores. Everyone wanted this uprising to be clean and not to be accused as a bunch of rioters and hooligans who have no respect for the law and human decency. Years after I arrived at this country, people were telling me how surprised they were of the positive behavior of the Hungarian people during the uprising. Their comments were based on what they had heard or seen on the newscast and read in the newspapers.

I was determined to go home; I did not want my parents to worry about me for days. The trains from the Western Railroad Station were canceled; I had to walk three more miles out of the city to find transportation that could take me home to Dunakeszi. I arrived home late. My Mother had been waiting for me on the street for hours; she did not know I was on my way home—it is the Mother's intuition. But she asked people arriving from different trains and buses if they saw me; she was very worried about me. She was very happy and relieved to see me when I arrived home.

For several days, the Soviet tanks and the military moved out from Budapest. The new government was established, headed by Prime Minister Imre Nagy who promised free elections and announced it in the radio that the fighting was over and asked that the people return to work.

The next day, with my Father, we took the train to Budapest to go to our respective offices together, which were a couple of blocks away from each other. Upon arrival in the city, we started walking because there was no public transportation. Across from the Western Railroad Station where we arrived was a butcher shop where approximately eight-to-ten-inch-long hooks were attached to walls behind the counter. When the store was open for business, this was where they kept the half of pigs or cows for the consumers to select the meat they wanted to purchase. But this time, it was members of the Hungarian secret police, the AVO, hanging there; the hook pierced through their backs, hooded, facing us, lifeless in their officer's uniforms. The AVO, the Hungarian secret police, was an elite military unit terrorizing the public, same as the KGB in the Soviet Union (USSR). From here, we walked toward the river Duna going by the Parliament building when shooting started and tanks rolled down the street in our direction. We had to run for cover under the gates of buildings or into courtyards. The renegade AVO units tried to pick a fight with soldiers and tank units, which sided with the freedom fighters and protected the Parliament building. Thirty minutes later, the fighting was over; the AVO unit lost. Buildings were riddled with bullet holes; a lot of damage was from the tanks firing the adjacent office and apartment buildings. We were safe; we continued our walk to our offices. We saw office buildings used by the Communist party and military barracks, where the AVO stationed and lived, were destroyed. In normal times, this trip from the railroad station to the office by streetcar with one transfer took thirty minutes. If you walked it, it was one hour in a good weather. This time, it took us three and a half hours. As soon as we arrived at the office, we checked in, drank some water, visited the toilet facilities, then we turned around and started walking back to the train station in a different way. We didn't know how long our return walk would take; we wanted to leave early to get home in a reasonable time. After a two hours' walk and a long train ride, we arrived home safely.

After this day, it appeared that everything was almost normal and routine. People were happy they got rid of the extreme Communist government. This happiness did not last too long. In the early morning hours of November 4, the Soviet tanks surrounded the city and began a counterattack despite the heroic resistance by Hungarians, some of whom were in their early teens. The overwhelming Soviet military power crushed the revolution and brought the country into outward submission. Almost fifty thousand Hungarians (civilians) were killed. Prime Minister Imre Nagy and his government officials, when they attended a meeting with a Soviet military, were arrested and executed. János Kádár headed the new moderate pro-Soviet government; he was the new chairman of the Hungarian Communist Party.

Under one of Stalin's purges, Mr. Kádár was in jail because he was too moderate at the time. During his confinement, he was tortured; they pulled all his fingernails. Now, tens of thousands of people were fleeing Hungary.

The 1956 uprising was over; it lasted thirteen days before it was crushed. On December 10, the country was put under a Soviet martial law.

After October 23, a family friend and old neighbor of my Mother—they lived in the other half of the duplex where my Mother grew up in Nagytétény—was asked to organize a new security guard to act as a new police in Nagytétény. He was in the process of organizing when the Soviet forces reoccupied Budapest on November 4. Shortly after he was arrested because of his activity, a military court in an unknown location sentenced him to death and had him hanged. The family had to pay for the rope and the coffin; he was buried in an unknown location. In 1995, the family was notified of the location of his remains, and he was allowed to be reburied properly. This took place several years after the Communist dictatorship ended. Meantime, his wife and his son passed away; only his daughter was living. She arranged his funeral.

The military help from the West, which was promised if there were an uprising in Hungary, never materialized. Recently, Defense Secretary Donald H. Rumsfeld made reference to it in his briefing on Iraq in the Pentagon, that this government does not want to do to the Iraqi people what the world did to the Hungarian people by not helping them to liberate themselves from a dictator. Then, the politician's preoccupation with the Suez Canal in Egypt was more important to the world than to help a country with ten million population that was fighting for its freedom, its life, and its welfare. The majority of the United Nations members were a bunch of spineless old men with no imagination and ability to see the future. That has been proven many times in the past forty-something years. Over a thousand-year hatred in Europe toward each other; it is so strong they prefer for a nation, a country, to disappear from the earth before they would help. This hatred toward other people can be seen in this country now, created by some extreme American politicians. They are for their own personal gain instead of the overall welfare of this great country; it was not this way in the late '50s and early '60s. The United Nations as an organization was a good idea when it was conceived. Now it is a dead-vested organization. It should be dismantled, and the headquarters building in New York should be demolished—the property to be used for a park or build a low-income housing on it; that way, it gets better use out of it.

Since October 23, the conversation came up several times with my parents that if I wanted to leave Hungary, I should do it now. The news we heard was that the border to Austria was open, no border guards; it was very easy to cross. You could take a train to the border and walk through to Austria without any interference. My parents tried to feel me out on what I was thinking regarding leaving Hungary. Since I applied to emigrate from Hungary several months ago, now was an unexpected opportunity to leave. The time had arrived for me to make my decision. My parents did not want to push me, but they encouraged me to leave. I will have a better life anywhere than in Hungary. I was hesitant to leave because if things changed back to the way they were before October 23, then I won't see my family again for the rest of their lives. I recalled all the conversations I had with my parents many times about a better life they had when they were living outside Hungary and in Hungary before Communism.

The following days and weeks after November 4, we were listening to different Western radio broadcasts, which was illegal again; we learned that less and less refugees were reported to be leaving Hungary due to the new rein posed tighter border controls. In the end, two hundred thousand refugees left Hungary, almost 2 percent of the population.

I decided that I wanted to leave after seeing what was happening. The police were rounding up teenagers of my generation. But it appeared it may be too late for me to leave. We tried through friends to get on as a volunteer on one of the last International Red Cross trucks returning to Austria. The effort failed. By then, it was early December. One evening when my Father came home from work, he mentioned it at dinner that a small group of people wanted to leave from his office. Should I be interested in joining them, he would help me to be part of the group. My answer was yes. I was not told the extent of the group for safety reasons; my contact was a thirty-something coworker of my Father's, whom I knew from the past. He would travel with us, helping his older brother Imre Reiner and his wife, Iren (Iréne), and their daughter, Andrea. If we were successful, he would try it with his family. We decided after a long discussion that the easiest time to cross the Austrian-Hungarian border was on New Year's Eve, but it was the most dangerous. The easiest because the Hungarian and the Russian border guards would sneak into the close-by farmhouses or group together to celebrate the New Year's, and there would be less military personnel to guard the immediate borders. The most dangerous because by the evening, they could be drunk, and then they are more likely to be trigger-happy. In preparation for the trip, we needed several things. One had to secure "special travel document," which would give us the purpose for our travel and take us close to the border. This document was needed in addition to the "identification card," which everyone had. You could not go out to the street without it. Then to line up guides, which we would need on the last fifteen or so miles (25 km.) of our trip when we are walking, and to have enough money with us to pay them. We didn't know the exact amount, but we could guess. Also, we were to have with each of us several bottles of hard alcohol such as homemade brandy for the Hungarian and the Soviet guards and useless old wrist or pocket watches for the Soviet guards to use it as a bribe if and when we get captured and "travel document" authorizing us to travel into a restricted zone, which is several miles from the border. Because of my job with the state's surveying office and I travel a lot, I had access to some of the documents that we needed and could be used for our trip. We needed the copy of the "authorizing travel" paper on the company letterhead, with the company seal over the authorizing signature. The two items were relatively easy to obtain, but the seal was impossible; it was kept in a locked cabinet. I collected and filled out the forms; somebody else signed it to be different, using a fictitious name. The problem was how to transfer the seal from my old travel papers, which was issued to me before the uprising and never asked to be returned. After some investigation and experiment, the seal was transferred from the old documents with a raw potato cut in half. I put the cut side of the potato on the seal of the old travel document, let it soak in the ink, and then transferred the potato soaked in ink on to our papers; the seal was transferred. It took a long time. With this process, I could make only a limited amount of forged documents. The seal was fuzzy, but acceptable.

It was decided that if we wanted to cross the frontier to Austria on New Year's Eve, we had to leave Budapest on December 29, in the early morning, by train.

This was my last Christmas at home with my family. In the past, even when we were financially poor, we had joyful holidays because we had one another. This time, as it was in the past three Christmases, I was the "Santa." I brought the presents for everyone in the family, but this time, the "Santa" was more generous because it was his last. The routine was the same; we decorated the tree on the afternoon of Christmas eve, put on our Sunday best, and the Santa arrived at six in the evening. His arrival was announced when my Father rang a small bell. We came in from the next room, sang some Christmas songs, and prayed, with no mention of my pending departure. In the end, we huddled; we hugged one another like we never hugged one another before.

We opened the presents and had dinner—vegetable soup and fried fish with mashed potato and, for dessert, rolled walnut and poppy seed cake, a typical dessert for Christmas in Hungary. After dinner, like every year, my Father read to us one of his favorite chapters from a book he read during the past year. He read a lot of books during the year; some of them were the same books in several languages, borrowing the books from friends.

This Christmas was on the surface like any other Christmas in the past; but the words were less, the looks were longer, and everyone was concentrating on me. It was very hard to take it, but I understood it. I could see it, that it was also very hard on my parents and on my sister.

After Christmas, I collected and packed what I needed for my journey; everything had to fit into a briefcase: for clothing, a warm shirt, one extra under shorts and shirt, several warm socks; soap; hand towel; shaving soap and blades; metal cap; and toothbrush and paste. Also, I had with me two bottles of homemade brandy and several nonfunctional wrists and pocket watches. I did this quietly when my parents were not around. On the last minute, I added food for the road for three days: fresh bread, Hungarian smoked sausage and bacon, some of my Mother's Christmas dessert, a bottle of water, and candies from the Christmas tree. I still have one of the candies. In addition to the above, I had with me a small 4"x2" 3/4"x1" prayer and songbook; it fit into my pocket. I received this prayer book from my Mother. The inscription reads,

In happiness and in sorrow
this book
shell be your devoted companion
throw out of your live journey.

Christmas, the year of 1947
(signed) your *Mother*

This book helped me out many times in the bumpy road I traveled during my life's journey.

It was December 28, 1956. The time had arrived for me to say good-bye; it was maybe the last time in our life. It was a big possibility we would never see one another again. My Father stayed home from work that day; and my Mother made the biggest lunch, what they could not afford, for my last home-cooked meal. During the meal, everyone was very quiet. It was a somber event, like the *Last Supper*. The food was excellent. My Mother outdid herself. She made one of my favorite meals—potato soup with sour cream, fried chicken with home fries, and walnut-chocolate cake for dessert.

After the meal, my Father, with tears in his eyes and a broken voice, tried to give me his encouragement, his last wisdom, and his last advice:

We raised you the best we could,
you are mature and old enough now
to stand on your two feet.
Life is short.
Do well to others, respect others, be polite, and be
considerate.
Be conscientious; be a hard worker.
Consider all opportunities
because the same opportunity seldom repeats itself.
If you follow this, you will survive and succeed out there,
and you will make it in the world.

When he finished, he got up from the dinner table and went outside.

These last words and wisdom of his are etched in my mind and guided me throughout my life's journey and brought success to my life.

The rest of us—my Mother, my sister, and I—started clearing the table. When I looked outside, my Father was clearing the snow from a small area in the yard. Then he came in with a fistful of dirt; he put it on a piece of paper and rolled up the paper with dirt in it and gave it to[9] me with the following words:

*When you leave this country, your homeland, and
when you die, your remains cannot be
laid to rest in the Hungarian soil.
At least, this way you will be resting with the
Hungarian soil when you are in your final resting place.
God will be with you; he will watch over you in
your journey.
You will do well; your family will
be with you all the time.
You will not be alone. Our prayers will be
with you all the time.*

My Father was not a religious person, but I knew he meant it.

I found out later that after I left, my Mother cried for weeks before she could acknowledge and accept the idea that maybe she wouldn't see her son again. It is a big sacrifice for a parent to give up their child forever and send him to the unknown. Sometimes, a parent's love and sacrifice have no limits for a better life for their children.

I took an early afternoon train to Budapest and spent the night with my aunt Zsuzsa, my Mother's younger sister, and my uncle Nándi's home. The

---

[9]   I have my Father's "gift," the Hungarian soil. And if I cannot be buried in Hungary, then I want to be buried with it according to my Father's wishes.

decision was that no one would go with me to the railroad station. It was a good decision because I was crying all the way there. I was very numb; at the same time, I was excited and sad. The following thoughts were going through my mind: will I survive, will I be captured, and will I end up in prison for years or the rest of my life? Will I survive the trip? What will the future bring? It was a good idea that I left that day and spent the night in Budapest; it was easier for me emotionally. I hoped I could have a good night's rest before my long trip and I could get to the train station early morning tomorrow. On the way to my aunt and uncle's place, I stopped by my office to borrow some surveying equipment. That would make my false documents seem more legitimate. That evening with my aunt and uncle was emotionally hard for all of us, knowing that we wouldn't have this opportunity again. They didn't have any children of their own; we the cousins were their children. We had a nice, quiet dinner; and for me, I was early to bed for emotional rest and, hopefully, some sleep.

The next day, I arrived at the train station very early in the morning; it was December 29. To my surprise, I found out that the group had grown to twenty-four people. Many of them were not dressed properly with proper shoes and working clothes to complement the "travel document" from the state's surveying office. We were spread throughout the train, to not be too conspicuous. During our train ride, our papers were reviewed and verified several times by the Hungarian and the Soviet police. I observed at some train stops that people from our group were removed from the train and detained. After several hours on the train, we arrived at our destination, the city of Kapuvár. Upon arrival, I made arrangements at the railroad station to return the surveying equipment to my office in Budapest.

To my surprise, sixteen of us made it. I found out later that people from our group who were removed from the train were sent to prison between five to eight years because they tried to leave the country. The prearranged guide, one of the group member's relatives, met us in the station. He was the first of three, one for each night. They were familiar with the specific area of our "travel." We started walking in small groups about four thirty in the afternoon to the westerly direction. At the edge of the town, we met and continued walking together in the dark. We walked all night in the fields; it was very cold, windy, and the snow was approximately twelve inches deep (30 cm.). It made our walk slow and treacherous. We walked behind one another, which made it easier. This way, we had fewer footprints. The last person carried a tree branch and covered our track by sweeping the snow with the branch.

On December 30, about five in the morning, we arrived at a small farm settlement. We were told that we had to hide during the day because the Hungarian border guards and the Soviet military inspected the area several times a day. I found a large haystack, about twelve feet in diameter and about the same height. I dug a hole to the middle of the haystack close to the ground. This way, when the guards stuck the rifle with the bayonet into the haystack, the blade won't reach me. After I crawled in, someone filled in the hole and compacted the hay to the consistency of the original haystack. I spent my first day there hiding. Everyone found some hiding place on the farm. In the evening, when darkness set in and after dinner, everyone reappeared from their hiding places; we visited the outdoor toilet, washed ourselves in the snow, and continued our second night's walk with a different guide through the night. This guide was somewhat familiar with the border patrol's routine. Today's journey was more dangerous than the night before. We were closer to the border; the guards on trucks and on foot were more frequent and used floodlights from the vehicle. We walked in a row like ducks, and the last person with a large branch brushed over the snow to eliminate the footsteps like the night before. We tried not to walk in open fields. The night was cold and windy again; almost a full moon on the sky was somewhat of a problem for us because we could be seen from a distance in our dark clothes with the white background. We walked by trees, scrubs, or by a grove. We crossed a road about two hundred yards back, walking on the inside edge of a grove. It was about two in the morning. When the sky lit up from several flares, we "froze" on the spot. Some of us hid behind a tree or lay flat in the snow. We were this way for about thirty or forty minutes. No one moved, coughed, or even breathed. The flares came from the direction where we had recently crossed the road.

When the flares stopped and we determined that there was no more activity from that direction, we waited for a while and then looked around to make sure that everyone was all right. Irene Reiner had been lying on top of her daughter, Andrea, in the snow to keep her quiet. Andrea was about five years old.

We were lucky that this episode came to an end because the child was turning blue from the cold. We returned life and warmth to her by putting her hands and feet into our mouth to warm her up. The rest of the night was relatively quiet.

On December 31, early in the morning, we arrived at our next destination, again a farm settlement. It was apparent that they were expecting us because the dogs were inside the barn so they will not bark on our arrival. Everyone had to hide again during the day. My hiding place was a stall with the cows in a cowshed. The people living there suggested this was one of the hiding places because the border guards generally didn't visit there. The building had about 150 stalls and housed 120 to 130 milking cows, 10 to 12 in a row. The passage through the building was at one end of the rows. My place was by the opposite wall from the walk. The majority of the time, the cows were standing, but when they decided to lie down, then I had to follow them and lie down too. It became a bit messy. The stalls were not very clean. The day went by very slowly; I could not sleep, and I was thinking about what tonight and tomorrow would bring. Will I spend the next day in a place where I could breathe freely?

Until then, our trip was, relatively speaking, uneventful; and everything was going smoothly. Based on the weather and circumstances, no one was injured or died. When darkness arrived, I felt very tired and sleepy. In the past sixty hours, I had slept maybe eight to ten hours, and a long walk was ahead of me. I was wearing old boots from my working days when I was surveying the countryside in the fields. But now, I thought the water had penetrated through and frozen my ankle on my right foot. It hurt when I move my foot or when I walked, and we could not remove my boot because the leather had shrunk. When we tried to, it hurt too much.

We left the farm as soon as it turned dark. Our goal that night was to cross the frontier to Austria by midnight. Our guide told us before we left that the border between Hungary and Austria was a small creek.

The border guards were more frequent, loud, and they appeared to be intoxicated. The areas where we were, were hilly and rocky, having large, ten—to twelve-foot boulders (3-4 m.). We had to be very careful, never knowing what was around at each turn. Our progress was slow. We were so close to our destination, and we didn't want to jeopardize it by getting captured, shot, or killed. These thoughts were short-lived. At one of the boulders, there were three Hungarian border guards sitting and drinking, celebrating the New Year's Eve early. When we saw one another, everyone was surprised. Luckily, their rifles were not near them. They were not expecting "visitors." After some conversation, we saw that they were slightly intoxicated. We offered them our supplies and joined them in the celebration. They were enjoying our brandy, and in no time, all three fell to the ground unconscious. To make sure, we "knocked" them out by "tapping" them on the head with a "stick." During this time, we were worried that additional guards or people would show up.

Having lost a good hour, we left in a hurry and moved fast the rest of the way. After a good hour's walk, we saw, in a distance, a flicker of light.

We anxiously started walking in that direction. When we got closer, we heard German conversation from that direction, and the light turned out to be a campfire on the other side of the border. It was in Austria! Between the campfire and us was a small creek. My heart beat so fast and loud in the silent night that I was afraid that the border guards would hear my heartbeat wherever they were.

We started crossing the creek, and in no time, the ice broke. It appeared that this crossing was used before. We were lucky that the water in the creek was shallow with large rocks. I was the only person with boots on. I volunteered to walk in the creek to help the others cross the creek walking on the rocks. It was New Year's Eve of 1957, thirty minutes before midnight, when all of us were on the "free" side of the creek. Every one of us had tears in our eyes, hugging one another; we took a minute to thank God for his help and his guidance in this journey. The feeling I experienced then, I cannot describe even today, because I don't know how. A person had to go through and live the past ten years as I did to understand it and to have that feeling. From the creek, the campfire was about fifty yards; when we arrived there, we were warmly greeted and had a Hungarian-speaking personnel, and they were waiting for us. They asked us to move away from the fire to give a "guiding light" to others if any more people were following us. We were escorted to a close-by building where we were greeted with hot chocolate, warm food, dry clothes, and blankets. We spent the rest of the night there; and the next morning after we received breakfast, a bus took us to a refugee camp. My right foot now was hurting even when I didn't walk or even if I didn't move it. When I had to walk, I was limping from the pain.

Upon arrival at the refugee camp, everyone received a brief medical examination. Because of the pain in my foot, we tried to remove my boot, but we could not do it. The leather had shrunk too much. The doctor cut off my boot; we discovered that my foot was infected. I lost the majority of my skin and flesh on my ankle. The shrinking leather from my boot cut into the flesh on my ankle, causing the infection and the pain. The surface was yellowish white, and there was not much feeling in my left foot. The doctor's diagnosis was that I had lost circulation and had a small frostbite. With medication under a doctor's care in the infirmary, rest, and a new pair of shoes, I was well again in no time.

The refugee camp called the *Ungarisches Lager*, administered by the Austrian and the International Red Cross, was located in the town of Kaisersteinbruch—a suburb of Vienna, the capital of Austria. The camp was located on an old military base; the housing was an old refurbished military barracks where several thousand refugees were housed in many buildings. Generally, the buildings were one story with ten to twelve rooms per building, with four to six people in a room. At the end of a corridor, there were the bathroom facilities. The occupants of each building were responsible for the cleaning of the building's inside and the outside surrounding areas. Three meals a day were served in a separate building in shifts. On a rotation basis, we were assigned to help out in the kitchen or in the dining room for one day, which happened once every three weeks. The rest of the time was ours. The camp provided everything we needed, including free hair-grooming service. Some nations had representative offices in the camp.

They were encouraging us to contact the country's embassy where we wanted to emigrate. They tried to help us find employment in Austria. Now the opportunities were very limited. The early refugees found employment while they were waiting for their travel papers to the new destination.

When I left home, my Father gave me a letter addressed to my half sister, Gisela, who lives with her husband, William Alexander Campbell, in Beirut, Lebanon, asking her to help me select a country to immigrate to. This letter was sewn into the shoulder pad of my overcoat. Hopefully, if the police searched me in my trip, it wouldn't be found. Shortly after my arrival, I mailed this letter to her from the camp. Approximately two weeks later, I received a response to my Father's letter. She was surprised that I was in Austria; she was indicating in her letter that she planned to visit me; furthermore, she would arrive in a couple of days. I was surprised of her pending visit, and at the same time, I was excited that I will meet my sister for the first time; she is twenty-one years older. When the day of her visit arrived, the loudspeaker in the camp announced that I had a visitor and to go to the camp office where she was waiting. The meeting was very emotional; it was the first time we saw each other. After some time, I showed her the camp and my room, then we went to Vienna, to the hotel where she was staying. She planned to stay in town for several days. We talked a lot. She was interested to know everything about our Father. It had been close to nineteen years since they talked or saw each other. She has never met my younger sister, Maria.

My sister Gisela told me that when my Father's letter arrived from Austria, they were surprised. Her husband questioned the legitimacy of the sender. Maybe it was a trick to lure his wife to Austria, because during World War II, he was a colonel in the intelligence unit of the U.S. Army. Maybe this was somewhat related to his past. They decided that my letter might be legitimate and she would travel to Austria. She was cautious and kept contact with her husband every day. After some lengthy conversation, she suggested that the best place for me to immigrate is the States. I needed a sponsor.

Both of them are U.S. citizens. With this in mind, we visited the U.S. Embassy.

We were told there that because they were not living in the United States, they could not be my sponsors. She relayed this information to her husband as soon as we returned to the hotel. We tried to figure out our next step. The next evening, she received a call from her husband and informed her that he had talked to his sister in Washington DC, explaining to her the situation. She indicated to him that they were willing to sponsor me. His sister was married to the Honorable Walt F. Horan; he was a member of the U.S. House of Representatives. We returned to the embassy the next day. The sponsorship was acceptable, but the immigration quota for Hungarians to the United States was filled up. The U.S. Congress was working on an emergency immigration program to increase the quota. The program was initiated by President Eisenhower based on Vice President Nixon's recommendation, from his findings during his visit late December of 1956 to several refugee camps in Austria.

We filled out all papers, providing all the necessary information to the embassy. With my sister's help, all the paperwork was accomplished fast. Now the waiting had begun. Before she returned home to Beirut, she gave me $30 spending money. That amount represented more than one month of my salary in Hungary.

Life in the camp was boring and depressing.

The public transportation in Austria was good and inexpensive. I decided to use some of my newfound fortune to spend some time in Vienna. I did some window-shopping; I visited the historic churches, buildings, and parks I read about. Even the air smelled different than in Hungary; the people didn't look depressed, and they dressed nicely. I felt like a sponge; I wanted to absorb everything, so much to see and to learn. I had to catch up with the rest of the world, which went by when my part of the world was standing still. The police did not stop me to see my identification papers. If only my accomplishment was to leave Hungary and only travel this far, it was worth it. I also visited the Schönbrunn Palace, the summer place of the Royal Habsburg family. The gardens of the palace grounds were magnificently well taken cared of. In the weekends, they had concerts in the garden. I spent lots of time there.

It took over two hours to get there, but it was worth it. To save money, I had a big breakfast and a big dinner in the camp and skipped lunch. The garden was free; the mansion was a museum and has an entry fee, which I could not afford.

Also, I used some of the money from my newfound fortune to send home to my parents a package of clothing—with the Red Cross's help—which they can wear or sell to have some supplemental income. During the following months when I was waiting, I was in touch with my sister in Beirut and updated her with the latest happenings. She periodically sent me some spending money.

Several years later, in one of my return trips to Hungary, I stopped in Vienna for several days to visit, and I spent one day in Schönbrunn, walking around in the garden and recalling the circumstances and time I spent there. This time, I went inside and visited the Palace.

The day of my departure from Austria came on a sunny Thursday, April 18, 1957, after three and a half months in the refugee camp outside Vienna. From here, we traveled to Eisenstad, Austria, to a "clearing" camp, by a bus provided by the International Refugee Organization, where I spent the Easter holiday. On Tuesday, April 23, at four forty-five in the morning, we left by bus to Munich, Germany—through Vienna, Linz, and Salzburg cities in Austria. We spent the night in the U.S. military base there. On the next day, Wednesday, April 24, at one forty in the afternoon, the military transport plane left to the "Promised Land" with sixty refugees aboard. Before we left, they gave us the opportunity to notify our families. I sent a telegram to my parents on the pending departure, in cryptic language, which we had agreed ahead of time.

During our trip, we stopped for refueling and to eat for one and a half hours each at Scotland and in Newfoundland military bases. I was very fortunate to be seated by a window. This was my first time in an airplane. The view was unbelievable; the houses below us were so small. When we were flying between and above the clouds, it was like floating in a bubble bath; you could almost reach out and touch it. The trip took over twenty-five hours; during the flight, only two people got sick because of the airplane flying through a storm.

This detailed information is from my notes I kept of my life's historical journey.

Besides the clothes I wore, I had two of the following in my small suitcase: a shirt, a T-shirt, under shorts, three handkerchiefs and socks, soap, shaving cream, razor blades, a razor, and one hand towel—basically the same things with which I left Hungary. The last two items and the small suitcase, I received in the Austrian refugee camp. I still have those items as mementos of my past to remember where I came from if I needed to be reminded of it.

A difficult chapter of my life had come to the end, and a new beginning of a new life, with unknowns, but full of new hope and possibilities had started. Anything had to be better than the past eighteen years. I was free! I was free! I was free! I was now the master of my own destiny!

Street scene during the uprising.
Budapest, Hungary, October 24, 1956.

Last picture of me taken in Hungary.
I am almost eighteen years old.
Dunakeszi, Hungary, Spring 1956.
This was the picture I gave to my parents to remember me by on the day I
left home on December 28, 1956.

VI

Beginning a New Life in the USA

(Spring of 1957 through 1959)

I was on a military transport plane that landed at Newark Airport in New Jersey on Thursday, April 25, 1957, at eight forty in the morning. I was eighteen years old. I was very fortunate to arrive at the land where my Father and millions of other people all over the world dreamed of all their life, to live in this great country.

We were taken by bus to Camp Kilmer refugee center in New Jersey; we were housed in military barracks. The welcome at our arrival was unbelievable; everyone was very friendly. The majority of the people spoke Hungarian. For breakfast, we received cereal, scrambled eggs, juice, coffee, milk, with different types of bread, butter, and jelly; it was so overwhelming—all these food for breakfast! I could not imagine seeing that much food in one place. The lunch and dinners were the same—plentiful, overwhelming, unbelievable selections and quantities. The refugee center had television and reading rooms, bowling alleys, and tennis courts. I stayed here for six days. During this time, we received several orientations about this country in general and on the customs specifically. We received a small Hungarian-English dictionary, which I still have. It was prepared for the U.S. military during World War II. We received additional clothing. We were interviewed and questioned several times about our past—where and

86

how we lived, where we worked, and how we got out from Hungary; they wanted to know everything.

I gave to the interviewer my "identification card" with my picture; it was like a passport with more information. It provided everything about the person—location of employment, your occupation, work assignment, membership to any organization you belong to, information about your family, and personal information about you. You had to have it with you all the time in Hungary, had to show it when the police or the military stopped you for any reason on the street or anywhere, including in your home. Also, I gave them my office identification card with my picture in it. I received documents for permanent residency and the green card; my name was changed from Károly Landesz Jr. to *Karl J.* Landesz.

When I had some free time, I reminisced, looking back on my short stormy life, that about eleven years ago I was begging on the street in Germany for the survival of my family. Now I was so happy. I cried. I couldn't believe I was here, that I came this far in such a short time. I knew someone was looking out for me from above. Thank you, God. Thank you.

On the seventh day of my stay in the refugee center, on May 1, 1957, I received a train ticket to Washington DC and twenty dollars, and they provided transportation to the railroad station of Newark, New Jersey, and they put me on the train to Washington DC. They told me someone would meet me there, no name; no other information was given.

I was very nervous about the train ride and what kind of impression I would make when I get there! Would they like me? To me, it was like to be an orphan from a different world with different background and finding a new home with a new family. It was very strange on the train with everyone looking at me; I did not understand what they were saying. The train ride took four and a half hours; I arrived in the mid afternoon to the Union

Station[10] in Washington DC. I got off the train and followed the rest of the people. A lady approached me and called out my name. Besides my name, I did not know what else she was saying. I spoke not one word of English. We walked to her car. After driving some time, we arrived in a residential neighborhood with beautiful big homes.

Big trees were lining both sides of the street. She stopped in front of a big house at 2729 Daniel Road, Chevy Chase, Maryland, where several ladies were leaving and wearing different costumes. We were sitting in the car for several minutes until all the ladies left, and then we went inside. I was introduced to Helen "*Sally*" Horan and Lira, the person who helped out with the cooking and cleaning. I was very confused. I was shown to my room on the third level of the house where the Horan children lived when they were growing up. Only the youngest son, Walter Horan Jr. (nineteen years old), was living at home. He was staying in one end of this large dormitory-like room; my bed was in the other end. The room was the full length of the house. We shared the bathroom. Several days later, I met the other two Horan children and their wives: Scott Horan (twenty-four years old) and his wife, Joan Blackstone, and Harold "Hal" Horan (twenty-two years old) and his wife, Dolores "Del" Sanders. Mr. Horan was in the hospital, the National Naval Medical Center in Bethesda. He served in the navy during the First World War. I met him on the next day; we visited him every day till he returned home. The two older children I met later; the oldest was Kaye (thirty years old), Mrs. Douglas Paauw, with her husband and with their two young sons living in Indonesia. Doug was a consultant at the Indonesian government on economics. I met them in 1959 when they came home for a visit. Mike Horan (twenty-seven years old) and his wife, Jan, and with their three daughters lived in Wenatchee, Washington.

---

[10] Years later, I had the privilege of managing the restoration and renovation of the station (1984-1988).

He was the manager of the Horan Brothers orchard. They grew apples and pears. I met Mike and his family in 1958 on my trip to Wenatchee. The orchard was owned by Mr. Horan and his late brother John's family; they inherited it from their father, Mike Horan Sr.

Everyone in the family and all the neighbors were very warm and very friendly. I was very lucky to end up in here. The family who lived across the street on the corner were Joseph and Louise Michalowicz. Every Sunday, they took me to church with them; they were Catholics as I am. The Horan's are Presbyterians. Mr. Michalowicz is the dean of engineering in the Catholic University of America in Washington DC. They also took me to the dedication service of National Shrine of the Immaculate Conception, located in the Catholic University grounds.

The communication was difficult and slow during this time. I didn't speak one word of English, but I had two dictionaries: one English-Hungarian for them and the Hungarian-English for me. We looked up one or two keywords from the sentence of what we wanted to say and showed it to each other, and for the rest of the words, we used sign language or pointed to things, like playing charades. I still have these well-used dictionaries. I received the dictionaries from my parents when I was living in the refugee camp in Austria, after they found out that I was destined to the States.

The combination of the flavors of the food, particularly the breakfast, for me was strange at the beginning. For example, sometimes the breakfast consisted of scrambled eggs (okay) with sage-flavored sausage (?), toasted cinnamon-raisin bread, and unsweetened grapefruit juice. This was one of Mr. Horan's favorite breakfasts. In time, I became used to all the new food flavors and their combination; everything was new to me.

Later, I found out that the lady who met me at the Union Station and drove me to my new home and to my new family was Helen Grindle Fuchs, Mr. Horan's secretary. The reason she recognized me in the Union Station was because no one wore an overcoat in May in Washington DC. The ladies in the different colorful dresses in the time we arrived at the house were the members of the International Ladies Club, and they were wearing their country's dress.

In June through August of 1957, I took an all-day language course in the American University Language Center for six weeks. Upon completion, I signed up to attend the Americanization Center for six weeks of morning classes and, at the same time, Coordinated Hungarian Relief Inc. for six weeks of evening classes. Scott Horan, every morning before he goes to work, picked me up and took me to school in downtown Washington DC. During my free time, I watched television; it helped me to get used to the sounds of the spoken word. The Hungarian sentence structure is different from the English. The Hungarian is similar to the Spanish language's sentence structure. In the early '60s, I took some language-related courses at the Montgomery Junior College.

According to the educational organization in Washington DC who credits degrees from different schools in the world, my technical school degree is equivalent to two years of university studies in this country.

By late August, I spoke and understood sufficiently to look for employment. I had interviews in private and government engineering and architectural offices. Finally, I found employment in the office of Jack C. Cohen, AIA Architect, in Silver Spring, Maryland. I started working on September 15, 1957. Jack was the first generation of American; his parents came from White Russia. The office had six employees when I started to work there. My first assignment was to organize the office—flat files and the bookcases and keep the office organized, then as draftsman, drawing single-family homes. In my free time, I visited construction sites to learn more about residential construction. My work also included processing projects through building departments and securing building permits. I prepared building site grading plans. The office grew, and the name changed to Cohen, Haft, Holtz Architects, then to CH2K. I became a section head for single-family homes' design production, managing eight architects. The plans we prepared were used to build several thousand homes in Maryland and Virginia. Sometimes in weekends, I accompanied Jack to inspect the construction of his new home in Potomac.

My starting salary was the minimum wage of one dollar an hour. The cost of a gallon of regular gas was sixteen cents and a gallon of milk, eighteen cents. A cup of coffee or Coca-Cola was five cents each. The first-class stamp was three cents. The maximum Social Security withholding for a year was ninety-two dollars. The annual salary for members of the U.S. House of Representatives was ten thousand dollars. The median family income was $4,966. The price of the 1957 Chevrolet Bel Air Convertible was $2,611; the Chevrolet Nomad station wagon was $2,857, and the 1957 Volvo PV445 Duett was $2,490. At the end of the year, the Dow Jones industrial average closed at 435.68. The Academy Award movie in 1957 was *The Bridge on the River Kwai.* Here are some of the milestones in 1957: Soviet Union Launches Sputnik I and New York City Retires Its Last Trolley Car. Some of the above information were published on different times in the *Washington Post* newspaper.

I worked in this office till March of 1962; by then the office employed twenty-six people, and I was making $4.50 an hour.[11] When I started working,

---

[11]   I saved all the payment stubs for the past forty-three years.

I gave one week of my gross salary to the Horan's. This was voluntary. At first, they were hesitant to accept it, but I insisted. They already gave me so much, and I was working now, wanting to contribute to the household expenses. I received lots of clothing for the holidays from the family and their friends. I bought additional clothing from various thrift shops: a very nice used jacket for 50¢ and suit for $1.50. I wore these for several years.

In the spring of 1958, I learned to drive; my teachers were Nagymama and a neighbor lady, Ann Whemyer. My driving lessons were in Rock Creek Park. The parking lessons were in the Carter Barron Theater parking lot in Washington DC. By summer, I bought my first car, and I paid cash for it; the car was a 1954 Studebaker Land Cruiser. The car's title was on Nagymama's name; I was added to their insurance. I reimbursed them for the additional cost of insurance. Doing it this way, I could drive the Horan's car if it was needed, and I saved some money in the meantime. The car insurance for a young man under the age of twenty-one was very expensive if it was not on the family insurance policy. When I turned twenty-one, the car's title was transferred back to me.

When my parents found out about my car, they were very excited and proud of my accomplishment in such a short time. They shared their happiness with their neighbors. One of the neighbors was a well-known cartoonist in Hungary. He drew a cartoon of my parents, illustrating when they were reaching out over the Atlantic Ocean and shaking my hand. My parents sent me this drawing.[12]

In the summer of 1958, my sister Gisela with her husband, Sandy (William Alexander Campbell), were here to visit his sister and his brother-in-law, the Horan's, with their son Andy from Beirut, Lebanon,

---

[12]   I have this drawing in a black frame and displayed in my home.

where they lived. Their other son, Rolland, joined them from Switzerland; he was here to join the U.S. Marines. They took us all to the circus, then we went to see two movies, one was *The Seven Wonders of the World* and the other was *Around the World in Eighty Days*, based on the book of Jules Verne, starring David Niven. During their visit, they traveled to different cities and places in the States. They also traveled to northwest Canada to visit the ancestral family ranch. When they returned, they had with them an old Winchester rifle, with several notches on the rifle butt. According to Sandy, his ancestors used the rifle to hunt and to fight the Indians. Sandy passed away in Beirut, Lebanon, on December 24, 1963, at the age of sixty-three. He was buried in Washington DC. My sister eighty-seven years old, and she is living now in Villa Rica, a suburb of Atlanta, Georgia.

The Horans had lots of friends in and out of Washington DC area; frequently, they had out-of-town overnight guests. I called the house jokingly the Horan Hotel. The family friends were notable when their youngest son, Walter, married Helen Barden in August of 1958. The newlyweds received a large amount of gifts, and lots of people were invited to the church wedding in Georgetown. The reception was held at the Army and Navy Club in Washington DC. Helen's father was a retired army colonel.

The Horans' social life was very active. They were out to dinner several days a week. Mr. Horan was a member of the Congressional and Burning Tree Country clubs, where he played golf and cards and conducted some business.

On certain occasions, I was invited to go with them to dinners or receptions. I had an opportunity to meet all the cabinet secretaries from President Eisenhower's administration, President Eisenhower's son, and the president's brother, the director of the CIA. I was introduced as their fifth "son." With their permission, I called Mr. Horan Dad, and his wife, Sally,

"Nagymama," Hungarian for *grandmother*.[13] I felt that I was accepted when I became the fifth "son." All of a sudden, I had four new *brothers* and a *sister*.

On one occasion, I was invited to a reception for the vice president and Mrs. Richard M. Nixon held at the Republican Women's Congressional Club. Going through the reception line, I was introduced to the vice president; with my accent and broken pronunciation, I thanked him for his help and told the vice president that because of him, I was in this country. He wanted to know more about it; he indicated that later we would continue this conversation. When the reception was over, one of his aides tapped me on the shoulder and indicated that the vice president wanted to see me. By then, I was a little bit more collected. I explained to the vice president that after his return from Austria, visiting the Hungarian refugees in late 1956 and his report to President Eisenhower, it resulted to the president increasing the immigration quotas by 6,500 for the Hungarian refugees. I was one of those 6,500 refugees. He was very interested in what I had to say. We were interrupted several times by other well-wishers. The vice president asked one of his aides to find a room where we won't be interrupted. A short time later, the aide returned. The only room he could find was an oversized janitor's closet. So the two of us continued our conversation there. He was very interested and asked lots of questions about Hungary and the Hungarian people. He wanted to know more about me and my past. The conversation lasted about thirty minutes. I had the opportunity, on another occasion, to see him again. He recognized me and asked how I was doing, and we had several minutes of conversation. On both occasions, I found him to be a very informed, very pleasant, personable, very caring, warm, and down-to-earth person.

---

[13]   *Nagymama* is pronounced *"Nodgmama."*

The Horan's were a very caring, family-oriented people, which reminds me of my family. They celebrated holidays, birthdays, and anniversaries together with the extended families, the sons-in-law and their families, and sometimes with the office staff from Capitol Hill.

In this gathering, we had as many as twenty to twenty-four adults and two to four children. In one of these occasions—which was celebrating my nineteenth birthday—I met the sister of Del Harold's wife, sister, the shy thirteen-year-old Jean Sanders.

Several years later, the summer when she graduated from high school, before she left for college, we went out the first time; we had dinner at the Roma Restaurant on Connecticut Avenue. We were seated outside in the courtyard underneath the arbor with hanging grapes. I think we had shish kebab. I found her attractive, but very insecure, and still a shy person; but we had a good time. Walking back to the car, we stopped in front of a furniture store, and each of us were to select what type of furniture each of us liked. The next time I saw Jean again was in a church on her wedding day in 1966.

When President Eisenhower delivered his last State of the Union speech in front of the joint session of Congress, I was sitting in the House Gallery, two seats away from Mrs. Mamie Eisenhower. It was an honor; I was very excited, and it was an overwhelming experience to be an observer of how the democracy worked. Be part of our history. This picture was published in the *Life* magazine; unfortunately, I don't have a copy of it.

John Foster Dulles, the secretary of state, passed away. He lay in state in the Washington Cathedral in Washington DC. I went there to give my last respect. I heard a lot about him from the Western news broadcast in Hungary. He was the most traveled secretary of state this country ever had at the time. He served one of the hardest and most difficult times in the world history, during the cold war with the Soviet Union.

On August 31, 1959, I applied for the *declaration of intention.* It is part of the process to become a U.S. citizen.

On December 17, 1959, I volunteered and signed up to join the U.S. Army Reserve for six years. The tour consisted of six months active duty, followed by five years and six months reserve training. I took my military medical examination in the Pentagon.

My Father retired on December 31, 1959, after his sixty-fifth birthday, but he secured a contract and continued to work in the same office till December 1964 to the age of seventy. His retirement income was small for him and everyone in his generation; the years for retirement started from 1945 after the end of the Second World War. The working years before that didn't count. Specifically for him, the years for retirement started from fall of 1947 when he began work after recuperating from his stomach surgery for ulcer. I started supporting my family in 1957 when I sent home the first package from the Austrian refugee camp. My support is continuing today by providing all my sister's living expenses. My sister is over sixty years old; she is mentally slow. She only worked eight years in her life, and you have to have ten years of employment to receive retirement or any support from the government.

I made a reference in an earlier chapter that my Father's friend and his sixteen-year-old son, when they lived in Tehran, were sent to a labor camp in Siberia. Several years after the war ended, they were released from the Soviet labor camp, and they returned to Iran. The son's name is Ernö (Ernest) Kurucz. My parents found out from his mother in Hungary that he immigrated to this country with his wife, Rozi, and with their daughter, Magda. They lived in New Rochelle, New York. Upon receiving this information, I got in touch with them; on the first opportunity, I drove up to New Rochelle to meet them. We became good friends; I spend a lot of weekends and holidays with them. They took me to Coney Island, several times we visited New York City, and on one occasion, we celebrated New Year's Eve in Times Square. It is a once-in-a-lifetime experience, all those people in one place at the same time. Ernö and Rozi in 1959 had a son, Peter; they asked me if I'd like to be his godfather, which I accepted. I taught him how to play chess when he was very young; he was a fast learner, and in no time, he beat me. In the later years, he became a chess master, competing in nationwide chess competitions. He joined the ROTC program, received a scholarship, and graduated as an aeronautical engineer. After graduation, he joined the air force. He retired as a major in 2002 from his last assignment in the Pentagon. He was part of the team that negotiated disarmament with the Russians. He is married; his wife's name is Eileen, and they have three children: Jim and Doug—the twins, and Clair. Peter and his family lives in Northern Virginia. His father, Ernö, and his mother, Rozi, are living in Florida.

In the last thirty-two months, I felt I'd grown and matured a lot with the help and guidance of the Horan's, my new adoptive parents. I felt I was now belonging to this country, and I could call it my home now. The people who had the privilege to be born in this country, they don't know how lucky they are.

I am with the Horan's.

My first picture in the United States, July 1957.

My family I left behind.

My sister, sixteen; Mother, fifty-three; and Father, sixty-two years old.

They sent me this picture for my nineteenth birthday.

Picture was taken in Budapest, Hungary, May 1957.

My first car, Studebaker
Land Cruiser, 1954.

A cartoon of my parents congratulating me for my first car.
Reaching over the Atlantic Ocean.
Chevy Chase, Maryland, USA, Dunakeszi, Hungary, 1958.

I am twenty-one, Washington DC, 1959

My sister Gisela's visit with her family.
Summer of 1958.

Standing (*left to right*): Sandy *(William Alexander Campbell, PhD, Gisela's husband)* Harold, Del Horan, Christian Oesch *(my sister's son)*, Oma *(Gisela's mother)*, myself, Dad, Nagymama, Helen Grindol.
Sitting (*left to right*): Gisela *(my sister)*, Joan Horan, Andy *(Andrew W. Campbell, my nephew)*

VII

The Turbulent '60s

I started my active duty in the U.S. Army on January 24, 1960. (My service number is BR 13652558.) The basic combat training took place in the U.S. Army Training Center, Armor Fort Knox, Kentucky, by Louisville. I was assigned to the Third Platoon, Company A, Tenth Battalion, Fourth Training Regiment. The training consisted of classroom lectures; firing range with M1 rifle; first aid; field fortification; camouflage; chemical, biological, and radiological warfare (CBR); and close combat. I participated in military drills, marches, and bivouacs.[14] One cold winter night, I was scheduled to guard the "Bullions Deposit Building." It was so cold and windy that the usual four-hour shift was reduced to two hours. Holding the bottom metal part of the M1 rifle, my hand, through the double gloves, froze to it. Before the guard duty, I showered; I think some water stayed in my ear. Ever since, I've had a draining problem in my ear. On March 26, 1960, I graduated from basic training in Fort Knox, Kentucky, and received the rifle marksman award for rifle firing.

During the training in Fort Knox, I befriended John Plater Jr. who is from Washington DC. We were in the same platoon, and he was also a volunteer, a pleasant, hardworking person with a degree in pharmacology. His service number was one digit higher than mine. We had the same unit assignment

---

[14]　I have the "training yearbook" from Fort Knox. In the book, my picture is in several locations.

101

in Texas. I suggested that we drive together in my car. He was not very receptive to the idea and did not explain why. He is an African American.

When I returned home, it was explained to me about the segregated south, the separate hotels, bathrooms, restaurants, and so on. It was a big surprise and eye-opener for me—about the "other side" of this country and its people. It was hard to believe these prejudices; this was not the way I was raised. In the end, I drove alone and took his duffel bag with me.

I spent a week at home in Chevy Chase before I reported to the U.S. Army Medical Training Center, Brooke Army Medical Center, Fort Sam Houston, Texas, by San Antonio. I was assigned to the First Battalion, Company D. First, I received a medical specialist training (MOS 911.1) as a basic nurse in the hospital. Then as a combat first aid provider with a lot of classroom and field classes and field training. For training, we watched movies for days, showing treatments for different types of injuries and surgeries from different field hospitals from the Korean War. These movies sometimes lasted five to six hours each. During the time, when they were showing the movies, we could not leave the room; some of the trainees fainted because of the subject.

Unlike in Kentucky, the temperature here was very hot, like the tropics. Our uniforms were shorts, short-sleeved shirts, and a tropical hat. At times, it was so hot that you could fry an egg on the concrete sidewalk.

The saying in the army, "hurry up and wait," is true. Many times, we had time to spare when we hurried to a place, and then we stood on the street or sat in the shade and waited for our next class or the next assignment. This was the time when I started smoking; the army provided us free cigarettes. Many of my buddies did the same thing. I smoked for almost forty years; the habit was hard to break, but after several tries, I stopped smoking in January 23, 2000.

I met new people and we became friends. When we got passes, we went to San Antonio to see the Alamo, took trips to Nuevo Laredo, Mexico, to see a bullfight, or to Austin, Texas, to see the capitol building and the sites.

In our last trip to Mexico, we bought several different bottles of alcohol. At the army base, we kept the bottles in my parked car's trunk. No alcohol was allowed in the barracks. One day, it was so hot that the bottles exploded from the heat; it made a big mess. It took a long time to clean up. I had to wash the contents off the trunk. It was where I kept my nonmilitary, civilian clothes.

Approximately seventy bottles were broken. In addition to mine, almost everybody from the barrack had some bottles in my car.

We graduated on June 23, 1960, from the U.S. Army Medical Training Center, Brooke Army Medical Center, Fort Sam Houston, Texas. We were discharged at one minute after midnight. We decided that the three of us, Vincent, Ted—my two new friends—and I, will drive back in my car to Washington DC. We arrived in Chevy Chase on June 27. From here, Vincent took a train to New York City and Ted, to Boston, where they lived. Since then, we periodically kept in touch. Vincent is now a parole officer in New York City, and Ted is a vice president for an insurance company in Boston.

At home, the army reserve unit I was assigned to—the Maus-Warfield USAR Center located in Rockville, Maryland—was the 472nd Medical Detachment (supply). My assignment was a medical specialist (MOS 911.1, later 910.00, then 767.10). The reserve training was for five and a half years, and it took place in the Center. We met every Wednesday for two hours in the evening, one weekend a month, and three weeks in the summer, assigned to different military training camps.[15] In time, with training and several promotions, my last assignment in the unit was a medical supply sergeant (E-5). During the Vietnam War in 1965, my reserve unit was put

---

[15]   Fort A.P. Hill, Camp Pickett, Virginia; Fort Indiantown Gap Military Reservation Annville, Pennsylvania; New Cumberland Army Depot, Pennsylvania; Fort Myer, Virginia; Fort George G. Meade, Maryland.

on a twenty-four-hour notice for activation. I sold my car and notified my landlord on the pending possibility. I arranged space for storage for my furniture. Then for several months, nothing happened. During this time, some of my friends provided transportation for me to my office.

I was honorably discharged from the Army of the United States as a sergeant E5 on December 10, 1965. I was told later that my reserve unit, the 472nd Medical Detachment, was activated and sent to Vietnam six weeks after I was discharged.

I was interested in this country's history. I asked Dad a lot of questions in evenings when everything was relatively quiet. Some evenings, he received several business-related calls at home. I learned a lot from him about this country's past and the constitution and the separation of the state and church. This subject was close to his heart because of the Catholic Church and his Irish ancestry. Because of the religious persecution, his father had to leave Ireland when he was a teenager. He left Ireland alone and settled in the Northwest Territories and became a Presbyterian.

He believes that today, some priests and ministers are hiding behind their collars to advance their political beliefs and are not spreading the Gospel, which is what they are supposed to do. He strongly believes the state should stay out of religion and the church should stay out of politics. We have many similar conversations, including international politics.

In the evenings, we watched television together; the Horan's favorite shows are *Gun Smoke*, *Ed Sullivan*, and *Jack Benny*. They also liked Jackie Gleason, Art Carney, and Jean Meadows in the *Honeymooners*.

This was my first presidential election (1960). The Republican Party was represented by Vice President Richard M. Nixon and the Democratic Party, by John F. Kennedy, a senator from Massachusetts, the first Catholic presidential candidate in the nation's history. I found it very interesting and educational to see how the process works. The presidential campaign was sometimes heated with different concerns and accusations about the candidates and their past, but the campaign was civilized. They had the first televised presidential debate.

The Horan's flew out to the West Coast, to Wenatchee, Washington, for their campaign. He was representing the Fifth District in the U.S. Congress. They asked me to drive their car to Wenatchee. I started my trip in early August. My plan was to spend some days in Yellowstone National Park. Unfortunately, early in my trip in Pennsylvania, close to Pittsburgh under the mountain in Laurel Hill Tunnel on a two-lane highway, an oncoming tractor-trailer's tire exploded with a loud sound and jackknifed. Several cars from both directions crashed into the track or into the tunnel wall. I ran into a car in front of me, and a car ran into me from the back.

My car was towed to a gas station in a nearby small town. The station was owned and operated by a father and son, without any other help. My car repair took several weeks. For parts, they had to drive to the city. They also had some previously accepted repair work to do, and one of them had to pump gas. To help them out, I volunteered to pump the gas without compensation. This gave me an opportunity to talk and meet other people and listen to their comments on the upcoming presidential election, which was a popular subject this time. In the evenings, I replanned my remaining trip without stopping over and spending time in Yellowstone Park. The plan was to drive four hours and rest for one and to drive through Chicago at night.

At the end of ten days, the car was ready. I followed my plan to drive twenty-four hours straight ending up in Fargo, North Dakota, just over the Minnesota border. I spent the night there. On the next two nights, I spent in Billings and then Missoula, Montana, close to the Idaho border. Before driving over the mountains, the police inspected the car in a roadblock for its worthiness for the winding, steep, and slippery roads ahead. The countryside was so beautiful; at times, I stopped by the roadside and enjoyed the big open spaces to see the sunset over the mountain, the rolling hills, and the gold-colored countryside before the harvest. I was glad I had this opportunity to see this big beautiful country. Throughout my trip, I ate at truck stops. They had a reputation to have good inexpensive food, and I had the opportunity to listen to the truck drivers' conversation and get a cross-country opinion of the people's concerns about the candidates and the election. The next day, I arrived at Spokane, Washington, where the Horan's were waiting for me. From here, we drove to Wenatchee, to their home. My arrival was announced in the local newspaper with a photograph showing me turning over the car key to the Horan's. The trip, not counting the delays because of the car accident, was an unforgettable, beautiful six days.

During my stay in Wenatchee, Mike Horan, the oldest son, took me to the *Horan Brothers* orchard. The orchard was located on the bank of the Columbia River; they also had a *"cold house"* on the property where they stored the fruit. I helped Mike to load a truck for shipment.

On one campaign trip, Dad showed me his dream and pride, the Grand Coulee Dam, which provided public power and irrigation for that part of the country. It was an overwhelming structure that provided a magnificent view when we drove over it.

I participated in the campaign. During his campaign speeches, Dad used short stories about his family or about himself or jokes and sometimes one-liners. In the later years, President Reagan made it to an art form. On some days, we started so early in the morning that it was still dark outside to attend a Grangers'—local farmer's organization—meeting. At one of these campaign rallies, I was asked to say a few words on "the living conditions in Hungary before the uprising." It lasted about fifteen minutes, with a big response and with lots of follow-up questions. This was the first speech of my life. I stayed in Wenatchee for three weeks and returned by plane. After returning to Washington DC, for many months I received "fan mail." Helen Grindle Fuchs from Dad's office wrote the response. I hope that in a small way, I contributed to this campaign and to Dad's reelection.

The campaigns were based more on substance and who was the better person to represent the people in the district, then on which party the person was affiliated with. For my effort in driving the car to Wenatchee, the Horan's gave me a portable stereo record player, which I still have.

The campaign was over. The 1960 election results were in. Dad won his ninth term in the U.S. Congress, and our new president was John F. Kennedy. This was one of the closest presidential elections in history to date. The president won by a majority of the popular vote by one-tenth of half of 1 percent, the narrowest margin of the century. President Kennedy was the first Catholic and the youngest president. His opponent, Vice President Richard M. Nixon, conceded the election late, the next day. He was not standing on a street corner in Washington DC and making speeches and encouraging his followers to riot like Vice President Albert Gore did when he lost his presidential election in year 2000. Vice President Gore was and is a sore loser. Mr. Nixon was a dignified person. He and his followers accepted the majority of the people's decision even if it was a very small majority. They did not hold a grudge against the duly elected president like some of the Democrats after the 2000 presidential election.

During my stay with the Horan's, I tried to make myself useful by helping around the house, cutting grass with a push mower, and helping out with the yard work when Frank, the caretaker, was not available. On one occasion, I had to find a way to stop the water from seeping into the recreation room on the lower level every time it rained. After exhausting every possibility to stop the water penetration from the outside on the surface, I dug a trench adjacent to the house, down to the foundation, put in gravel, and installed perforated drain tiles on top of it to divert the water from the house. This solved the problem, and the water stopped seeping into the house. After the walls inside were dry, Harold and his wife, Del, and Walter Jr. and his wife, Helen, had a painting party to paint the room and, in the process, painted one another.

In the past three and a half years, I saved my money with the hope that someday I would have my own place, my own apartment. I liked living here, but I didn't want to abuse my adoptive parents' generosity. In addition to my credit cards, I took out a personal loan for $300 for a six-month duration from my bank, the National Bank of Washington, to establish good credit rating. I found a nice one-bedroom apartment close by in the Rock Creek Gardens apartment complex at 2223 Washington Avenue, Apartment 201, Silver Spring, Maryland. In the small shopping center in this complex was the dry cleaner, which the Horan's and I used. This was about a five-minute drive from the Horan's home. I knew the neighborhood. The three-story apartment buildings were very nice, well maintained, and with a lot of mature trees. The rent was $88 for a month,[16] including electricity with a one-window air-conditioner unit; the apartment was heated with radiators. I moved in on February 1, 1961, and lived there till March 1965. I used the money I saved to furnish the apartment. The bedroom had a sofa bed to make it look like a study, with desk, dresser, and several bookcases, which I made. Living and dining areas consisted of one big room, dining table with chairs in the dining area, royal blue sofa, two dark red armchairs, two end tables, a coffee table, gray rugs, and curtains. I bought it from a "model home." Some of the furniture I bought on the moving sale. In the kitchen, I added a small table that I still have and a storage unit for the pantry.

---

[16]   I have the apartment lease and some of the furniture.

I enjoyed decorating and living in my first apartment. The apartment had a concrete sub floor, with finished wood flooring. The walls separating the units were masonry. My apartment was on the second floor, a corner unit. The bedroom windows overlooked a nice courtyard. Soon after I moved in, Harold and his wife, Del, with their young daughter, Jennifer, moved in across the street in the same complex. I did some babysitting when they went out. When the baby was too restless and Harold had a lot of studying to do, he came over and studied in my apartment. When they moved to Pittsburgh to attend the seminary, I helped them move with one of their friends, Bill Jebram.

Around this time, I bought a sailboat with a trailer, jointly with a friend; we kept it in the Washington Sailing Marina on Daingerfield Island, Virginia. The sailboat was a racing-boat class "Jet 14." The boat was fourteen feet long made from fiberglass. The mast rose up to twenty-three feet; it is a light fest boat. I learned to sail, and we sailed a lot on the Potomac River. The sailing was new to me, and I wanted to learn it and experience it. One year, we participated in the presidential regatta; it is held on the Potomac River every year. We came in second place in our class. On long weekends, several of us from the office got into a station wagon, and we drove to Rehoboth Beach; one of my coworker's parents had a summer place there and let us use it. Each time when I went, we took the boat with us and sailed it there. On some other occasions, we stopped at this side of the Chesapeake Bay in a marina and sailed across the bay. It was scary sometimes when we had to dodge the big ocean liners. After some years later when the fun and excitement was over, I sold the boat; it was a good, exciting, and learning experience.

Early in 1962, two of my coworkers in Jack C. Cohen's office, Terry Horowitz and Walter Seigel, left. They opened their architectural office as Horowitz & Seigel Associates Architects Inc. located in Georgia Avenue in Washington DC, close to the Maryland line. The office was located in a small two-story office building in the second floor. They asked me to join them as a manager of production, and in a short time later, I become an associate. I started work there in March of 1962. The office designed single-family homes, office and apartment buildings, and a church. In the ground level of the building is Ted Lerner's real estate company. About this time, he started to develop properties. I befriended Ted's younger brother Larry, who had just dropped out of college and was now employed by his brother. Ted put him in charge of an approximately 140-unit single-family housing subdivision. The project was in both sides of the future Beltway, which was under construction in Maryland. Larry lacked contractor's experience. I offered my help, and every weekend, we prepared the next week's work schedule and reviewed the construction and the progress on the site with Larry. We did this for many months. Ted was pleased with Larry's work and the end result. Ted and Larry Lerner developed and owned Wheaton Plaza, White Flint Mall, Landover Mall, Tyson's I & II, and several office and apartment buildings with thousands of units. Years later when I had my own architectural office, they employed us as one of their architects for several of their projects. I worked in the Horowitz & Seigel Associates office till February of 1965.

About this time, my parents' water well in their home dried up. They had to carry in the water in the bucket from the public pump down the street, two blocks away. It was hardship for them. Shortly after that, the government installed the water pipe on their street. I paid for the connection to the house, and they deducted part of the cost each month from their rent.

It was five years since I had been a resident of this country. Now I could apply for citizenship. On June 24, 1962, I did just that. It took the Immigration and Naturalization Service more than two years to process my papers. The justice department told us later that the reason it took so long was because one of the departments lost my file. When the department moved, they found it behind a filing cabinet. The interview and the test were in Baltimore, in the federal building. Nagymama came with me to provide moral support. I studied hard; I had to learn a lot about the government of the United States, the constitution, the Bill of Rights, the Declaration of Independence, and how the state and local governments functioned. I did not want to fail.

On November 13, 1964, I became a U.S. citizen. Nagymama and Dad were there with me and also the staff from his office. At the ceremony, I received a small flag and a booklet about this country, which I cherish. This document also legally changed my name to *Karl J.* Landesz. I cannot describe the sensation I felt. Now I had a country where I belonged and call it my home. I was without a country for so many years. The Hungarian government took away my citizenship and for all the persons who left Hungary in the late 1956 and 1957 because we were "criminals" and "traitors" by leaving Hungary. I am now the citizen of the greatest nation of the world. I received congratulatory letters from Congressman Carlton R. Sickles of Maryland; the governor of Maryland, J. Millard Tawes; and Thomas B. Finan, attorney general of Maryland.

On the accession of my parents' twenty-fifth wedding anniversary on July 10, 1962, I found a way through an agency to send them a television. In Hungary, it was considered to be a luxury to have one in your home. The broadcast was only a couple hours a day. They were very excited and happy about it. They had television before I had; I could not afford this type of expense at the same time. I bought my television later. It was also a custom in Hungary in this occasion for the couple to exchange a silver ring like a wedding band. After my Father's passing, my Mother gave me his silver ring; and it was attached to his prayer book that his mother gave to him when he was leaving to serve in World War I.

My nephew Roland Campbell, my sister Gisela's oldest son, was getting married to Jane "Jenny" Shillington in Atlanta, Georgia, on December 22, 1962. They met in Savannah, Georgia, where she lived; and Roland was stationed in Beaufort, South Carolina, in the marine base. I was the best man, and Jenny's maid of honor was her twin sister, Joan "Jo." After the honeymoon, they moved to Silver Spring, Maryland, where Roland started law school at Georgetown University. Jenny found employment on Capitol Hill in Dad's office. Joan "Jo" and I got along well. I found her very attractive. We decided to "correspond" by telephone and then followed up with my weekend trips by car to Atlanta several times a month. I would start driving after work on Friday, drive straight through the night, and arrive in Atlanta early Saturday morning. I leave on Sunday afternoon, get home early Monday morning, sleep a few hours, and be in the office by nine thirty in the morning. The trip took about twelve hours.

In April of 1963, Dad ended up in the hospital again for several weeks. During this time, the Horan's received an invitation to the White House for President Kennedy and the First Lady's reception on April 25. Mr. Horan was a Republican; he was a member of the Committee on Appropriations and the subcommittees of Agriculture, State, Justice, Commerce, and the Judiciary. He had been chairman of the District of Columbia Subcommittee. By this time, he was the most senior member in both parties west of Mississippi. You cannot turn down a presidential invitation to the White House. Nagymama attended, and I escorted her to the reception. That was my first time in the White House.

On April 25, we drove through the main entrance of the White House and stopped under the entry canopy. The marines took our car and parked it. An honor guard escorted us on a red carpet into the White House. When all the guests arrived, everyone lined up in the large hall where the stairs descended from the second floor, where the presidential living quarters were located. Everyone cheered when President Kennedy and the First Lady slowly walked down the stairs. At the bottom of the stairs, Vice President Johnson and his wife joined them. They proceeded to shake hands with every guest. The ladies were in beautiful evening gowns and gentlemen in black tuxedos. We were walking around and visiting every room on the main floor. The dining room was where the food was set up in one end; the bar was on the other end. The rooms were beautifully decorated, with lots of flowers in each room. The president and the first lady were very nice. Because of my accent, they asked me where I am from. We had a pleasant conversation. The following Christmas, I received a Christmas card from President Kennedy and the First Lady. The Christmas card was donated to the Wenatchee museum to be a part of the Horan exhibit and to be displayed there. In contrast, I found Vice President Johnson's behavior as unbelievable. He was a rough and a loud person; his Southern drawl echoed through the rooms. It was an opposite behavior to the dignified president and the first lady. I met Secretary of Defense Robert McNamara; we exchanged some words, then Nagymama showed me downstairs and the White House library. The reason Nagymama was familiar with the White House was because she spent a lot of time there in different occasions during the Eisenhower administration. I was very honored to be in the White House and with these honorable people, the leaders of the free world. That day was the experience of a lifetime. In the end, we drove home and the "fairy tale" was over.

In early July of 1963, Jo visited Washington DC from Atlanta for a week; she was staying with her sister. This was her first visit to this city. We went out every day; we had a good time together. After eight months of courtship, we got married on August 24, 1963, at the First Presbyterian Church on 1328 Peachtree Street, NE Atlanta, Georgia.

The minister of the church was the Reverend Harry A. Fifilld, PhD, a family friend of the Shillington's. He officiated the wedding. The reception was in a country club in Atlanta. We had our honeymoon at Myrtle Beach, South Carolina, in the Caravelle Motel on the beach. After the honeymoon, we settled in Silver Spring, Maryland, in my Washington Avenue apartment. Jo found employment in Washington DC with a company that investigates and reviews the black boxes used in the airplanes. This company was affiliated with all the airlines in the world. As a company benefit, employees were provided with free airline tickets anywhere in the world. We took advantage of this benefit several times by going to France and Hungary. We were very happy, working very hard, planning and saving for our future.

In the meantime, slowly I found out how dominating my mother-in-law was; she put a lot of pressure on her daughters.

On November 22, 1963, a shot in Dallas, Texas, echoed throughout the world when President Kennedy was assassinated. We were listening to the radio in the office when we were working. I was sitting at my drafting board and drawing when a bulletin in the radio reported that President Kennedy had been shot in Dallas. President Kennedy's motorcade rode through the streets of Dallas; sitting beside the president was his wife, Jacqueline. The motorcade was rushed to the hospital. The first information was very sketchy and with lot of confusions; then we were told that the president was dead, killed by an assassin's bullet. No one wanted to believe the news; all of us were numb. We stopped working, and we went home to our families and watched David Brinkley's television broadcast on the latest information and happenings. Vice President Lyndon B. Johnson was sworn in on Air Force One to be our next president; by his side was Mrs. Kennedy. President Kennedy's remains were returned in the same airplane with the new president to Washington

DC. He lay in state for two days in the rotunda of the nation's Capitol. The entire nation was stunned at the president's death. Because he was so young and vital, the people mourned him as they had never mourned for a president since Lincoln. President Kennedy's interment was in Arlington National Cemetery, Virginia.

The year was 1964, the presidential election year. President Johnson represented the Democratic Party, and the conservative Barry Goldwater, a senator from Arizona, the Republican Party. President Johnson was a seasoned and old-fashioned Southern Democrat from Texas with a reputation as a "smoke-filled backroom, arm-twisting" politician. He was annoyed when a "young, upstart" senator from Massachusetts was nominated at the 1960 Democratic Convention and not him. Mr. Johnson also was a presidential candidate and the Democratic leader of the U.S. Senate. He resented it that Senator Kennedy was nominated. Before and during this campaign, a lot of protests took place against the Vietnam War. His campaign did anything so that he be elected and be the next president on his own right. His campaign, in my opinion, to date, was the first campaign to mislead the public with his intention, with his words, with his actions, and with his advertisement. He campaigned on the side of peace in Vietnam, and when he was elected, he followed Senator Goldwater's campaign pledge and expanded the war. He started and set the foundation, and he was the "godfather" of future misleading campaigns and lies in the advertisement during the campaign. I have a problem with individuals who misrepresent things and out rightly lie for their own benefit and for their own personal gain.

The November 4, 1964, election results were in. Dad was defeated in the congressional election after twenty-two years in the U. S. House of Representatives representing Fifth District from Washington State. He was ill during the campaign. The person defeating him was Thomas S. Foley, a Democrat. Mr. Foley, in his book *Honor in the House,* made reference to his 1964 campaign.

> *One of the things that were interesting about it was that I had really found Walt and Sally Horan to be truly delightful people. Walt was a very warm and generous personality . . . . This was not a race to discredit a very popular, and deservedly popular, congressman who had served the district well. It was a race about an argument that, after twenty-two years of good service, the time had finally come for a change. So, I praised Walt Horan's record, which I thought was praise-worthy, and pointed out some differences. It was largely, a very positive campaign. He, in turn, said he'd known me, and my family, my father and mother, and that I was a fine young man.*

Following the election, Mr. Foley told the *Spokesman-Review,* "*I follow an incumbent of many years who has served with dignity and honor, and I wish to extend to him my high regards and best wishes.*" Horan issued a statement saying, in part, "*To the new man in Congress, Tome Foley, goes my sincere congratulation and best wishes for a successful session of Congress.*"

> Mr. Foley continued to say, *I was sworn in on the fourth of January 1965, and Walt came on the floor, which was quite unusual, and took me into both the Republican and Democratic cloakrooms and introduced me as his successor as if we were members of the same party. People were flabbergasted by it. I learned something interesting about Congress. I was received with greater equanimity in the Republican cloakroom then by some of the Democrats. People like Democrat John Rooney of Brooklyn, who had come to Congress with Walt, and served with him on the Appropriation Committee, viewed me as an enemy of his friend, and therefore, as his enemy.*

As I remember, Walt leaned down to this crusty, bald-headed, tough-minded Irish pol from Brooklyn, and I heard him whisper, "John, it's all right."

Years later, Mr. Foley was elected by his peers to be the Speaker of the House of Representatives in the U.S. Congress. After his retirement from the U.S. Congress, he was appointed by President Clinton to be the U. S. ambassador to Japan.

After the election, the Horan's returned to their Chevy Chase home. They asked me to design a house for them based on their needs, ideas, and requirements. They planned to build their retirement house in Wenatchee. They took with them the house plan I prepared for them on their next trip to Wenatchee. There they talked to some contractors and with a real estate agent who helped them find a new house with a similar floor plan.

After many farewell parties and reception given by friends, relatives, and his friends and colleagues in the House of Representatives, Dad and Nagymama moved back to Wenatchee on the summer of 1965. After settling in their new home, the following year they took a trip to Manila, Philippines, to visit their daughter Kaye and her family for Christmas. Dad got sick there and passed away in Manila on December 20, 1966. He was sixty-eight years old, born October 15, 1898, in Wenatchee, Washington. The funeral service was on March 12, 1967, two o'clock in the afternoon at the First Presbyterian Church in Wenatchee. The interment was in the Wenatchee Cemetery. I attended the service. In my adult life, this was the first family member I lost, my adoptive father to whom I am very grateful for the rest of my life. During my stay in Wenatchee, I shared a bedroom with Harold. In the morning, when I opened my eyes, I can see the top of the snow-covered Cascade Mountains from my bed. This was my first trip there since they returned to Wenatchee. It was interesting to see the similarity between this house's floor plan and the house plan I designed for them. During my stay, we visited a park in nearby Cashmere where all the old remaining log cabins from the surrounding areas were assembled and turned into a museum. It was called the *Pioneer Village*. One log cabin was called the Horan Cabin, where Dad was born. Other log cabins from the early days of the territory were all furnished with some original furniture. In the museum was an H-shaped branding iron that Mike Horan Sr., Dad's father, used on his cows and a lard can with the Horan name on it, which goes back to the days when Mike Horan Sr. owned a butcher shop. Nagymama was holding up well and looked good. She is "Nagymama" even now as she looked after everyone, assembled for this sad occasion. It was nice to see all the family again.

The U.S. Congress on August 17, 1999, passed Public Law 106-48 that the federal building and United States courthouse located in Spokane, Washington, shall be known and designated as the Thomas S. Foley United States Courthouse. The plaza where the courthouse was located shall be known and designated as the Walter F. Horan Plaza. *"Between them, Foley and Horan spend more than a half century in the House representing Eastern Washington . . . . They were lionized in person and by videotape by judges and current members of the state's congressional delegation* (from the *Spokesman-Review*). The dedications took place on April 6, 2001, with three hundred invited guests, including his daughter Kaye Horan Paauw, who represented the family; she gave a short speech. The invited guests included several of his grand—and great-grandchildren, as well as former ambassador Thomas S. Foley with his family.

In the past years, I sent the support money monthly to my parents, but during the early '60s, I changed it to quarterly with my parents' concurrence. When this change took place, they did not receive money from me for two months. The Hungarian secret police, known as the AVO, visited my parents, wanting to know what happened to me and why didn't I send the money. My Father explained to them that my support was changed to quarterly payments. They instructed him to write a letter and ask me to send the money immediately. If I did not comply with their request, then *"it will have serious consequences,"* they told my parents. The government desperately needed Western currency, specifically the U.S. dollar. The secret police read all incoming and outgoing mail. They knew if my parents relayed to me their request and their wishes. They censor your letters and cross out words if it is sensitive, in their opinion. I received a letter from my Father where he indicated his preference for the monthly support. I found out later the AVO visited my parents and that was the reason for his letter. This was everyday life over there then. The Communist government, through the secret police, controlled and knew everything about you. I continued to send my support every month; without it, their day-to-day living would be very difficult, if not impossible.

In late 1964, with one of my coworkers, Andy Supplee in Horowitz & Seigle's office, we decided to open our own architectural office. We invited Andy's old classmate from the Catholic University, Madis Valge, to be our partner. We named the office Madis Valgi Associates, Architect AIA and opened our doors for business on March 1, 1965, at 850 Sligo Avenue, Silver Spring, Maryland. We put $10,000 together to establish a credit rating with Dunn & Bradstreet. We had no specific projects when we started, but each of us had contacts and a reputation to perform fast and provide good work. My assignment was to line up work and to maintain the office books, and also to do drafting. In a short time, we got our first project, a housing subdivision. Larry Lerner came through with several projects for us. We designed for the Lerners a high-rise apartment building in Alexandria and second floor additions to Hecht and Woodward & Lothrup Department Stores in Tysons Corner Shopping Center in McLean,

Virginia. We also worked on the Landover Mall in Maryland and on several housing subdivision projects in Maryland and in Virginia. We were busy in no time. We also got contracts to do master plans for a small fishing ship factory in Japan and for the proposed Jean Dixon Children's Hospital and Medical Complex and a large shopping center in Florida. After the 1964 riots in Washington DC, we did building survey with police escort and prepared reconstruction drawings for the insurance companies and for the owners of the burned down and scorched buildings on Georgia Avenue and Fourteenth Street.

We were lucky to get work so fast because none of our families had contacts in the industry. In this business, it was important who you know; the competition was high. Andy was single, a hard worker, does very nice work. He was from this area, from a middle-class family. Madis and his parents came from Estonia. They left before the Soviet occupation; his father was a furniture carpenter. Madis had two brothers—structural and electrical engineers. He was married with two children. His wife was a teacher. And then there was me—the new refugee. We worked well together; our staff increased to seven architects and a secretary. My time was divided to three parts: one-third to get a job, one-third to do the work, and one-third to collect the fee. We had some slow-paying clients. I was restless and impuissant. The office was not moving as fast in the direction I would like it to be. I wanted to try some other things.

The anticipation that our office would do even better and Jo's substantial pay increases for her good performance at work made possible a move to a better, larger, and nicer place. The apartment complex was under construction, consisting of several four—and five-story buildings, with a swimming pool, basketball and tennis courts, and a putting green. The complex was located in Adelphi, Maryland; our new home was located at 1830 Metzeratt Road, Apartment 22. We moved in on April 1, 1965, and lived there till May of 1967.

The apartment had two large bedrooms and two bathrooms and central air-conditioning and heating. The kitchen had a dishwasher and disposal and a large balcony off the living room. Our apartment was on the second floor from the front, and the third floor from the back of the building was overlooking a small park with a playground and with mature trees. We furnished the apartment very nicely. We wanted to have a nicer place because we invited my sister, Maria, from Hungary to visit us.

At the same time, Jo and I were planning my first trip to Hungary since my escape in 1956. The reason I could return now was because the Hungarian parliament reclassified the 1956 refugees, and they were not "traitors" and "criminals" anymore. At the same time, they reinstated the refugees' citizenship. It was taken away in 1957. So now we can return to Hungary with no harm to us. The Hungarian government needed Western currency for international trade, and the best way for the government to get the money was for the refugees from 1956 to return and visit their families after eight years. When applying for entry visa, everyone had to buy ten days of hotel room coupons, even when you were staying with your family. You had to register with the police within twenty-four hours after your arrival, and you received temporary identification card for the duration of your stay. We were skeptical, and with Dad's help, we contacted the Hungarian desk in the State Department for information regarding my return trip to Hungary on what we could expect during our visit there. We got cases but somewhat a positive answer. Then we applied for visa and started our trip in late spring of 1965. This was Jo's first trip outside the USA. Our first stop was Paris. We stayed for a week in a small hotel downtown. We were very busy during our short stay. We visited the National Opera House, Notre Dame Cathedral. At the cathedral, in one of the towers was a narrow stairs leading to the roof. I climbed up to the outside roof area and took close-up pictures of the gargoyles and the sculptures decorating the exterior. The cathedral was built on the Roman temple's site. The construction started in 1163, and it lasted about 250 years. We walked in Paris at night to see the famous City of Lights. We took a walk on the beautiful Avenue des Champs-Élysées to see the chestnut tress in bloom. We took the elevator ride up in the Eiffel Tower to the top observation area and visited the Arc de Triomphe and the Louvre. In the Louvre, we found my brother-in-law William Alexander Campbell's excavation from the ancient Syrian city of Antioch; it is on a permanent exhibit there. One evening, we saw a show in a dinner nightclub. We visited unique small stores and ate fresh French bread with cheese and wine for lunch in a park. We took a side trip to visit Versailles, the royal summer palace, and walk in the garden where Marie Antoinette and Napoleon Bonaparte walked. The Versailles was restored after the Second World War with the Rockefellers' help.

We left Paris on May 28 and flew to Budapest. Going through the customs there, I was very nervous. Not because of the procedures we had to go through, but because of my parents waiting on the other side of the door. How they will look after eight years and how they will react and if they would like Jo.

I found out in the past six months that my Father has prostate cancer, and he retains excessive amount of water in his body. When we came through the doors, I saw my parents were waiting for us with flowers. When our eyes met, tears got in our eyes. When I left in 1956, we thought we would never see one another again. I saw that my parents showed the time, which has passed more than I anticipated. My Father was a thin, slender person then; and now it appears he gained a lot of weight, but it was all water in his system. Also waiting for us in the airport were my aunt and uncle, Zsuzsa and Nándi. I spent the last night with them in Budapest before I left in 1956. We took a taxi to Dunakeszi, the northern suburb of Budapest, where my parents lived. In their home, everything looked so nice. They outdid themselves for our visit. It was nice to see my old home again. We had my Mother's home-cooked dinner. I ate very slowly, wanting to enjoy every bit of her meal after all these years. After dinner, Jo and I returned to Budapest where we spent the nights. In advance, I rented a room from Uncle Nándi's sister. This way, we had more privacy, and I could spend some time with Jo, and she won't feel left out as much.

I rented a car for two weeks. During that time, we were very busy. We arranged for a professional photographer to take a family portrait and individual pictures of all of us. Later, the photographer's shop window displayed Jo's picture for over a year. Every time my parents were in Budapest, they made an extra effort to visit that window to see Jo's picture.

Now the Hungarian government allowed private small businesses to exist; it was limited to one-person operation and ownership. The spouses and their children could help in the business, but no employees were allowed. In the past, the government owned everything. This was a big step; it was considered a big freedom at the time. During our walk when we were sightseeing in the city, I found a small jewelry store, the size of a large elevator cab, where some silver jewelry were displayed. After looking at it closer and talking to the owner, an older gentleman, I decided to buy several pieces. Later, I found out the bracelets and necklaces were made of old silver battens and decorations from old military officers' uniforms—the *Huszár's* from 1840s. (The Huszárs are the old Hungarian cavalrymen).

This was Jo's first time in Hungary. I wanted to introduce her to the family, but we didn't have time to visit every one of them. To remedy the problem, I invited everyone to dinner in a well-known restaurant named Gundel. This restaurant only catered to foreigners. Here, you can order the kind of food that a public didn't see and could not purchase in the stores. All the forty-six invited guests showed up from both sides of the family. We had a private room with one long table. The American and Hungarian flags graced the table with several flower arrangements. At the end of the room was a small gypsy orchestra. The seating was so arranged that next to Jo were seated some of the English-speaking relatives, including my cousin Öcsi's wife, Hajnalka. She told Jo during the conversation that she was expecting Cicka. We were the first in the family to find out the good news. This seating arrangement gave me the opportunity to visit everyone. I was trying to catch up with the happenings in the extended family in the past eight years. The dinner lasted over five hours. We had a five-course dinner. Everyone could order what he or she wanted. Before, during, and after dinner, we had wine, beer, or soda water. In the end, we had a big selection of dessert and espresso. We consumed three cases of beer, four cases of wine, and a case of soda water. The service was excellent; the staff brought the food to the serving waiter. Every four guests had a serving waiter; they stood behind you about three feet away. In this kind of exclusive restaurant, each waiter had to speak a minimum of two other languages besides Hungarian. We had a good time; the food was excellent. Many of my guests had not been in a restaurant for fifteen or so years. For them, restaurants were so expensive, they could not afford it. I paid about the same amount for all these food, drinks, including the tip here as I paid in Paris ten days ago for two of us in the dinner nightclub at *Mole-Rouse*.

My Father tried to come with us when we went sightseeing; he had to use the toilet facilities a lot because of his illness. He took us to the area in Budapest where he lived and grew up to show it to Jo. This was in the Castle District in Buda of Budapest. As children, we visited this every year and spent a lot of time here with my Father.

During the same time when we were in Hungary, the city of Budapest had a world exhibit. All the major industrial countries were invited. United States also participated. I took my parents and aunt and uncle to see the exhibits. In front of the U.S. pavilion, the line was so long you had to stand in line for several hours before you could get in. I did not want to stand in line. I went directly to the entrance of the building; I showed my passport to the guard. He suggested we try to go in by the exit. He told me last time he let someone in, in turn he had a small riot in his hand. At the exit, the police let us in. The corridor was lined wall to wall with people. Slowly we tried to move forward against the people who were trying to exit. At the same time, I was explaining what was exhibited in each location. Very few signs were provided to explain the items that were exhibited. All of a sudden, we couldn't move forward; it turned out the exiting people turned around and followed us and listened to what I had to say. They were so eager to understand and learn what was exhibited. We were asked to leave. We ended up not seeing the majority of the indoor exhibit. Outside by the exit was a large clearing. It was roped with lots of people around it, and in the middle, several Chrysler, GM, and Ford cars were exhibited. The distance between the people and the cars was a hundred to a hundred fifty feet. I also tried to get next to the cars; with my passport it worked. The guard let us in. By the cars was a person from the Sates; he let my parents sit in the cars. He and I started talking, and he explained the lack of signs on the U.S. exhibit. The reason was that the Communist government did not want the United States to overshadow the Russian exhibits.

In anticipation of my sister's visa application, I took my parents to the American embassy in Budapest to inquire what documents and information we needed and how long it took for her visa application. To my surprise, the embassy staff were informed about my visit to Hungary. When I introduced myself at the front desk, the receptionist made a phone call. We were asked to wait; in a few minutes, we were escorted to a large nicely furnished room. Then a gentleman appeared and escorted us to the ambassador's office. We were treated with coffee and dessert. We had a long conversation about my parents and my visit. After leaving the ambassador's office, we stopped by the library, borrowed the *Look* and *Life* magazines for my parents to see, and in the PX store where I bought some chocolate and tropical fruit.

I found out upon arriving home to Washington that the Horan's were concerned about my visit to Hungary. Through his friends in the State Department, they notified the embassy of my trip. They had the complete transcript of the conversation and what had taken place during our visit in the embassy in Hungary. By this time, Dad was not a member of the House of Representatives, but he had lots of friends.

After seeing what my parents needed, we went to the only self-service food store in Budapest for grocery shopping. Only baskets were available in the store. This was the first visit for them to this type of store. I went through every aisle and filled up four baskets with different types of canned and dry goods, sugar, flour, salt, and different brandies and several bottles of different good wine. At the cashier, everyone was amazed at the quantity of my purchases and asked me when I was ready to pay, "which bank I robbed and when," because the bill was so high for them. We had to pack it ourselves. I did not know that you had to bring your own bag. Finally, the manager of the store found some bags and gave it to us. When we got home, my Father displayed the brandy and wine bottles at the top of his bookcase, savoring the moments of his "wealth."

In the meantime, we found out that the Hungarian government rejected my sister's application for the passport. No reason was given, but through the grapevine, we learned that the local comrade, the commissar, gave a negative recommendation to the Hungarian Interior Ministry Police, the AVO, about my sister. The reason was of her lack of interest in his lectures on Communism in my parents' home. She was not willing to sit through his two hours of brainwashing lectures every several months. Unfortunately, there was no appeal.

On the last day before we left on June 15, my Mother informed me of my Father's true condition. He was diagnosed with prostate cancer several years ago, but they did not want to tell me before because they were not sure I could come home. If not, then I would just worry about it.

Hungary had free social Medicare. The rules at the time for a person with cancer was that the medicine was rationed from the day of diagnosis. The patient received a limited amount of painkiller medication and limited dose of morphine in the end. My Mother asked if I could send medication even if it was Bayer aspirin. It was better than what he was getting then. Then he didn't have to start using his allotment. I promised I would do everything to provide what he needed.

Another government rule was if the person was being terminally ill, like cancer, and needed hospitalization, the government would only provide a dormitory room with twenty to twenty-five patients in a room, with one nurse to care for all the patients. My Mother told me she would not let this happen to my Father, to end up in a place like that. It would be very depressing for him and for everyone; she indicated she would take care of him at home till the end. It was very hard and sad to listen, talk, and think of my Father's future.

We ran out of time. Our stay was over; we had to leave. We had a good time. We were very happy that we were all together again, even for a short time.

My Father's condition was deteriorating. The medicine for pain I sent for him was not helping him anymore. He was too weak to see the doctor in his office. The doctor had to make house calls. The doctor's visit by law was free, but he only visited patients who paid him the most. In his district, he had too many patients. He was the only doctor, and he was selective of whom he visits. My Mother found out that he had two young children, and they liked chewing gum. I sent some; when the doctor visited my Father the next time, they asked him if he wanted money or chewing gum for payment; he selected the chewing gum. From here on, he got paid for each visit with a small pack of chewing gum. He never missed an appointment. I never paid so little for a doctor's visit anywhere anytime in my life.

In the meantime, in June 1967, we moved to 8107 Tahona Drive, Apartment 103 in Silver Spring, Maryland, close to the intersection of New Hampshire Avenue and University Boulevard and one block from the Langley Shopping Center. We lived here through July of 1973.

In the late summer of 1967, my Mother asked us if we could come home for a visit. My Father's condition was rapidly deteriorating. We again checked with the State Department. This time, the news was not good. The international politics between United States and the Soviet Union was different now. They anticipated that we will be searched and harassed. We decided to have separate passports; this way if I was detained, Jo can return. That time, you had the opportunity to have one passport for the family. We scheduled our trip for early September in 1967. We planned to have two weeks in Hungary with my family and the last week in Venice, and Rome, Italy. We traveled from Washington DC through New York with Pan American airlines to Vienna, Austria. For the excess weight, we sent a box air freighted in the same flight. It was gifts for my parents—what I saw they needed the last time we were there. We rented a Volkswagen "bug" in Vienna. On the way to the Austrian-Hungarian border, we stopped to buy some food and items you could not buy in Hungary, like Coca-Cola, orange, bananas, and so on. We were allowed to bring in to Hungary food for one week for ourselves.

Before we started our trip, we checked again with the State Department, and their prediction came true. At the Hungarian border, upon reviewing our passports, I was asked to move the car to the side in a remote location where it was thoroughly inspected, removing all hubcaps, inspecting the space behind the dashboard by reaching in, and by doing so, severing all wires. I lost the use of the speed and mileage indicators. I didn't know what they were looking for, but they did not find anything. The border guard asked me to accompany him to the office. Jo stayed behind in the car. She did not understand a word of Hungarian. She did not know what was happening; it was upsetting for her. I was not permitted to translate. In the office, they were asking me to sit down and wait; I waited.

It felt like hours went by; meantime, they watched me. Then I was escorted into a private room, asked to empty my pockets, and then to remove all my clothes. I was as naked as a newborn. They checked everything, every square inch of my clothes. They watched me again to see my reaction. About a half hour later, I was permitted to put my clothes on. The ordeal in the border took over three hours. Later, Jo told me they watched her all that time when I was away. When we are allowed to leave, we did not talk for at least thirty minutes; then I told her what happened to me inside the office. The shock for her was overwhelming. This kind of experience was new to her. Indirectly, she had a taste of what could happen to you when you were in a totalitarian country. The drive took over five hours, not counting the delays in the border in the two lanes called the international highway, between the two capital cities—Vienna, Austria; and Budapest, Hungary. In the evening when the cows went home from the field, they took over the road, and you're stuck in the "traffic." You know the saying, "You wait till the cows go home"? That's what happened to us. When we arrived at my parents, they were worried. We were running several hours late, but everything was fine when we arrived. My Father was in bed; he had been that way for several weeks, according to my Mother. This time, we were staying with my parents. My Father needed my Mother's attention. We could help her and spend more time together. Father had lost his appetite and was losing weight. The doctors visited him twice a day now. He would like to eat cantaloupe, yogurt, and goose liver with boiled potato. We went to the Farmers Market at Lehel Square in Budapest. To find the cantaloupe was relatively easy. For the yogurt, we located the farmer who makes it and sells it; and for the liver, we had to buy a live goose. We took it home, and someone in the neighborhood killed the goose for us; we plucked the feathers and then cleaned it. My Father had his wish, and we had a roasted goose for dinner and several more meals after. Majority of the time we stayed around the house. Jo helped out in the kitchen, taking notes of my Mother's recipes and learning the Hungarian way of cooking. My Father and I had some time alone to talk and reminisce about his life, his life experiences, and life in general. He told me that he felt that he was coming to the end of his life's journey, and he expressed it to me how short a time we humans spend in this earth compared to some other life-forms and happenings around us.

He expressed it this way:

Time we spend on earth
is the time it takes to blink of an eye,
enjoy life and appreciate every minute of it,
because some day you will wake up and discover it
that it went by.

Now I am coming to the end of my life's journey, and I am looking back, and I see it now how correct he is. He also told me some of the major inventions and happenings in his lifetime—the invention of the airplane, and it can carry passengers. Now there were movie houses and televisions to enjoy. The year after he was born, the first motion picture premiered in Paris on December 28, 1895. Then he talked about the streets where he grew up, in the Castle District in Budapest. He was amazed how the big articulated buses can maneuver, turn, and not hit anything. The street he was talking about was narrow—from the medieval time. Even then, two carts pulled by a horse could hardly pass by each other.

He asked me to take care of my Mother and my sister after he was gone. Unfortunately, my sister is "slow." Mentally, she was about twelve to fourteen years old, and she had a very difficult personality. She is now sixty-three years old. She only worked eight years in her life; ten years was required to receive pension. He also asked that we look after his parents' and grandparents' graves. In Hungary, you had to repurchase the graves every twenty-five years. Otherwise, the remains are removed and put in a common grave, and the plot was resold. He felt that he would die in the early part of October. This was very hard for me emotionally. I left the room and took a long walk in the neighborhood. The subject of his "pending departure" was never mentioned anymore. Jo and I took some time to visit aunts and uncles and other relatives. I showed her my old schools where I attended. It had been only eleven years, but to me, it was a lifetime since I graduated. I didn't know when I would be back in Hungary again. My Father's health was deteriorating; we canceled our trip to Italy and stayed with my parents through September. It was very hard to leave when you know you wouldn't see your Father anymore. It was a very emotional good-bye, and it was hard when you had to keep the emotions to yourself. We returned home to the States safely.

My Father passed away in his home in my Mother's arm in Dunakeszi on October 18, 1967, five weeks short of his seventy-third birthday. His remains stayed in the house for days because of a bureaucratic mix-up. My Mother used this time to properly dress him. Then the casket was taken to north, twenty kilometers to the county seat, the city of Vác; then the casket was put into a second casket; and finally, it was then returned to south, thirty-five kilometers through Dunakeszi to Budapest to the cemetery where he wanted to be buried. All this transportation took place with a horse-drawn wagon. He wanted to be buried in the cemetery where his parents and grandparents had their final resting place. My Mother had to bribe several individuals in different government agencies. Öcsi, my cousin, was a big help; my Mother could not go through these obstacles by herself in her condition. The funeral was on October 23, two o'clock in the afternoon in the Farkasréti Cemetery in Budapest. I did not attend the funeral. I was there with my thoughts and prayers and in spirit. Öcsi took and sent me pictures of the inside service in the chapel, the procession to the gravesite, and the graveside service. After the funeral, my Mother, at home, discovered that the last time the doctor was there, he gave two injections of morphine to my Father for his pain. Each injection was in a separate capsule, and the empty capsules were left behind. When she discovered it, she questioned the doctor why two doses were given at the same time. His answer was simple and to the point—that was my Father's last two morphine shots, which was available for him; he used it to overdose him, and that was what killed my Father, not the cancer. Otherwise, without the morphine, he would suffer a lot. This was the first of the many problems and difficulties I had with the social medicine and the Hungarian medical system.

Looking back on my Father's life and his accomplishments, I am extremely appreciative of how he raised us, with his example, his teaching with his discipline, and with his work ethics. He provided us with everything and more than what he could afford based on the circumstances and the politics at the time in the world. In 1947, after the secret police confiscated our passport, which was our freedom, what an emotional pain it was for him, and it was followed by the mental restrictions he had to endure. In his younger days, he was an inventor; several patents are to his name. One of them is a lock of which I have the first production piece. He was very artistic; one of his works is the head of Christ on metal, which I inherited from him after his passing; I keep it in my bedroom. He was a partner in two different companies in different times with his brother; one was a sheet metal plant and the other, a construction company. I saw in the early fifties some of the railroad cars they owned with the *Landesz Brothers* name on it. The cars were used to transport the heavy construction equipment. By then, the cars were confiscated by the government. He traveled a lot, worked ten years in Turkey, and ten years in Iran. He spoke six different languages. He was one of the design engineers for the Trans Arabian Railroad project in Iran. In the last twenty years of his life, to forget the present and keep his mind alive, he read a lot, gardened in the summer, which he enjoyed; and in the winter, he used his hand to build different things, like frames for photographs. I have some of it. He built a birdcage with wires, then we had a bird; it was the only pet we had when we were growing up. Before the war, he designed a house for us; it was never built. In later years in his life, he built a small-scale model of it. I have the drawings of the house and the photographs of the model.

I can understand now why sometimes he got upset with us and disciplined us. In the end, he was proud of me for what I accomplished in my life. Thank you for everything. I am sorry if sometimes I misbehaved. I am sorry that I have only a limited vocabulary to truly express how I feel. Unfortunately, we children only appreciate our parents when they are gone.

In the spring of 1968, we found out that Jo was expecting, and she was due in early November. We were happy and looking forward to the big event and counting the days to be parents and for our pride and joy to arrive. We planned how we would furnish the baby's room, which now is our guest bedroom/den. We started to buy things for the baby's room; we already had the crib from Aunt Fran, Jo's aunt. She sent us the crib; her grandchildren used it when they were young, when they were visiting them. We didn't know the sex of our child, and we won't know it till it is born. This was a very exciting time in our life; finally, I will have a family, which I wanted very much. To me, to have a child or children was very important; I wanted to have a happy, close family like I had when I was growing up.

We invited my Mother for a visit, to rest, recuperate, and to gain some weight; we were very concerned about her health. The last years were hard times for her, and it was a difficult circumstance taking care of my Father. She lost weight; she was less than ninety pounds, and her stature was about five feet. Because of lifting my Father, she strained herself and had a hernia. She arrived on May 2, 1968; she was sixty-four years old, and this was her first trip to the States. My Mother was very concerned of taking this trip. This was her first time flying, and she didn't know what to expect. She didn't speak English, and she worried how she would ask for help if she needed it during her trip. We prepared for her about twenty-five English-Hungarian cards with individual phrases like "Where is the toilet?" or "May I have a glass of water" and so on. She had to transfer airplanes in two locations during her flight. The itinerary was from Budapest with Malév Hungarian Airline to Vienna, Austria; and from there, she had to transfer to Pan American airlines to New York, go through customs, then fly to Washington DC. We requested assistance for her at each airport. The cards and the promised help during her trip helped her to be excited and to accept the invitation to visit us. When the Malév airline landed in Vienna, a passenger car waited for her by the plane and transferred her to the Pan Am flight, and in New York she received a wheelchair and assistance going through the customs. She was very grateful and surprised to all this attention she received during her trip. During her visit, Jo and my Mother got along very well. We went shopping together. She wanted to be active and helpful. Sometimes, we made a grocery shopping list for her; she walked to the store when we were at work and bought what we needed. By now, she was familiar with the store and found her way around. At the cashier, she gave her money in an envelope; they took out what was needed to pay for the purchase; then they returned the change into the envelope and gave it back to her. She didn't speak any English. Many times, she cooked, and when we got home from work, a nice dinner was waiting for us. We took her to different restaurants, and Jo cooked meals for her to taste some American food. We took her sightseeing in Washington DC, visited the different museums, the national zoo; and we visited Mount Vernon in Virginia. We went to New York City for several days; she was amazed of the tall buildings. The temperature during our stay in New York was very hot, with no air movement outside; it was hard for Jo and my Mother to breathe, but we had a memorable time. All of us enjoyed the trip; this was Jo's first trip to the Big Apple.

We found out from my Mother that her retirement income after my Father was one-half of what he received, which was about $65 a month, and two people—my Mother and my sister—cannot live on that amount. During the time when she was visiting us, the Hungarian government kept her retirement for the duration of her stay. My sister remained in Hungary because the government at this time did not allow all the same family members to leave the country at the same time. We had a happy time together. The sad time arrived when we had to say good-bye; she left on August 18, 1968. We enjoyed her visit, and we would miss her. She was rested and gained some weight; we were very grateful for that and for her visit.

In the past years, each time when Sara—Jo's mother—calls or visits us, more and more she talked about how nice it would be if her daughters would be living in Atlanta. In time, the calls became more frequent, and the pressure was increasing. Jo now received daily calls from her mother; she was pressuring her by using false illnesses, telling her how sick she was and how much she needed her daughters by her side, that they all should move to Atlanta to be close to her. Both of her daughters were over thirty when they got married less than a year apart and moved out from her home and from her "guidance." The "girls," as she called them, had to give her their income when they live at home, and then she gave them allowance. Sara lived alone now; she divorced her husband when the girls were six years old, and she was legally blind. She only can see the outline of a person or an object if she had the contact lens on.

After her divorce, her sister Fran supported her and the two girls. By then, Fran was an independent, wealthy lady through her investments in her husband's company. Sara was a very dominating person. In the past years, she visited Jenny or us several times a year; the sisters were very devoted to their mother. Sara favored Jo; she was weaker of the two, and Sara can influence her more. Sara could not understand that her thirty-year-old daughters with their husbands can make their own decisions. They had their own life to live, and they didn't need to consult with her and get her approval for everything. Sara could not accept the idea that Jo was happy, maybe for the first time in her adult life, and had control over her own life. Jo took several trips to Atlanta to see Sara's doctors, but everything was a false alarm. The doctors' conclusion was that she was a hypochondriac.

Rolland, the husband of Jenny, Jo's twin sister graduated from the Georgetown University law school and found a job in Atlanta with the Federal Trade Commission as a young attorney. They moved to Atlanta. We were hoping this would solve the moving problem for us, and she would be satisfied with one of her "girls" by her side. Jo did not want to move back; she was happy here, and I had my own architectural office now, which was doing well. We didn't want to give it up. The constant phone calls and pressure—sometimes she called Jo twice a day—had its consequences. Jo spent a lot of time in isolation; she was withdrawn, depressed all the time, walked to a close-by park, and stayed there for hours. According to her doctors, these condition created a chemical imbalance in her system, which can impact the unborn child's health. No medication can be provided for her depression this time because of her condition being with child. During the last six weeks of her pregnancy, we saw the doctor at least once a week for a blood test; we had a packed suitcase with us because if it became an emergency as a result of the blood test, we had to go to the hospital immediately from the doctor's office. In our October 22 doctor's visit, we were told that early in the morning the next day we should go to the hospital, and they will induce the labor; the blood test reached the critical level.

Our son William "Bill" Charles Landesz was born after over ten hours of labor on October 23, 1968, at six fifty-eight in the evening in the Sibley Memorial Hospital, Washington DC. He weighed 6 lb. 15 oz., and he was 20 inches long. It was a difficult birth, using clamps on the baby's head to pull him out. In the beginning, he would not breathe; he had to be "encouraged" by being slapped several times and sticking needles in his heel. His head and heel were bruised for a long time. But he was alive, healthy, and we had a son. Bill was born one year from the date of my Father's funeral, twelve years of the 1965 Hungarian uprising, and fifty years of my maternal grandfather's passing. He was named after the husband of Fran, Jo's aunt, Bill (William), and his middle name, Charles, is the English name for *Karl*. Jo and Bill came home to Tahona Drive on October 26. We were so happy; I could not find words to express it. Jo was nursing Bill every four hours; he was in his room and slept a lot. After the first days, we established a good routine; this way, Jo could rest between nursing. When we ate and Bill was awake, he sat on the table in his "carrying seat," which he got used to very fast; and he liked to sit in it. Bill's first big outing was on November 4 to the nearby voting place to vote for our next president. President Johnson withdrew his name for the presidency "for national unity" because with his politics, he divided this nation. The candidates were Mr. Nixon, a Republican, and Vice President Humphrey, a Democrat. The president-elect Nixon declared victory the next morning.

We invited my mother-in-law, Sara, to visit us and to meet her grandson; she arrived on the second week of November and stayed with us for two weeks. On the first day, she insisted she would take care of Bill during her stay because we didn't have any experience in childcare. When Sara diapered Bill, every time, Bill cried, which was unusual for him because he was a very quiet, adjusted baby. When we first looked, we didn't find any reason for Bill to cry; but when we picked him up, his cry increased and became louder. After more investigation, we found that when Sara diapered Bill and when she used the safety pin (the safety pin was about two to two-and-a-half-inch long) to pin the diaper, she included part of Bill's skin; that was the reason for his crying. From then on, every time Sara diapered Bill, Jo or I checked Bill and corrected the problem. Jo at first didn't want to say anything to her mother, but when it was happening too many times and after a lot of consideration in Jo's part—after a lot of crying by Jo, the concern of her mother, and Bill in pain—she decided to talk to Sara about the situation. Jo diplomatically said to her maybe the reason was because she cannot see well what she was doing. She denied it even after Jo showed her the bloody diapers. Sara accused us that the reason we were saying that was because we didn't want her to diaper Bill, which was correct; we didn't want her to diaper Bill. She refused our request, and Jo gave up on her. Jo and Bill had to suffer a lot because of her unreasonable attitude. Jo told me later that her mother told her that I fabricated all these because she did not do it and the red spots on the diapers were not blood but that it was a dirty diaper. We had a diaper service. When Jo tried to tell her that she saw it firsthand, Sara indicated to her that Jo doesn't know what she was talking about. My mother-in-law also had other bad habits. She stayed up all night to watch television and slept all day. We could tolerate that for the sake of peace, except that she needed company, and she woke up Bill. Then when he cried, she bounced him on her knees, sometimes all night. This routine of hers gave us a problem later because we had to do the same thing each time when Bill cried. This was the only way Bill wouldn't cry; we had to bounce him on our knees. Sara also wanted to know if Bill had been baptized. When we told her no, she stated that Bill had to be Presbyterian; this was her final decision. When Bill was born, he had blue eyes; but as everyone knows, it can change when a child gets older. Sara insisted that we get eye drops to make sure Bill's eyes stay blue. These two weeks went very slow. It was supposed to be a happy occasion, but it turned out to be a disaster. We were very glad when she left, and it took us several weeks to get back to our routine with Bill. I don't know what else Sara told Jo, but after she left, Jo was a different person. The renewed happiness as a new family slowly disappeared, and she was more depressed and refused to see a doctor. Christmas was approaching, and we decorated the apartment; she was cooking and baking nice Hungarian food and pastry. We were preparing for our first family Christmas. The holiday season was very joyful and happy. We were spending a lot of time shopping for Bill. He ended up with many gifts, toys, and clothing under the Christmas tree. It was fun to shop for him; there was a big selection and nice clothes and toys for children to choose from. We took him at dusk to see the lighted Christmas trees in the neighborhood, and you could see his eyes follow the lights.

It appeared that Jo, during the holidays, was feeling better and enjoying it. Quietly inside I felt that this was my Christmas present from Jo, that maybe she was getting better. We celebrated New Year's at home, the three of us, with a glass of champagne at midnight and thanked God that we were a family and we have a son; and it appeared Jo's health was returning to normal. This was a good feeling. The happiness did not last long. After the New Year, the telephone started ringing with calls from Atlanta again, and Jo's depression was accelerating. She spent the days in bed; she only fed Bill. Jo was losing her milk; we started using formula more and more. I got up early each day to prepare breakfast, lunch for Jo, sterilize the baby bottles, and prepare and mix Bill's formula. In the evening when I came home from work, I did the same things, hand-wash things for Jo and prepare dinner for us.

My mother-in-law succeeded. One evening at the end of January 1969, when I came home from work, no one was home. I found a note from Jo, informing me that she could not take any more pressure and had gone back to Atlanta to satisfy her mother's wishes and that she loves me and hopes she could work out things with her mother and she would return soon. I tried to call that evening and every day for several days. Sara intercepted all calls with different excuses as to why Jo could not come to the phone. Later, I found out that she never told Jo that I called. In one of the conversations with the Devil, I found out that she sent the airline ticket for Jo without Jo's blessing because, according to Sara, Jo in the telephone was very depressed and in *"her condition, she cannot raise a child."* I asked her if I had anything to say about this and if I could see my son. Her answer was, *"No, and Jo will not go back to you. I will see to that."*

After this conversation, I looked for a lawyer in Maryland. The local attorney indicated that the divorce could be handled here based on a desertion on her part, but the child visitation had to be petitioned in Atlanta. Then in Atlanta, I found a marriage counselor and, with her help, tried to get Jo to meet and talk and find out what was happening. All responses and denial came from Sara and not from Jo even though all correspondence were addressed to Jo. During all this time, I could not see Bill. It was suggested by the marriage counselor that I ask the court for visitation rights. After several months of hoping I don't have to take this step, I requested and received visitation rights. The "temporary order" dated May 9, 1969, gave Jo the temporary custody; and I can visit Bill one weekend a month, Christmas Day, and his birthday. I had to provide sufficient notice of my visitation intentions. Also, I had to be notified by Jo of any of Bill's major illnesses, the place and time of his christening, which I also can attend. I don't want to go into every detail what I had to go through to see Bill even with a court order. Sara decided she would fight everything every step of the way. She hated me, but I didn't know why. I did not give her any reason for it. Maybe because I was married to her daughter and she was not number one anymore. Here are some examples of what I had to endure: I sent thirty days' notice in writing of my planned visit to see Bill. The letter got "lost," and I didn't find out until I was in Atlanta. I could not see Bill because I didn't have proof that I sent the letter. From this point on, I sent everything through registered mail with return receipt. The next letter I sent, notifying my visit, was in thirty days in advance. The excuse this time was that thirty days was not sufficient enough according to Sara. I went to court, and Jo lost. Next time, I gave forty-five days' notification. The excuse was they forgot about it because the time was too long. I went to court, and Jo lost. I had a visitation right for Christmas day. I notified Jo that I wanted to exercise it. Upon my arrival at the hotel in Atlanta on December 24, I called the apartment where they lived to find out when was the convenient time for Jo and Bill for my visit on the next day. I was looking forward for this visit; that would be Bill's second Christmas. Sara answered the telephone, and she told me I could not see or visit Bill; no reason was given. Immediately I called my attorney, and she managed to have an emergency hearing in front of a judge on the same day. In the late afternoon, Jo's attorney was notified; and with her client, they were present. When the judge asked Jo why I could not visit Bill when I followed the requirements established in the temporary court order, Jo did not have any response. The judge ruled on my favor. Jo got very upset with her lawyer because she couldn't help her; she fired her on the spot in front of everyone. Jo started to cry, and the judge asked her why. Jo told the judge it was because her mother insisted that I could not visit Bill in her home. Jo and Bill were living with her. After some consideration and reviewing all the rulings from the previous court hearings, the judge told Jo that she was responsible for her son, not her mother. I have the right to see my son. Jo was to move out from her mother's home. Her mother had to stay out of their life, and she immediately had to stop interfering and challenging the court orders. Next time, the court removed Bill from Jo's custody, and I could petition the court for full and final custody of Bill, and I could raise him in my home in Maryland. From that time on, Sara was not there when I visited Bill, and everything was relatively better and smoother. Jo went through three lawyers—either they were fired or quit because Jo couldn't work with them. Bill was christened, and I was not notified. When I found out, I met with the minister, and he told me he specifically asked Sara of my whereabouts, and she replied that I was too busy to attend, which was not true.

One of my trips to visit Bill was on July 20, 1969. I just arrived at the Atlanta airport when the television showed astronaut Neil Armstrong stepping on the moon's surface at 10:56 p.m. and declaring it to the world, *"That's one small step for man, one giant step for mankind."* It was hard to imagine that this could happen when less than sixty years ago they did not even know how to fly. The Wright brothers flew the first powered, manned, and controlled aircraft on December 17, 1903.

For Bill's first birthday, I asked Jo if she would allow a picture of the three of us commemorating his first birthday. I arranged my visit to be that day, and we had a picture taken by a professional photographer in his studio. This is the only family picture I have of us together.

As a result of all this aggravation and lack of sleep in the past year, I lost over forty pounds. I now weighed 112 lb., and my height is 5'10''. Dr. Marks, the family physician, prescribed sleeping medication and a sedative for my nerves. Everyone was concerned about my health; I looked like a ghost.

This brings us to the end of the sixties; it was the best of years and the worst of years of my adult life. The best was my son being born and I had a family, at least for three months. On Bill's first birthday, I wrote a letter to him—hoping someday he can read it—expressing my feelings and my thoughts about him. It was written in Hungarian, and I did not mail it. I have it, and I am hoping he will learn Hungarian one day to read it. The worst was losing my son and the ordeal that followed because of one selfish, self-centered, manipulating sick person, my mother-in-law; she doesn't care if she ruins her children and their family's life as long as she had her way.

In this decade, the nation and the world lost three great individuals: a young president, a civil rights leader, the recipient of the Nobel Peace Prize, and a senator presidential candidate, because of misguided hatred for mankind.

I lost my Father and my Dad; both of them were big instruments in molding, influencing, and guiding my life in different times. What I accomplished in my life and what I am today is because of them. I am very grateful for that to both of them. It was a fascinating, happy, and sad decade all at the same time.

Turning over the car key to the Horan's upon my arrival at Spokane.

Spokane, Washington, 1960.

"BOX LABOL" from the *"HORAN BROS. Inc."* Orchard

The White House invitation.

Jo's visit to Washington DC, July 1963.

Left to right: me, Jo, Dad, and Jenny, Jo's sister.

My Father with the model he made from the house he designed.

The family picture taken in Budapest, Hungary, 1965.

Last picture of my Father.
He was seventy-one years old, June 1965, Dunakeszi, Hungary.

My Father's funeral.

Budapest, Hungary, October 23 1967

The Landesz family.

This is the only picture I have of us together.

October 23, 1969, Atlanta, Georgia.

VIII

The Decade of the '70s

I started this decade in a positive way and tried to forget my recent past; I invited my Mother for a summer visit to help me regain some of my weight with her good home cooking. This would be her second visit. I asked the airlines for the same assistance she received in 1968 during her first trip. This time, she had no concerns of traveling and flying. Her presence and her cooking did miracles for me: I gained some weight and I was more relaxed and I could sleep better now. We talked a lot about our past, the hardships we had, and lived through it. It helped me to see that this was not the end of the world; this was only a big bump on the road, and I had to continue on with my life. The past cannot be helped, but the future was in front of me, and I should look forward to it. The time we spent together and the conversations we had helped me a lot. We planned a trip to Atlanta on August on my scheduled summer visit with Bill and for my Mother to meet her grandson. We decided to drive to Atlanta; this way, she can see this big country and the changes in the countryside driving south. This was her first long-distance drive in the States. We stayed in the hotel, which my Mother enjoyed. Our visit with Jo was cordial and pleasant; we visited Bill several days in his home, and we went with Bill and Jo to different parks and to the zoo, which especially Bill and my Mother enjoyed. My parents used to take us to the zoo a lot in Hungary when we were growing up. My Mother was very happy to have this opportunity to meet, spend some time with, and get to know Bill. It turned out to be her first and only grandchild.

Shortly after returning from Atlanta, she had to leave and go home to Hungary. Her eight-week stay was a lifesaver for me. She helped me to look at life and my future in a different way, the positive way. A Mother traveled thousands of miles to help her child who needed her support even when that child was over thirty-two years old.

After my Mother left, I spent all my time in the office. I only went home to sleep. I became a workaholic, and I stayed that way for over twenty years. I learned one thing from this: you cannot trust and depend on anyone, except on yourself.

After over seven years of marriage, the final court decree of my divorce from Joan "Jo" Shillington Landesz was issued in Atlanta on October 15, 1970. The summary of the court decree was I have visitation rights one weekend a month, six days every Christmas, two weeks each in June and August, and on alternate years for Thanksgiving Day. I could not move Bill from the six-county metropolitan area of Atlanta till January 1, 1974. After that, I could take him anywhere; it was up to my discretion. I didn't have to pay alimony, only child support and the premium of the medical insurance for Bill, but no other medical expenses. I visited Bill every other month for over three years, and after that, four times a year. The reason I reduced my visits was because the emotions were too much to bear, to see Bill growing up and I could not be with him all the time, and all my money went to the expenses for air travel, hotel, and car rental. During the summer visits with Bill in 1974 and 1975, I flew to Atlanta in the morning, picked Bill up in his home, and we returned to Maryland in the afternoon. We did this twice a year, and each time, he stayed with me for two weeks. At the end of the two weeks, I took him home to Atlanta. Starting 1976, Jo and I agreed that Bill (seven years old) could travel by himself to visit me without my escort. The first time when he traveled alone, I met him in the national airport in Washington DC. He had tears in his eyes. When I asked him what was the

BLINK OF AN EYE 151

problem, he told me his mother told him, "You are a big boy now, and you will fly by yourself." He was upset because he wanted to know what all these people were doing on the plane and why he was not flying "by himself," as his mother told him. I explained to Bill what it meant when his mother told him "you are flying by yourself." It was not easy; it took some time, but I think he got it! During this visit and every visit, we had a good time; we went to different places and parks, and we saw different things. He liked the Smithsonian museums and the different exhibits there. He behaved well during all of his stays.

I decided to take a break from the everyday routine. On the evening of September 7, 1971, I left from the Washington Dulles airport to visit my Mother and my sister in Hungary. This was my third trip and the first since my Father's passing. I flew with Pan American airlines from Washington, Dulles, to London, then with British Airways to Budapest. I arrived the next day at one twenty in the afternoon. This time, going through the customs in Hungary was uneventful.

After a couple of days, I rented a car to get around easier. I hoped we could take a trip and go to see places where I have never been before. It was an unusually warm and rain-free September. I enlisted my uncle Nándor's help to plan the trip. He knew the interesting historic places to see and visit. We ended up selecting eight places or cities to visit. All were in the western part of Hungary. We did not set a time duration for the trip. All five of us—my Mother, sister, aunt and uncle, and I—started our trip on September 16. My uncle was the tour guide; he knew Hungarian history well. Our first stop after a two-and-a-half-hour drive was the city of *Hatvan* (Hot-won) Settlement; on this site, the time of the Bronze Age started. The present name of the city was given in the year 1170, when the monks settled in the area. From here, we drove through the *Mátra* (Ma-tra) and *Bükk* (Bick) mountain range to the towns of *Mátraháza* (Ma-tra-ha-za) and then to *Kékes* (Kay-kesh). These areas were sky resorts; *Kékes's* elevation was about 3,200 feet, the tallest mountain peak in Hungary. The peak had a radio-transmitter tower; my Father was a part of the team who designed it. For insulation, the tower stands on a large porcelain ball; it was one of a kind in Europe at the time. It was considered a very innovative design then. Our next stop was the city of *Eger* (Egger) to visit the ruins of a fort from the twelfth century; it became famous in 1552 when 80,000 Turkish soldiers kept the siege on the fort for 38 days against 2,100 Hungarian defenders in the fort. The Turkish army could not take possession of it; they retreated. Next time, the Turkish army attacked the fort 135 years later in 1687, when they succeeded and the fort fell. This area was also famous from the vineyards and their fine red wine, the *Egri Bikavér,* known in this country as Bull's Blood of Eger (Egger). The northwestern edge of the *Bükk* (Bick) mountain range was the city of *Miskolc* (Mish-kolls), our next stop; the original settlement dates back to the prehistoric times. Then our trip took us to the city of *Nyiregyháza* (Knee-edge-ha-za). People have lived in this area since the Stone Age according to excavation records of the area. The city got its present name in the year 1219. We continued our drive to the city of *Debrecen* (De-bret-sen), which was the center of the Reform religion in Hungary (similar to the Presbyterian religion in United States). In this city was where the seminaries and the universities are for the Reform Church. The first settlement for the city dates back to the twelfth century. The last three cities were major cities in Hungary. On our way home, we stopped at *Hortobágy* (Hor-to-badge), the "Great Plains" of Hungary; it is a national park, a working farm where they raise longhorn white cattle and wild horses. The park had a shallow lake. Over it was a bridge with nine arches; it was built between 1827 and 1833. Next to the bridge were a museum and an excellent restaurant, where we had lunch. After we ate, we continued our trip to the city of *Karcag* (Kart-sag). Here was where my uncle Nándi was the president of two flourmills before WWII. The settlement dates back to the fourteenth century. It was also known for its folk art, specifically the black pottery that I collect. One of the oldest and still-in-use high school buildings is located here; the building is over three hundred years old. The walls are over a yard thick. On our way home, the last city was *Szolnok* (Suol-nuk), which was settled in 1030, situated by the river *Tisza* (Tee-sa), the second major river in Hungary after the river *Duna*. This trip took us four days; it was very educational, and we saw and I learned a lot. To be in some of the old buildings was so overwhelming; you can feel the past as it took place in it, and you'd feel very small, like an ant. Everyone enjoyed the trip, staying in hotels and eating in the restaurants. For them, it was having food that you cannot eat at home because the government was saving it for the foreign tourists, which we were because of me. Every time we stayed overnight in a hotel, I had to register with the police in the police station. The hotel kept my passport till we left in the morning.

Before I left for my trip, a Hungarian family (Mr. and Mrs. Zoltán Körössy, PhD) asked me to visit and give Mrs. Körössy's mother—who lived in Budapest—a gift, which they were sending with me. They also asked me to visit their son Zoli's fiancée, Kati, in the city of Miskolc. The young engaged couple met when she was visiting her sister here. I met the Körössy family in 1957; I don't recall the time or the specific circumstances. We became good friends. Mr. Körössy graduated from a law school in Hungary; then he attended the elite police academy. After graduation, he became a district commander in a major city. He came with his family to the States in late 1945. They also have a daughter, Láli. We dated about a year till January 1963 when we broke up. Then I started dating Jo. Later, Láli met a cadet from the Naval Academy in Annapolis. After his graduation, they got married. They lived in the suburb of Chicago, and they have three children.

When I was visiting Mrs. Körössy's mother and her two siblings in Budapest, I was introduced to a twenty-three-year-old young lady, Ilona

Vigh. She was an architect, a recent graduate, and a distant relative. I found her very pleasant, smart, interesting, nice, and very attractive. Ilona lived and worked in Budapest. Her parents were separated; her mother lives with her sister, both of them teachers. They lived about three hours' train ride from Budapest. After this meeting until I left Hungary, we spent lots of time together. After her work, we went to restaurants or different places like museums or just walked on the streets and in the parks in Budapest. The last day before my departure, we discussed that if she could get a passport and the permission from the government to leave Hungary, then she will visit me.

During my stay, I visited Zoli's fiancée, Kati, and her family in Miskolc with my Mother. Shortly after my visit, she was granted an emigration exit permit because she reimbursed the government for the cost of her education; she has a medical degree. At this time in Hungary, the education was free, paid by the government. Shortly after she arrived in the States, they got married in December 1971. Now they have four children, and they live in Kensington. One of their sons is a fourth-year cadet in the Naval Academy in Annapolis. Her mother is living with them; she came to the States after her husband passed away in Hungary. Kati is a practicing physician; she has an office in Kensington and Silver Spring in Leisure World. She was one of Helen Grindol Fuchs's doctors. Helen was Dad's secretary. Zoli is an operating room nurse working for Kaiser Permanente. Mr. Körössy passed away in February 1995; he was eighty-three years old, and Mrs. Körössy, in January 2003. She was eighty-one years old.

This trip was different from previous trips because no one was sick. We traveled a lot; we went to places where I have never been before. It was the first time I had the opportunity to see this part of Hungary and unexpectedly met Ilona.

I left Hungary at eight forty in the morning on October 6. I traveled from Budapest to Paris by Malév, the Hungarian airline, and from there by Air France to Washington Dulles International Airport, arriving five forty-five in the afternoon.

In the following weeks and months, there's a lot of letter writing and weekly telephone calls taking place between Ilona and me. In one of her first letters I received, she let me know about her visit to the passport office. She was informed by the passport office that the government would only take her application papers for the passport and the visiting exit permit if she had a letter from a relative in the States, inviting her and taking responsibility for her during her stay, and she had to have a round-trip airline ticket. I relayed this information to the Körössy family; they agreed to send her the letter. I paid for the open airline ticket, and the Körössys sent it to her. With these papers, she now could apply for her passport and the exit permit. Now the waiting was on. The correspondence and the telephone conversations between us became more frequent. We became very fond of each other. I am not the type of person who can write romantic letters, but for my luck, in *The Evening Star*, the evening newspaper in Washington DC, every day it publishes a drawing with two small cartoon characters with quotations; it is called *Love Is . . . ? by Kim*. I cut it out and sent it to her. Here are some of the sayings: "*Love is . . . more giving than taking*," "*Love is . . . never holding back your affection*," or "*Love is . . . reading life's meaning in each other's eyes*." I have a collection of these drawings.

In the meantime, I found out that Mrs. Körössy is Ilona's second cousin.

The good news arrived on December 12; she had the passport and the exit permit. The next step was to apply for the visa. When she was submitting her papers in the embassy, no time was given to her when she can expect a reply. This was typical in Hungary; the waiting was on again.

I received a telephone call from Ilona in the morning of December 23,[17] letting me know the good news; everyone was surprised of the speedy approval. She received the visa that day. She told me she was packing to go home to spend Christmas with her family, and we would talk again about her pending trip after the holidays.

I received a surprise call from Ilona on December 26, letting me know that she was arriving on the evening of the twenty-eighth of December 1971. I was surprised of the fast movement of the events. I called the Körössy family and relayed the news to them. Ilona was staying with them during her visit.

When I was driving to the airport to meet her, different things went through my mind. I was a bit confused; maybe I was scared. Strange feelings came over me. I was saying it to myself, *Let's see what the future brings.* In the airport, when I saw her walking out the door from the customs area, her face was very radiant. She didn't look like she traveled all day; she appeared very happy. We drove to my apartment first to show her where I lived. Then I took her to the Körössys' home, where she was staying for the duration of her visit. Ilona knew about the Körössy family from her mother. They had never met. I was on vacation between Christmas and New Year. We celebrated New Year's Eve together. On New Year's day, I had dinner with the Körössys. In the following days and weeks, we spent lots of time together. We went downtown to show her the city and visit museums. I took her to

---

[17]   The time difference between Hungary and this country is six hours; 8:00 a.m. here is 2:00 p.m. there.

my office to meet my partners and showed her what we were working on. We explored different stores and malls. Her authorized stay in this country was for thirty days. During this time, we enjoyed each other's company. We were very fond of each other. We were now emotionally involved. We were falling in love. I asked her to marry me; her answer was yes. Ilona's visa would expire on January 28; therefore, we had to be married by then. The calendar showed it was January 15.

Our first trip was to the Hungarian embassy to find out what were the procedures and what approvals she needed to legally extend her Hungarian exit papers. If we got married without the Hungarian government's approval, then if someday she wants to return to Hungary, she will be arrested. Probably, as long as there is Communism in Hungary, she will not see her parents. The embassy was not very helpful; according to them, she must return to Hungary and start the proceedings from there. The permission from the government to marry foreigners can take several years, and it is not sure she will receive the permission. When we got home, we discussed it; it was her decision. She will lose a lot if she does not return to Hungary in time. After Ilona thought it over for several days, she decided we should get married without the Hungarian government's permission. Because Ilona lacked English language skills, I looked for a Hungarian-speaking priest to marry us. I found one. He was teaching in the seminary in the Catholic University in Washington DC. His name is the Reverend L. A. Irányi, PhD. He also oversees the order of the Piarist Fathers in North America. We made an appointment with him to explain our case and events that took place in the last thirty days. We expressed our desire to get married and asked if he would officiate the ceremony. His response was yes. He advised us, because I was married before to Jo in the Presbyterian Church, that I need to request an annulment from the Tribunal of the Archdiocese of Washington. He indicated to us this proceeding takes three days and what documents I needed to take with me when I applied for the annulment. He asked a priest friend in the St. Camillus Rectory in Silver Spring if he could conduct the ceremony there; he didn't have a church assigned to him.

I called the Tribunal in the Archdiocese of Washington DC for an interview and to file my papers. They gave me an appointment for January 22. The interviewer was a young Irish priest. He told us that she should return to Hungary and follow her country's law and apply from there even if it takes several years. He also indicated the paperwork in his office would take several weeks, if not several months, to process. We listened to what he had to say; I translated everything to Ilona. When he was finished, I brought it to his attention that in this country, the church and state are separate. We were not here to get his advice or his opinion. I also informed him that according to my information, the paperwork only take the maximum of three days and that I would be back on January 26 in the afternoon to pick up the approved document. I asked him to leave it with the receptionist in the lobby.

He was curious where I got my information. I also told him with or without the church's approval, we would get married. The papers were ready on time, and a copy was sent directly to the parish where the ceremony would take place.

We decided to invite to the wedding only the family, and it would be very simple. In the meantime, when all these things were happening, we were shopping for some clothes and a wedding dress for Ilona and a suit for me. Mrs. Körössy prepared the food and the dessert for the reception, which would be held in their home. The wedding was scheduled for January 28, 1972, but because of last-minute problems with the availability of the church, it took place a day later. My best man was Louis Fuchs, Helen Grindol Fuchs's husband, and Ilona's maid of honor was my sister Gisela. Mr. Körössy walked Ilona down the aisle and gave her away.

After the reception, we retired to my apartment in Silver Spring. Our honeymoon was postponed till the summer; we planned to combine it with a visit to Bill in Atlanta. Unfortunately, my savings ran out, and we still had more immediate and important expenses ahead of us. Ilona signed up for English language courses. After a couple of months, I started teaching her how to drive. Later, she took professional driving lessons, and then she got her driver's license. In the past, Ilona did not have to cook; now she had to learn that too. She even had to learn how to cut up a chicken. In a short time, she turned out to be a great cook. In her free time, she worked in my office to get some American experience, to learn the technical terms, and learn to prepare the architectural drawings in the American way, at the same time helping us out; we were very busy in the office. By end of July, she was comfortable to look for employment; after several interviews, she found a job as a junior architect with a nationally known large architect and engineer's office in Washington DC. When she started working in the morning, I took her to the bus stop in Silver Spring by my office. In the evenings after her work, she came to our office and she put in two to three additional hours helping us out. Everything was going so well in our life. We decided to make an extra effort to save money and to buy a house. In my office, she did not get paid; but by completing the project faster, the office got paid sooner. For compensation, the office decided to give her a *Barcelona table.* It is a designer glass coffee table; it was for our future house. After a few months, we saved some money; to ease her long commute by bus to downtown, we bought a car for her.

On our first wedding anniversary in 1973, Helen and Louis Fuchs gave us a numbered print by Agnes Mills called the *Mare and Stallion.* Now it is hanging in my dining room.

We saved a sufficient amount of money by August of 1973 to have a 20 percent down payment for a house. This large down payment would reduce our monthly payments, and we didn't have to pay a special insurance. I borrowed ten thousand dollars from a friend to have extra money in our account in the bank; it helped us to get a favorable loan. After a lengthy research, visits, and reviews, we found our house in the *Parkside* subdivision in Silver Spring, Maryland, of Layhill Road on a dead-end street on Alderton Road, not far from where I live now. I designed that house when I was working with my previous employer. The house was under construction. The builder now was one of our clients. We purchased it through his real estate agent; we didn't receive discount but changes to the house's floor plan were free. This house was the first real estate owned by any member in both of our families in any generation. It was a two-story house with one car garage located on a lot that was third of an acre, with some mature trees in the back of the lot. The house had four bedrooms; the master bedroom had a walk-in closet, two baths and a half bath, a spacious kitchen with breakfast area, large family room with fireplace, and a good-sized living and dining room. To save money, we left the walk-out basement unfinished. After we moved in, I mentioned it to the builder when he was in the office that I planned to finish the basement myself. He suggested making a list of what I needed, and he will buy it on the builder's discount and will deliver the materials to my house. It turned out later that the materials were a gift from him. I planned an L-shaped recreation room with a kitchenette by the stairs, with a laundry room and two storage rooms. I did all the construction work in the weekends; it took me a year. Someone else did the installation of the electric work and the installation of the carpet. As soon as the basement was finished, we added a large brick terrace from the recreation room. In the the family room, we replaced the window with French doors.

We built a deck from the family room, connecting it with a stairs to the new brick patio below. We were very happy here. We were working together and planning our future. We had a lot of good times in this house; we planted vegetable and flower gardens and added several evergreen trees and shrubs. We purchased a Scandinavian teak dining room set and a white sofa with a matching armchair and a rug called *Vesuv* made in England for the wall and the *Arco* floor lamp from the Italian designer *Achille Castiglioni*. It had a three-hundred-pound Italian white (curare) marble base. Now all rooms were completely furnished. All this furniture are in the living room now in my house.

I decided to leave the partnership with Madis Valgi Associates. I wanted to experience new opportunities. My last day was April 30, 1974. Part of the settlement from my office was a solid oak drafting board and a teak desk. The desk is now in my family room. The office still exists, owned and managed by Madis. Andy my other partner passed away in the late '90s.

I had no problem finding employment. I was asked to join the office of Chatelain, Semperton & Carcaterra Architects and Engineers as a project manager. The office was located in Washington DC. Mr. Chatelain's office is the oldest architectural office in Washington DC. They had a contract to prepare construction documents for the new headquarters building for Martin-Marietta to be located in Bethesda, Maryland. Martin-Marietta was closing their headquarters in New York City. They already canceled their lease and set the moving date. The production drawings in the architect office were not progressing, and they were more than six months behind schedule. The office lacked organization and discipline. The client was ready to go to court. The partners in the office called me into a meeting, and they asked me to prepare a plan how the project can be completed in twelve months. In four days, I prepared a schedule with man allocation with hours, including the same to all consultants because without their cooperation the project cannot be completed. After the presentation, they asked me to take charge and manage the project. I accepted with the stipulation that I don't get interference from the partners of this firm and the principals of the consulting firms and that I have a free hand to set office hours for every person who was working on the project. A short time later after discussing it between themselves and with their consultants, they gave me the green light for what I asked for. With this plan, the client delayed the lawsuit to see how things will progress. Martin-Marietta planned to review the progress in the office monthly. I streamlined and reorganized the staff on the project. Three men prepared all the details; the rest of the staff drew up the details and the plans, elevations, and other necessary drawings for the building. One person did all architectural coordination, and another person provided daily quality control. All the drawings, which were worked on during the day, were reproduced at night, reviewed, coordinated and commented on in eight hours, and returned to the person who prepared the drawing for correction. Everybody had to work twelve hours a day, except some of us who had longer days. I oversaw the production of all disciplines and coordinated with the engineers. The consultants had to move in to our office and had to work the same long hours as we did. In the evening when they went out to have dinner, including the principals who worked on the project, they had to leave behind the restaurant's telephone number. If they were not back in an hour, they received a call from me, and they were reminded of the schedule of the project and the consequences. On the first time, the principals of the consulting engineers were annoyed. I only had to make this call a few times. The dinnertime was not part of the twelve-hour workday. The project was completed on time and within construction budget. My next project in the office was to work on the restoration and renovation of the old Carnegie Library on Mount Vernon Square, Washington DC. When the new Martin Luther King Jr. Library was completed, everything was consolidated into that one location. The library moved out from the Mount Vernon Square location. The old Carnegie Library was restored and remodeled to a media center for the future expansion of the University of District of Columbia (UDC), which was to be located in the adjacent site.

The UDC never built on the adjacent site. Now the old library building was the History Museum of Washington DC. The adjacent site was where the new convention center is located now.

In early 1976, I started a taxi company, and managing it was an addition to my regular work. I bought used Chrysler cars. The space or area of the backseat in these cars is more than in any other cars. I had the seats reupholstered to comply with health regulations. I had it painted to the Washington DC Yellow Cab Company colors. Then I rented the cabs out to drivers. I engaged an older, experienced cabdriver to be my overseer and to find and check out reliable drivers for me. In a short time, I had ten taxicabs; nine were in use, and one was in reserve for replacement in case one of my taxis broke down. This way, I won't lose the driver of the car when it was in the shop. Every Friday afternoon between four and six, I was in the Cab Company's headquarters in New York Avenue. I collected the weekly rent and paid for the insurance and the repair bills. The repair shop was located on the premises. The drivers averaged a thousand miles a week of city driving. I paid for the weekly insurance and the upkeep on the cars, the driver's pay for the gas, and maintenance. I only accepted cash from the drivers. In the beginning, I got paid with checks; I found out later that the checks had insufficient funds in the bank, and some of them could not be collected. Because of my "cash" policy, the IRS audited me; but when I showed all the returned checks, which I could not collect, they waived their objection. I was the only white man in there with all that money, but everyone knew me there. Many times, I conducted business from a bench in a parking lot of the building. I did this till the fall of 1977, and then I sold all the cabs. I did not make profit, but it was very educational, not just the business point of view, but working with and learning from people from different walks of life.

My long hours in the office left Ilona alone at home in the house, so we decided to get a dog to keep her company, to provide some security and protection for her. One of my coworkers in the office offered us a puppy when his dog gave birth on January 19, 1976. We brought him home when he was eight and a half weeks old on March 20; we gave him a Hungarian name of *Muki*. The English translation is "fella." On the first night, he cried all night; he missed his mother and his siblings. On the next night, we put in his "bed" a hot water bottle wrapped in soft cloths and a clock. The ticking of the clock represented his mother's heartbeat, and the hot water bottle, her warmth. Then on, he was quiet and slept through the nights. He was a mix, border collie and beagle. Muki understood and took commands in both languages. He was a good companion, protector, and a good watchdog. He lived for almost thirteen years; he passed away on November 25, 1988.

We were very happy that our life was going so well. We discussed to start a family, but she would like to advance her career first before she would settle down. She wanted to stay home with the children. For my thirty-sixth birthday on June 5, 1976, Ilona prepared an elaborate dinner with all my favorite food and dessert. She gave me a beautiful carved jade chess set she bought in Georgetown. It was a big surprise. I have it displayed in my house.

I left the office in November 1976 of Chatelain, Semperton & Carcaterra after the library restoration project was completed. Then I took two weeks' vacation before I started at the end of November my new employment with DMJM Architects and Engineers (Daniel, Mann, Johnson & Mendenhall) in Washington DC. My assignment was to coordinate between architects and engineers and manage the production of a large office-building complex for the government of Saudi Arabia. It consisted of an eight-story office building, five-hundred-car parking structure, prison, mail receiving area, and repair and maintenance shops. The shops were for furniture/carpentry, electrical and mechanical systems, electrical equipment, and any other repair and maintenance. The shops were to provide maintenance and all the repairs for the complex independently, not using any outside help. All the shops were furnished with the necessary equipment and tools. The complex received two separate sources of electric power and water. It had a special air and water filtration system. It also had electric power generators for emergency, capable of providing power for the complex for ninety days. Over fifty architects and engineers were assigned to work on this project. Ilona also was employed in this office, but she was working on a different assignment. On my first day briefing, I found out this was a super secret project. Very few people knew the overall scope of the project and all parts of the design. In the evening after the working hours, all drawings were put away in a large safe. A handful of people only knew the combination of the safe. I found out later they were all from the CIA. Their assignment was to watch over us not to take home any scathes is a free hand drawing or copies of the progress drawings.

Each architect or engineer had a specific assignment and a task to work on and to complete. Someone else did the coordination between the staff. It was an interesting, but a difficult job to work on because of all the restrictions. The project was about 75 percent complete when it came to a halt one Friday. The Saudi prince who was the overseer and charge of this agency, for whom the complex was going to be built for, had fallen out of the king's "favor." The king stopped the project. All fifty people on the project were let go on this "black" Friday. As far as I know, the complex has never been built from those drawings. Therefore, let me add some comments to the design and the scope of this project. The scope called for a perimeter enclosure to be ten feet high and a yard-thick reinforced concrete wall to hold off a tank. Inside the perimeter was additional electric fence with motion detectors. The gates were two-inch steel plates with reinforcement. In front of and behind each of the gates were special security that rose up from the ground to stop any type of vehicles, including a tank. The windows between second and eighth floors were bazooka and tank bulletproof. The ground floor windows—because it was a large glass—in an emergency, a two-inch steel plate will slide in front of the windows and the doors. The roof had a heliport. It also had living quarters and storage space with food supply to accommodate three hundred people for ninety days. The prison cells were for one hundred special inmates. A separate wing was to accommodate the members of the royal family with their entourage if and when they are arrested. It was designed like a fortress and furnished like a palace. Each room in the complex can be visually and vocally monitored, including the toilet facilities. All elevator cab dimensions were like a small room to fit in a medium sofa for the royalty and a standing space adjacent to it for six people. No person can stand in front or at the back of the sofa. The length of time the elevator doors were to be open and the speed of the doors had to be carefully timed so that the long loose white clothes the men wore will not to be caught between the doors when it closed when they entered and left the elevator. In public areas of the building and some private offices, all the walls and floors were covered with a different type of marble. At one of the gates was where the "mail" room was located. All personnel, vehicles, deliveries, and mail came through this room and checked for explosives. The walls, floor, and ceiling of this room were made of four-foot-thick reinforced concrete, with no windows; the doors were like a bank's vault doors covered with reinforced two-inch-thick steel plate. Oh, one more thing, there was also a print shop furnished with all necessary equipment and accessories to print currencies for the majority of the countries in the world.

After the "black" Friday, I had two weeks off before I was rehired by DMJM as a senior architect/project coordinator in their Baltimore office for the design of the Baltimore Metro System. DMJM was in a joint venture with Kaiser Engineers Inc. on this project. My assignment was to work with the engineers on the aerial stations, coordinate and review the contract documents, and to be a technical adviser to the design architects. The work in this office was routine and uneventful. The director of architecture was Basel Acey; he was the first architect hired several years back by Harry Weese, the architect of the Washington Metro, to work on the metro design. Then the manager of the Harry Weese office in Washington DC was Stanley "Stan" Allan.

We invited my Mother and Ilona's aunt Csuri to visit us for the summer of 1977. Aunt Csuri was Ilona's mother's younger sister. Ilona's mother, Ila néni, visited us last year soon after the Hungarian government allowed relatives to visit defectors. Because Ilona did not return to Hungary in the specified time authorized by the government, she was considered one of those defectors. My mother-in-law stayed with us for several months. She was very proud of our accomplishments. We enjoyed her visit.

On my Mother's third, and it turned out to be her last, visit, she was in her seventy-fourth year. This time, the trip for her was like traveling in a car—according to her; she was very comfortable with flying. For Ilona, this was the first time she had seen her aunt since she left Hungary in 1971. We combined her visit with my Mother's to help my Mother during the trip because of her advancing age. This trip gave my Mother the opportunity to meet and know Ilona and for Aunt Csuri to meet me. They were the first family guests in our new house. Both of them were pleasantly surprised when they saw our home for the first time. Because of my Mother's age, we had to limit our sightseeing, but we had the opportunity to show them the church where we were married.

We visited Mount Vernon, the Kennedy grave in the National Cemetery, and took several trips to the Smithsonian Museums. We gave several parties and invited friends, particularly the Hungarians. During this time, Bill was visiting us for three weeks. We took a trip to Skyline Drive and had a picnic in the park. We planted two small pine trees in our front yard in memory of their visit. Their visit lasted over eight weeks, and we were sad to see them go.

At work in one morning on the second week in January 1978, Basol called me into his office. He informed me that Harry Weese & Associates was looking for a person in the Miami office to be an overall technical coordinator for the Metro Dade County Metro System, which was now under design. He recommended me to Stan Allan; now he was the president of Harry Weese & Associates. He already provided all the information on me to Stan. According to Basel, I had the job if I wanted it. Stan Allan was visiting the Baltimore office because he was the chairman of the committee who reviewed and oversaw the design of the system. The review board was hired by the city; it had a total of five members, all well-known architects and deans of architectural departments from different universities all over the country. They were to provide independent comments on the progress and the design of the project. The committee met every two months for three days, two days to review our work and one day to report their findings with recommendations in a joint meeting to the city and to the state. During these two days, each lead architect or engineer presented their group's recommended design in specific areas of the project, with some alternate designs. I generally sat at the back of the room to answer technical questions if they arose. That morning was the first day of the scheduled presentation. Ilona was the last presenter before lunch break. When she completed her presentation, Stan asked her to introduce him to her husband. I had heard of Stan Allan, but we had never met before. That day during lunch, Stan told us that he heard good things about me and he wanted to hire me for the Miami office. He also indicated that my position had been advertised in all the major newspapers and they did not find any qualified person. Stan mentioned this to Basol, and he recommended me to

Stan for that position. I figured this was an interview, and I tried to tell him my background and my experience.

After a few minutes, Stan indicated he had the information on my experience and my capabilities. He would rather tell us about the work and the people in Miami and the warm weather and the living conditions there. He also indicated that if I would like to have the job, it was mine; my position would be a project architect. He knew my present salary, and he offered me a 30 percent increase and a position for Ilona in the office there. Also he let us know that Florida didn't have state income tax, which was an additional 8 percent income. After the afternoon session, he visited Washington DC to see the recently opened first segment of the Washington Metro. I offered him a ride. After work, we met, and Ilona offered him the front seat, but he insisted to be seated at the back. I had a two-door Datsun 210 with a small backseat; the occupant had to be seated sideways. During our trip to Washington, he only talked about Miami and how much we would like it there. The project would last about five years. He liked to have the answer from us in two days, before he returned to Chicago where the Harry Weese home office was located. The next two days, Ilona and I discussed the offer and what we had to do if we accepted this opportunity. We met again for lunch on the second day, and we accepted the offer with some conditions. We wanted to spend a week in Miami and meet the people whom we will work with, a reimbursement for this trip and one additional trip for house hunting, and when we move, the travel and moving expenses to Miami. Also, to be reimbursed for living expenses and furniture storage there until we can move in to our house and the expense resulted from the sale of the house we lived in then. Also to be reimbursed for all the expenses at the end of the project in Miami, for travel and moving costs back to Washington DC, and the expenses from the sale of the house in Miami, living and the furniture storage in Washington DC. Stan agreed to all of our requests. Harry Weese & Associates would reimburse all these expenses.

Stan suggested that our trip to Miami be coordinated with him because he wanted to be there when I presented my salary request to the office manager in Miami. Ilona and my employment in Miami had to be approved by the client, Dade County.

On this transit project, Harry Weese & Associates was a part of a joint venture with four other firms, and it was called the Kaiser Transit Group. During our visit to Miami, we looked and priced out some houses. We tried to gauge, get the feel how it will be, and how it will feel living here because of the warm temperature and high humidity most of the year. We received good information from Harold and Del Horan as they were living in Miami for several years. He was the minister in the Pinecrest Presbyterian Church there. During our stay, the office manager invited us to a party given for the office staff, with the senior staff of the engineering departments, and some people from the client. This was a good opportunity for us to meet and talk to some people who were transplanted here from other parts of this country and find out their impressions and the living conditions in Miami. Our visit lasted for a week.

Upon returning home to Maryland, we prepared and sent our résumés to Miami to be submitted to Dade County for our employment approval. The waiting was on. We were not putting the house up for sale until I had a letter confirming our employment. After four weeks of waiting, I decided to give a call to Miami; I gave them three days to respond to our employment or we were staying in Maryland. I relayed the same information to Stan in Chicago. In two days, I received a phone call in the morning and an express letter in the evening confirming our employment. We took a second trip to Miami to find a house for us and to sign the contract. We put up our house for sale, started packing, and giving items away we won't need in Florida. The house was sold before the sale sign was put up. A young couple with a small child bought it. They were moving from New York as he was employed by the *Wall Street Journal*, and he was transferred to the Washington office.

We were invited to several good-bye parties. Many of our friends requested that if they visited Florida, they would stay with us. Our moving day was on the ninth of May 1978. The furniture was going to storage in Miami, and we were staying with Harold and Del Horan.

The last time we left our first house, it was emotional; in Europe, people lived in their homes for generations. We put a lot of personal touches into this house as we planned to live there for a long time. The circumstances in this country were different. Using a Hungarian expression "Humans plan and God decides," that's what happened to us.

Now we were on our way to the South to different and new surroundings. It was almost like 1957 repeated itself by relocating; but this time, I was not alone, and I had a family where we were going.

We left on the tenth of May. We took the Auto Train from Lorton, Virginia, to Orlando, Florida. We arrived in Orlando in the midmorning. From there, we had several hour's drive to South Miami where the Horan's lived. On the Auto Train were our two automobiles, Muki our dog, and for us, we had a private stateroom with bunk beds and a toilet room with a shower. Before dinner, we had cocktail in the "dome" car and saw the sunset. We had dinner and breakfast on the train's dining car. In the evening, the porter made our beds. Late in the evening, the train stopped for thirty minutes for people traveling with dogs to take them out and walk them. This was a nice accommodation for people traveling with dogs.

In our first day in Miami, we visited our house—it was under construction—to see the progress, to find out when it will be finished and when we can move in. We were staying at the Horans' in their guest bedroom. They have three children; two were living at home: Sandy, fourteen, and Tom, twelve. Jennifer, the oldest, was eighteen years old. She was living with some of her friends. This is the young lady I used to baby sit when we were living in Rock Creek Garden apartment complex in Maryland when she was less than a year old. Harold and Del also had a dog and a cat, so Muki, our dog, had some company; but he should watch out for the cat. In the evenings before dinner, we took a swim in their pool. It was easy to get used to this kind of living. Ilona and I started work for Harry Weese & Associates on May 15, 1978. Over 250 people worked for the joint venture on this project. Everyone including the client was in the same building in downtown Miami across the street from the old courthouse. In the first several months, I worked long hours. The project was under design in the last two years. I had to read lots of correspondence to learn how and why some decisions were made. The project had twenty aerial stations with twenty miles of aerial track and a train yard with several buildings. The design had three main materials: reinforced concrete—white from the coral stone used in the concrete, stainless steel, and glass brick. The platforms had red tile flooring with granite edge.

We moved in to our new house on June 15, 1978, ten days after my fortieth birthday. The house was located at 8440 SW 178th Street, Miami, Florida 33157, the area called Perrin. Our house was five blocks away from the Biscayne Bay. It was an L-shaped one-level house, which had an entry foyer, living, dining room, and four bedrooms, two and a half baths. The kitchen had a space for a table, and it was adjacent to the family room. The back of the house had a domed screened area of forty-by-fifty feet and twelve feet high, with a twenty-by-thirty-foot pool with a diving board. This area had built-in planters with lots of lush tropical vegetations. This screened-in pool area can be accessed through the master's bedroom, living and family rooms, and one of the full baths. The kitchen also had a pass-through window to the pool area. We used this large area for our everyday living and dining. The house also had a laundry room and two-car garage. The garage entry was from the side of the house. The front of the house had a circular driveway, nicely landscaped with tropical plants, and it even had a palm tree. Some of the outdoor plants I brought back with me are now in my living room. Outside, adjacent to the screen, three-foot-high "majesty" palms were planted about five feet on the center. In about three years, they grew to about nine feet and gave us privacy in the screened-in pool area. The backyard was fenced in with a four-foot-high fence for Muki where he could run around freely. The property also had orange, grapefruit, and Key lime trees. The topsoil was only six to eight inches thick, below was coral stone. The grass here looked like crab grass from the north. No storm pipes were installed in the streets. If it rained, water flowed through the cavities of the coral rock and dissipated. The furniture we had fits perfectly into our new house. We had professionally made curtains especially for the large sliding doors and windows. Now our home was complete.

The first party we gave was the housewarming party; we invited every one of our new coworkers from the office and some of our new friends. One of the housewarming gifts was a spider plant, which I still have, with lots of descendants hanging from it.

During the summer, some of our friends from the north were descending to visit us. The Abrahams, we know them for over seven years, have two children, Andrea and Tom. Luis was an electrical engineer, and we worked together in the DMJM office.

They lived in McLean, Virginia. His wife, Elizabeth, had a business making custom curtains. She made the curtains for us. Their son was about Bill's age. Luis passed away several years ago. The children are married, and they are living in the Atlanta suburb.

Our second summer guests were the Csiszár family. Alex was a mechanical engineer; he was one of Ilona's professors in the university where she graduated from in Hungary. They had a son. Now they live in Derwood, Maryland. In time, I lost touch with both of the families.

During Bill's summer visit, we could not get him out of the pool; at the end of each day, he was so wrinkled he looked like a dried prune. We took him to see the Parrot Jungle and the Monkey Jungle. In the Parrot Jungle, the parrots were free; they came and stayed on your shoulder. The jungle was situated on several acre sites, very close to the city. In the Monkey Jungle, the monkeys were free, and the visitors walked in the caged-in walkways. It was strange to be a "monkey" caged in like that. We also went to the beach and took him to see the Sea Aquarium in Biscayne Bay. He liked to come and spend his summer vacations here. In later years in one of his summer visits, we took a trip to Orlando, Florida, to see Disney World; and we spent several days there. We stayed in the hotel where the people mover had a stop in the hotel lobby. He liked it here very much. I took him each year to the construction sites to see the progress of the Metro construction.

For the rest of the summer into the fall, Ilona in her free time during the week and all weekend enjoyed the pool; she likes water and sun a lot. It appears Ilona missed our friends from up north. She felt she was alone here. My time and my mind were in the office. I was involved too much with my work. We didn't spend enough time together. She was alone too much and bored. The firework in our life was now a flickering spark. Our first Christmas in Florida was different as the days were sunny; the temperature was warm. The Xmas trees were sold in air-conditioned tents so they don't dry out from the heat and sun. The neighborhood got together and hired a snow machine and, in one neighbor's front yard, made about a fifteen-foot-high "snow mountain." In the afternoon, the children played on it. Then in the evening, the adults took over sliding down, in shorts or in their bathing suit, with drinks in one hand. The Christmas Day was a warm sunny day, and I took a swim in our pool. This was so different for me, to have this opportunity to do this, knowing my past circumstances and where I came from—the cold snowy north central Europe.

We celebrated our seventh wedding anniversary by going out to a nice exclusive restaurant in Coral Gables. The reservation had to be made several weeks in advance. In the restaurant, before you were escorted to your table, the ladies received a long-stemmed red rose. When you were seated, they put a pillow under your feet to be comfortable. The food was out of this world, and the wine selections were excellent. We enjoyed it, and we had a good time. Ilona gave me a special card she made, illustrating the major events in our seven years of marriage—from her arrival at this country, buying our first house, furnishing it, finishing the unfinished lower level, building a new brick terrace and a wood deck, our car accident by the DC line, having the yellow cabs, commuting to Baltimore, my Mother and Ilona's aunt's visit, selling our house in Silver Spring, taking the Auto Train to Florida and, with our house in Florida, illustrating our life's story in the past seven years together. In the end, she drew a baby in a blanket with a question mark for our future. It was drawn on a long brown paper; it was rolled up and tied with a ribbon when she gave it to me. This gift made me emotional and very happy.

In early February in 1979, we traveled north to visit our friends, the Csiszár family, in Rockville, Maryland, for a week. During our stay, the area had a big snowstorm with over twelve inches of snow with big drifts. It was a pleasant change and an unexpected surprise for us, and we enjoyed it a lot. It was strange to see two adults like kids playing in the snow, and we had lots of fun! I missed the feel of these cold ice crystals in my hand.

The following weeks after returning home from our trip, in one of our conversations, Ilona told me when she attended the university and after graduation that she did not date; she did not have the opportunity, and now she realized how much she missed that time and that kind of experiences in her life. She wanted to catch up on that and wanted to experience different things, which was to go dating, and she also wanted to go and to experience being in a nudist camp. After more conversations, reasoning, and explanations, she stated she wants a divorce. I asked her if she was willing to see a marriage counselor, hoping maybe it could help to sort things out. She stated that her mind was made up and planned to look for a place to live. That day, she moved out from our bedroom to the guest bedroom. I tried to reason and talk to her several times in the following days with no results. I did not intend to go through a dragged-out emotional divorce. We sat down and went through our furnishings and assets and divided it. Ilona wrote it up; it ended up as a four-paged detailed list. We called it "Property settlement between Karl J. Landesz and Ilona V. Landesz." We signed it on April 2. It was to be effective in April 4, 1979. This way, if she wanted to change her mind, then she had the opportunity to do so. We had it notarized. We also agreed to have only one attorney. We would see the lawyer together. In the lawyer's office, we would flip a coin and that would decide whose lawyer it would be. The other person would not contest. She moved out from the house on April 4. I helped the movers to load the truck. I wanted it to be over fast. It was hard to hold back the tears, but when the truck left with her, then the Niagara Falls had a competition.

We found an attorney; we explained to him our plan and showed him the notarized list of our settlement. He didn't see a problem with our plan. I flipped a coin; Ilona called it. She had an attorney. The separation agreement with the list as part of it was issued and dated on April 26. The divorce hearing was scheduled for three in the afternoon on April 29, 1979. Ilona attended the hearing; I didn't have to be there. The divorce was granted. My marriage to Ilona lasted for seven years and four months. Overall, it was a very happy, exciting, and unforgettable seven years. Four months before that, she prepared and gave me the anniversary card indicating our happy life together and our future to come. Now everything was over, and my life had fallen to pieces again. Looking back, it was my fault that I was not as attentive as I should have been in the last months. I probably should have spent more time with her and helped her to work out the problems.

In the office, I was not her immediate supervisor, but it was difficult to see her every day in there; and sometimes we had to communicate because of some work-related business. By the end of fall, she asked to be transferred to the Washington office. She remarried in 1985 in Washington. Her husband teaches economics in George Washington University, and they are living in Alexandria, Virginia.

After the divorce, I spent more and more time and effort with my work, using this as an escape from the world and what happened to me.

This fall, Alan and Edna Sanders, Del Horan's parents, spent a couple of weeks in my home before they went to Sanibel Island on the Gulf Coast of Florida for their winter retreat. Each day during their stay, they went over to see the grandchildren in the afternoon after school and stayed for dinner. This way, both of the families had some time to themselves. It was good for me to have someone in the house besides Muki and not to be alone. Alan and Edna repeated the same visit on the following year.

I didn't want to spend the 1979 Christmas alone. I took three weeks' vacation and spent the holidays in Hungary with my Mother and sister. That was to be my first Christmas with my family since 1956. In the past twenty-two Christmases, every time I was there and Bing Crosby sang, "I'll Be Home for Christmas," my eyes get watery; and I recall my last Christmases with my family. But for this Christmas, I would be home for Christmas, and it would not be in my dreams. It had been over two decades since we were together in this joyful occasion. I was forty-one years old. This was my fourth trip home. Unfortunately, this time, there were only three of us in the family.

I left Miami on the afternoon of December 20, 1979, traveling through Frankfurt, Germany. I arrived in Budapest on the next morning. It was a rainy, cold day; it felt like I landed in Siberia coming from warm, sunny Miami. Going through customs was routine. If travelers didn't have an entry visa, now they could get it in the airport when they arrived. The government even provided a place where your picture can be taken for your entry visa. In the airport, waiting for me was my Mother; her sister, Aunt Zsuzsa; and Uncle Nándor. It was nice to see my family again and nice to be home again. My luggage weighed the maximum I was allowed to carry. This Christmas, I wanted to be the Santa again, the same way it was on my last Christmas before I left home in 1956. When I was shopping in Miami, it was hard to find warm clothing, but I found things that they would like. The home where my Mother and sister lived was nicely decorated for the holidays. My Mother was cooking and baking constantly for the next several days. She was preparing the same meal and desserts that I had for my last Christmas before my travel started to the "other world." We bought the Christmas tree on the same day and the same place from the same people where we bought it in the past when I was living at home. Here, the time stands in place. We decorated the tree in the afternoon of Christmas eve day. The items we decorated the tree with was very similar to this country; we also added special Christmas candy. We lit the tree with lighted candles. That was the reason we put up our tree until Christmas eve; that way, the tree was still fresh, and there is less danger of catching fire from the candles. (This custom goes back over four hundred years. The legend is that the Reverend Martin Luther started this custom in the 1500s. He was looking up at the winter night sky, wondering at the beauty of the stars. He decided to put lighted candles on the family's Christmas tree.)

When the time arrived to ring the small bell announcing the arrival of the Santa, as customary in our family, my Mother asked me to do the honors. First, I was not sure I heard it right. It was the first time it truly hit me that my Father was not being here with us and how I could step into his shoes. It was a small thing, but symbolized a lot for me. Ever since I could remember, my Father rang the small bell, announcing Santa's arrival. After some emotional pause, I reluctantly went into the other room and rang the bell. My Mother and sister came in; we sang the same Christmas songs what we were singing over two decades ago; then we prayed. We thanked God we were together again in this joyful occasion. In the end, we hugged, but this time for me, it was an incomplete hug. All of a sudden, I felt very warm inside; I know my Father was watching us from far, far away. The dinner was unbelievable, and everything was so nice. It was hard for me to see an empty place on the table next to me. After dinner when my Father used to read to us, we spent the time talking about him, the times we had with him. When we were clearing the table after dinner, I looked outside to the area when my Father cleared the snow over two decades ago to collect that fistful of dirt, which he gave to me twenty-three years ago. My Mother and sister opened their presents one by one that Santa brought for them; they liked everything.

In the end, my Mother took several small packages from under the tree and gave it to me. When I opened the packages, I recognize it were some of the Persian items we had around the house. This time, my Mother provided background information to each of the items. One was a hand-carved silver matchbox case with matchbox and matches in it. According to her, the match from this box was used last time when I was born. The other gift was a silver cigarette case, my Mother's gift to my Father when I was born. She purchased two plain silver cigarette cases lined inside with gold and two different postcards. The pictures on the postcards are the ruins of the ancient city of *Persepolis*. *Darius I* founded the city about 518 BC. It was rediscovered in 1924 by archaeologist Ernst Herzfeld. She took these items in Tehran to an artist who carved the pictures from the postcards to each side of the cigarette case. She gave one to my Father and the other to the doctor who helped me on my arrival. Only two of this design exists in the world. I also received some other Persian and Turkish artifacts, which were in my family's possession since the late 1920s. The items they had were purchased in antique shops or from the artists in Istanbul, Turkey, or in Tehran, Iran. In the past, in each of my visits, they give me different items from their collections. The last day before I left, at dinner, my Mother gave me one more gift, the small bell that my Father used to ring on Christmas eve, signaling Santa's arrival; and I used it this Christmas eve. This bell was never used since then. We had beautiful, memorable holidays, and I was glad I came home to spend the Christmas together with them.

It turns out this was my last Christmas I'll have with my Mother. Every minute you spend with your loved one has to be cherished because you never know what the future will bring.

The winter weather did not allow us to visit and see places or take trips. Most of the time I was home with my Mother, and this gave us the opportunity to go over my parents' photograph albums and their old documents and papers. Looking through the albums, my Mother gave us the background story for each picture. It was nice to find out and to learn about my past and the early years of my life. Going through the papers, I found things that were very interesting. One was a stack of old Hungarian paper currencies from year 1944 through 1946 in different denominations. It was printed during the inflation and the Russian military occupation. My Father inherited the old money from his older brother in 1948 when he immigrated to Argentina, South America. Some of the banknotes were in two languages, Hungarian and in Russian. Some were only for the use of the Red Army (Soviet forces occupying Hungary). Some had expiration dates on them. The banknotes' face values were from one pengö to one hundred billion pengö. (Pengö was the name of the Hungarian currency then.) Some were with postage-stamp paper stamped on the banknote, indicating additional devaluation of the currency. This helped the government without printing more money to keep up with the rapid inflation. During this time the inflation was so great the workers got paid twice a day, lunchtime and at end of the workday. The half-day income may be worth the price of two eggs. The money they got at lunchtime, they had to spend it right a way because by the evening, it was not worth anything. Each day, you go to work carrying a suitcase with you; this was where you put your pay. All this information was from my Mother, family members, and older friends and neighbors of my parents. Much of this Hungarian money was framed, and I have it in my family room. When some of my guests were complaining of the hard conditions in this country, I showed it to them and gave a short explanation of the history of the currency, letting them know how lucky they were they didn't have to go to work with a suitcase six days a week to collect their pay twice a day; and the only enjoyment they get from it was when you burn it, it gave you some warmth for a short time.

I also found an old newspaper called the *Magyar Nemzet* (Hungarian Nation) dated July 12, 1959. The article reported about a unique television tower construction in Hungary. The tower was six hundred feet high, six feet in diameter, with a two-person elevator in it. At the top of the tower was a sixty-foot television antenna. The article described the unique design of the tower and its anchoring. It gave the names of the design team, and it included my Father's.

To that date, I was not aware of this project of his.

On this trip, I learned a lot about my past, when I was young, and the happenings in Hungary when we were in Germany.

I returned to Miami on January 10, 1980.

Looking back and trying to summarize this decade, it had its ups and downs like a roller-coaster ride. During this decade, several major happenings took place in my life. I resigned from my architectural office, started up and managed and sold my taxi company, worked for other architectural offices on very interesting projects, and moved to Florida for a new, challenging job. Between all these was my divorce getting finalized, then getting married and divorced again. The life was not boring. I learned a lot.

Trip to Atlanta.
August, 1970, Atlanta.
My Mother and Bill.

Silver Spring, Maryland.

On our wedding day, January 29, 1972,

Our new house in Silver Spring, Maryland, August, 1973.

With my mother.
Summer 1977, Silver Spring.

My mother with Bill.
She is seventy-four years old.
Summer 1977, Silver Spring.

Our house in Miami, the pool area.
June 15, 1978.

Christmas eve, my Mother and sister.
Dunakeszi, Hungary. December 24, 1979

Ilona's seventh wedding anniversary card,
illustrating our seven years of marriage.
Miami, Florida, January 29, 1979.

(Starting from top, left to right). Her arrival by plane. Our wedding. Commuting to work together. She worked evenings in my office. Our first house. Christmas in our new house. Ilona's and my Mother's visit. I resigned from my office partnership and started working in Washington DC. Furnishing our house. Our dog, Muki's, arrival. Finishing the basement. Ilona cut her finger with the lawn mower. I built a deck and terrace. We had a car accident at the DC line. Our taxi company. I started working for DMJM. My mother and Ilona's aunt's visit. Commute to Baltimore to work on the Metro there. Sold our house and moved to Miami. Traveled by Auto Train to Florida. Bought a house in Miami and started working on the Miami Metro. Closing it with a question mark for a future baby.

IX

The '80s

Every weekend on Sundays, I had dinner with Harold and Del and their two children, Sandy and Tom. Before dinner, we had a cocktail. I kept a small bottle of Southern Comfort (bourbon whisky) in her kitchen cabinet. I have it on ice with ginger ale before dinner. After some time, I noted the contents of the bottle was losing its strength. I found out many years later from Tom, their son, that he'd added water and/or tea to compensate for the amount consumed by him. Harold liked to have dinner at six. After dinner, we watched the *Masterpiece Theater* on television. When I left, I helped Harold take out the garbage and put it by the sidewalk. It was nice to see their children Sandy and Tom growing up. She was becoming a young lady, and he, a young gentleman. The other daughter, Jennifer, got married; and they had a son, Bill. Sandy was so popular with the boys that when her sister was visiting them, she became Sandy's "appointment secretary" and "traffic cop." When Sandy's dates were ringing the doorbell at the front door and Sandy went to greet them, Jennifer lets the previous date out the backdoor. This time in Harold and Dell's lives was a lively time period. I had many good and nice memories of the times we spent together. Sometimes Harold, in his Sunday sermon, made references to my past or items in my home. He gave me a copy of the sermons for me to save.

Meantime in the office, work was progressing. The design team members in the joint venture were experts in their field on mass transit.

We were the general consultants to Metropolitan Dade County Office of Transportation Administration, the owner of the Miami Metro system. As a general consultant, we were to prepare for the project the following: general plans, directive/design and standard drawings, and the master specification. These documents established the design and standards for the project. The general plans showed the station's location and its design on each site. Directive drawings developed the meager areas of the design. Standard drawings established the interface details with the procurement contracts, like for example, the elevators and escalators in the system. Each procurement contract was one contract for the entire system; it provided uniformity and simplified maintenance for the project. The master specification established the construction requirements and the quality of the materials to be used in the project. Upon completion of the above documents, the section designers were selected; they were architects and engineers who prepared the construction documents the system will be built from. These documents were based on the established criteria, design, and standards for the project. We also prepared construction documents for the University of Miami station. The contract documents for this station established the minimum content and the requirements of the drawings for the section designers when they prepared the drawing for the other stations. My assignment in the office was to manage the production of the architectural drawings for the architectural department (Harry Weese & Associates) and, as a technical coordinator with the other departments on the project, to see that Mr. Weese's design intent was carried out by all disciplines. Mr. Weese provided us with the conceptual design for the system from his office in Chicago. In the Miami office, the local designer worked out the concepts and faxed it back to the home office for Mr. Weese's approval. Sometimes, he visited our office in Miami. We also provided periodical on-site review visits for the project during construction.

In the summer of 1980, my cousin Egon Landesz with his wife, Andrea, were visiting from Buenos Aires, Argentina. This was the first time I'll see them in thirty-three years. They arrived in New York City several weeks ago; they rented a car, traveled to Boston, then to Atlanta to visit my sister Gisela, then to here. He was a general contractor there; he built custom homes and small shopping centers, as well as some road construction. He worked with his father; they were partners until he passed away at age seventy-eight in May 1969. This time in Argentina, they had 1,000 percent inflation a year. He explained to me how it worked and how he paid laborers or bought or sold anything. The beginning was establishing the base rate or price of an item; then at the end of each day, based on the government statistics, it got adjusted with the reported percentage. This way, hopefully everybody had a breakeven. We had a nice visit. I showed them the sites of Miami and visited the Everglades. They enjoyed my swimming pool; they spent a lot of time in it. He returned the following spring to invest some of his savings in this country. He also made arrangements with some doctors for his son, Patrik's, treatment. Patrik arrived in the fall and stayed several months with me. Egon passed away in Argentina after three strokes at the age seventy-five on December 19, 1995. He was buried at sea.

During Bill's 1981 summer visit, we traveled to Hungary to see and to visit his grandmother and his aunt Marika whom he never met. He was twelve years old. To cover the trip's expenses, I borrowed on my life insurance. I'd like to show him how people lived in other countries and, specifically, how people lived under the "improved" Communism. I wanted him to experience the everyday chores for him to see what you had to do to accomplish the cooking each day, doing laundry by heating water on the wood-burning stove, and hand-washing the clothes in a wood tub or just going to the stores and buy the food for a day. I took him to meet all the same relatives his mother met sixteen years ago, plus some additional second cousins arriving since then. He met Aunt Zsuzsa and Uncle Nándor; we had lunch with them when we were in Budapest, sightseeing. We took a train from Dunakeszi to Budapest. In the city, we walked everywhere; this way, I could show him from close-up several-hundred-year-old buildings or to pop into stores for him to see what merchandise were available. We visited the Castle District in Buda. I pointed out to him the house where my Father lived when he was his age, where he took us in the summers for a day trip when we were his age. In this district, the buildings were under restoration, and each layer of stucco was dated when it was applied to the buildings in different centuries. I pointed out to Bill the layer of stucco dated when the country he was born in was discovered by Columbus. We walked where the Roman emperors and the Turkish sultans walked, ruled from, and then left behind. We visited old buildings, roads, and the ruins of viaducts that they built centuries ago and the ruins of a coliseum where killing Christians was used for entertainment. We visited the zoo, and my Mother walked with Bill like she used to do it with us when we were his age, explaining the different animals, which countries they were from. My sister and I stayed in the background and watched and listened how they communicate and pointed out different animals to each other. This was the high point of our visit for my Mother. She was so happy that she could communicate with Bill directly and they could understand each other.

I was glad she had this time and the opportunity to spend with him. If 10 percent of what he saw during our stay stayed with him, then he learned a lot. Very few children have this opportunity to see and experience different things firsthand.

He played with my old toys; he liked them. Before we left, my Mother gave it to him. He took it back with him to Atlanta. We played in the yard; he climbed the same tree I used to climb when I lived there and sat on the branches and daydreamed of a better life. That daydream came true, and it was real now—I have a better life. He also crawled in the pit where the water meter was located. It was a damp hole and full of slugs, which he became fond of. The day when we had to leave, we got up early. Bill got ready first. He went outside to wait for my cousin Öcsi to pick us up and to take us to the airport. In the meanwhile, I was getting ready and doing the last-minute packing. We safely got to the airport; it was a sad good-bye as all good-byes are. From here, we flew to Frankfurt, Germany, and from there to Miami. When we were waiting in the international transfer terminal in Frankfurt, I noted Bill's blue blazer had white streaks on them in several locations. I asked him if he knows how the streaks got there; he had no idea. I did some investigation, and I found out every pocket in his blazer had several slugs in it. Probably some of them crawled out in the overhead compartment coming here on the plane, and that made the marks. We went to the toilet room and emptied all his pockets and flushed the remaining slugs down the toilet. I was glad I found it there because no animals were allowed to be brought into the States. If it was found out there, it could have complicated our reentry to the United States. We returned home to Miami without any additional incident. This brings us to the end of his three-week visit with me.

In April of 1982 during the spring break, Jean Sanders, now Mrs. Owen Chambers, with her two children—Jeanette, twelve, and Owen Jr. (his nickname is *Gipper*), six years old—were visiting her sister Del Horan and her family for a week from Gaithersburg, Maryland.

It was the first time I saw Jean since her wedding sixteen years ago. I found her more attractive than ever before. During their stay, they came to my house for dinner one evening. Jeanette and Owen were very pleasant, intelligent, and smart children, behaved like grown-ups. Jean met her husband when she was in college. He graduated from Virginia Military Institute (VMI) in 1965 and served in Vietnam; he was a retired marine officer, a major. Now he is working for an agency affiliated with the federal government; the office is located in Maryland.

In the office, we completed the contract documents for the University of Miami station. We also prepared a large-scale colored landscape drawings of the station and the surroundings area; we mounted on several four-by-eight-foot foam boards and sent it to Mr. Weese to Chicago to be displayed in the office there. In less than a week, it was returned to us with several markings on the landscape design. We had to revise the drawings, and it was reissued to the contractor. The station was publicly bid for construction in the end of 1981. The lowest bidder was a general contractor from New Jersey. Locally, no contractors were capable of handling large contracts like the station. The Dade County Office of Transportation was the overseer of the construction; they provided full-time inspectors for the duration of the construction. The inspectors were to observe that the contractor was complying with the requirements of the approved contract document. In other words, to see that the contractor was building it right, and everything was done the way it was supposed to be. Things went smoothly in the first several months of the station's construction. On one of my regular site visits, I observed cracks in the rainforest concrete structure where an expansion joint post was to be installed; the expansion joint was missing. I pointed this out to the county inspector who was on the site full-time and to the contractor's superintendent, requesting that this problem be resolved with a recommendation for a substitution in a timely manner. Two weeks later, I returned with structural engineers to see the resolution of the missing expansion joint. Nothing had happened to remedy the problem, but the contractor was allowed to proceed with the placement of the reinforced concrete the rest of the way without providing the required expense joint. When we approached the construction trailer, I observed a meeting was taking place between the county representatives and the general contractor.

When I was entering the trailer, I was stopped and turned away. I was not allowed to enter and report my findings or attend the meeting. Florida had a Sunshine Law. All meetings where the government or their agent was a participant in a meeting was to be open to the public. I requested to be included in the meeting; it was denied. I let them know that I will notify the *Miami Herald* newspaper and the local television station to look into what was happening with the construction, why the meeting was in secret, and why the county inspectors let the contractor construct an inferior product, by doing so, wasting the taxpayer's hard-earned money. I called my office and let them know what had taken place. Then I left and returned to the office. As soon as I arrived, there was a phone call from Chicago, wanting to know what happened. The client, the Dade County, called and was upset that I threatened them by calling in the media to investigate their action. It appears I struck a nerve. The county requested the joint venture to call an emergency meeting and discipline me for my action. In the joint venture, Harry Weese & Associates (HWA) was represented by Stan Allan, the president of our company. In two days, the meeting was held. The client insisted that I was to be suspended for three weeks without reimbursement for my pay from the client and for the duration I have to stay out of the office. In addition, I cannot do site visits for three months. I was informed officially about their action. In private, all the principals of the joint venture one by one let me know they appreciated my action. They had a concern that some employees in the county were taking the wrong road in this project. Now they felt things were more open. They also let me know I will get paid and the joint venture will reimburse Harry Weese & Associates for my salary. In the first two weeks, I worked from home. At the end of each day, someone from the office stopped by and gave me the work and picked it up the next day. For the third week, I was already scheduled to start my vacation and to visit Hungary.

My trip to Hungary was scheduled several weeks before my Mother was diagnosed with glaucoma. Every one of her siblings has or had cataract or glaucoma or both. The doctor who examined her requested that she be operated immediately.

Because she was a widow of a retired worker, she was at the bottom of the priority for the surgery. When the time came for the operation, a month later, by then she was blind. This happens when the government manages and reasons health care. The government, this way, wants to reduce the old people's life expectancy in the long run to save money. In this country, some insurance companies do the same when they don't pay for lifesaving treatment for their patients or they act very slowly on the process for its approval.

I received a letter from my sister on June 3 that my Mother turned yellow all over her body, including the white of her eyes, and she had pain in her side. The doctors concluded that she has problems with her liver or bile. The doctors decided to operate on her and see what was causing the pain and the discoloration on her skin. She was taken to the hospital in Budapest on May 27 and was operated the next day.

I left on June 15, 1982, at four thirty in the afternoon. This was my sixth trip to Hungary. My trip became an emergency leave. When I arrived on June 16 at one fifty in the afternoon, my cousin Öcsi was waiting for me in the airport and took me to the hospital to see my Mother. I found out from Öcsi when we were driving to the hospital that according to the doctors, she has a tumor in the bile duct and this was the reason she turned yellow. The surgeon who operated her thinks the tumor has cancer; therefore, he closed her up without doing anything to her. It was customary in Hungary not to tell the patient that he or she has cancer. But in a short time, she figured it out. She found out from the nurse that during the operation, nothing was removed; this was also the practice in Hungary if they found cancerous tumors. She was very happy to see me. All these years, she was the strong person helping me when I needed help. Now it was my turn to be with her and try to help her. She was in a room with nine other patients with one nurse per shift to take care of all. The nurses were on a twelve-hour shift. One nurse took care of everything: bringing the food; cleaning the room, including the bathroom; bringing the bedpan; checking the temperature; giving of medicine; changing of bandage; and giving of a sponge bath if you cannot get up and do it yourself. Generally, the patients got washed and cleaned at night because then the nurse has the time to do it. If you were strong enough to wash yourself or take a shower, then you clean the bathroom after yourself. These things were typical in the Hungarian hospitals. For my Mother to get some special attention, I talked to the day and night nurse and gave each in Hungarian standards a large amount of money to look out for her and give her special attention when she needed it. It was customary to give some money to the doctors who cared for your loved ones. I located the sergeant; when I tried to give him some money, he refused it. Instead, he requested for plastic bags like the Ziploc bags for his patients. He knows that I am from the States. These plastic bags were not available in Hungary. The hospital reused all the plastic bags and tubes for the patient's needs. It was used to hold drainage after the surgery. I saw that some of the bags on the patients were in sad condition; some were leaking and dripping when they walked in the corridors.

One of the patients in my Mother's room was a young lady. She had two small children, and she has been in the hospital since Easter. She had been operated three times. First for appendectomy, the second time for the infection from the first operation, and the third time to remove a pair of scissors they left in during the second surgery. She was still recuperating, and we were now close to the end of June. It was a warm summer; the windows were open, no screen on the windows, the flies were all over the room, including on the patients and on the food. The food was—let's put it this way, my dog, Muki, received better food than what was served in the hospital. Every Sunday morning at six o'clock, when the breakfast was served, they gave you your lunch and dinner for that day. It was two slices of bread with a slice of cold cuts and a slice of cheese. The kitchen was closed on Sundays; this was the day off for the staff. My cousin Öcsi brought her home-cooked food every day three times a day, before he went to work in the morning, in his lunchtime, and in the evening. He did this with all the family members when they were in the hospital. My Mother stayed in the hospital for over thirty days. We took her home on June 25; she was very weak. She was in her seventy-ninth year of her life. She had no appetite; she didn't want to eat. With the local doctor's help, she got medication to help her appetite and some vitamins. I bought all the vitamins on the black market. Slowly, she was regaining some of her strength. I returned home to Miami on July 1; this was the first time she has not come to the airport to wave good-bye. I had a feeling that my next trip to Hungary would be different.

Through the telephone, I was in close contact with Aunt Zsuzsa and Uncle Nándor and with Öcsi to monitor my Mother's condition. She didn't have a telephone in her home. One of them visited her every other day. Her health was slowly deteriorating. On November 12, 1982, she passed away at her home in my sister's arms; she was seventy-eight years old. When I received the news, it was not unexpected, but still it was hard to bear. I curled up in one corner of the sofa like a butterfly in its cocoon and let the emotions go wild. It took me a long time till I settled down and regained my composure. It was hard to think that she has left us and I won't see her again.

The last glimpse I have of her was when I looked back from the street in front of the house before I got into the car the day I was leaving, and she was standing inside the door of the house and waving. She was so frail; she could not see me that I was waving to her because of her lack of eyesight.

Now, looking back, it is hard to find words to properly summarize her life among us. She was the calmness during the storm. She was our guiding light during the times when it was needed the most. She was our Mother who took care of us no matter what. She was our teacher, more than one way, in the turbulent times in our lives and in our history. She never complained about anything. When we did not have enough food for all of us to eat, for herself she boiled a cup of water with a dozen or so caraway seeds in it for flavor, and she had it with a slice of bread. I recalled she did this more than once when we were growing up. Her stature was small, but made up for it by giving her heart. She left her mark in this world in her children. "We are sorry if in our life's journey together, we upset you or gave you any hardship. But we loved you very much." She was buried in the Farkasreti Cemetery in Budapest, next to my Father, on December 6, 1982. The funeral was at two o'clock in the afternoon local time. I did not attend. I was there in spirit. Next time I visited Hungary again, it was seven years later in 1989.

When I returned from my trip to Hungary, I found out that during my trip, Jean's husband, Owen Chambers, and the father of Jeanette and Owen Jr., unexpectedly passed away on Father's Day on June 19, 1982, fifteen days shy of his forty-first birthday. He was a Vietnam veteran; he committed suicide when he visited his widowed mother who was in the hospital in Beaufort North Carolina.

In early October, I called Jean to see how she was doing; we had a long friendly, pleasant conversation. I called her again in the middle of the month to see how she and the children were. I mentioned to her I had to take a business trip to Washington DC at the end of the month and if we can we get together then and go out. By the end of our conversation, she offered if I wanted, I could stay in her home in the guest bedroom. I arrived on Wednesday late afternoon; she picked me up at the national airport. When we arrived at her house, the children were very excited. Edna, Jean's mother, was there; she was watching the children. It was nice to see her again since the spring when she was in Miami. After dinner, Edna went home to Leisure World in Silver Spring where she lives.

After the children went to bed, I told Jean my trip was not a business trip. I came up to spend some time with her and with the children. She was not that surprised; maybe I am not a good fibber. The next morning after the children left to school, we had a conversation; she was very nervous and talked a lot. We had lunch in the Normandie Farm restaurant in Potomac, Maryland. During my stay in the evenings, we went out to dinner; Jean enjoyed it. Edna or some other people babysat for the children. In the weekend, I spent time with Jeanette and Owen; we played inside and outside the yard. For the first time, they had an adult male to talk to and visit with. All other time, they only were associating with their mother and grandmother. They missed their father; it appears that Jeanette did more than Owen. She was older, more to remember by. Jean and I, we talked a lot. She talked, I listened. It helped her to express her concerns, her thoughts, her sorrow, and sadness. She had no one to talk to; Edna was not the person to talk about death or personal problems. She confided in me and talked about her life with her parents, life with her husband, and her marriage, specifically in the later years. Her husband was under doctor's supervision for depression. Her last conversation with him was on Father's Day; maybe it triggered his action. She recalled the telephone call; it did not sound that it was a diplomatic conversation, particularly with a depressed person. That conversation troubled her for years. She blamed herself for what happened that day. She was concerned of what is the future for her and for the children. This type of conversation followed for many, many months. At the end of my stay, we concluded that my next visit would be at Thanksgiving. I returned to Miami on Monday evening. In the following weeks, we spent hours on the telephone almost every evening; sometimes I called her from the office when I worked late. The office had an unlimited lump sum, long-distance telephone contract. It appears our telephone visits helped her to start sorting out her problems and face it one by one, one day at a time. It was a very slow process.

My next trip to the north was on midday Wednesday for my Thanksgiving visit. Jean met me at the national airport. This time, she appeared more upbeat and not as depressed as she was a month ago; her appearance was happier and relaxed. We had a nice Thanksgiving; Edna stayed with us throughout the weekend.

It had been over five months since Owen passed away. Jean asked me if I would go through the house room by room, including the master bedroom and bathroom, all closets, chest of drawers, and collect all her late husband's belongings and put it in plastic bags to be donated to charities. Some items were put aside and given to her cousins. Her husband's military uniforms, other military items, sign-in album from their wedding, family pictures, his two briefcases, his camera, and some other personal items were put into several footlockers in the basement storeroom. The military uniforms were saved for their son, Owen. It would be given to him when he grew up. Everything that was related to her husband was put away, except one recent small picture when he was with the children; it was left in the den on a bookshelf. This day was a very difficult and emotionally hard day for Jean. The next days were better, and in the surface, it appeared some of the wounds were slowly healing. For Jean, this was the first step in the positive direction. Again, we spent a lot of time talking. She mentioned that Christmas was approaching and she didn't want to spend it alone in her house. She talked to Del, her sister in Miami, and they spent the Christmas holidays with them. Edna was already scheduled to be there. During our conversation, she indicated that she never traveled outside this country. That gave me an idea what would happen if for Christmas I gave her a trip to Nassau, Bahamas, to spend the first days of the New Year there, start the New Year in different surroundings, in a different environment.

As soon as I returned to Miami, I made arrangements with a travel agent for our pending trip. When the airline tickets and the hotel were reserved, I called her and told her what would be her Christmas present from me and would she accept it; with no hesitation, she said yes. But first, she had to talk to her sister if she would look after the children during our trip. The response from Del was positive. I finalized our trip, and we were scheduled to leave Miami on December 30 at eight fifty in the morning and to return on January 4 at five twenty-five in the afternoon. The reservation was for us to stay in the Balmoral Beach Hotel on the beach in Nassau.

The time was upon us for Jean and the children to arrive for their Christmas visit. The first days, we went to the parrot and monkey jungles, which they enjoyed. We had good times together. They spent some time in my house; the children enjoyed riding my lawn mower, which each tried out. They also spent some nights in my home. After the children retired for the day, Jean and I spent time in the pool before we ended our day. Jean's Christmas present to me was a set of luggage that will be useful for the trip to the island.

We left for Nassau on schedule; the flying time was approximately forty-seven minutes. During our approach to our destination, we looked out the window, and the water below us was calm, clear, and had beautiful turquoise color. Our room was in the sixth floor, had a balcony, and overlooked the pool and the ocean. On the first morning, we had breakfast in our balcony. We spent a lot of time on the beach, where we drank fresh coconut juice from the coconut, which was picked in front of us from the tree; this experience was first for both of us. We took a boat ride and ended up in a small island by ourselves. The water was so clear you could see the white sand and the fish nibble on your leg. We went sightseeing, walking the historic part of Nassau. We visited the old fortresses and shopped in the straw market. Our five full days were unforgettable; I will remember for the rest of my life that we had fun; we enjoyed each other's company. The only problem we had was with the New Year's Eve dinner. The restaurant's capacity was not sufficient, even in shifts, to provide dinner to every guest. They had a no-reservation policy. The lines were very long. We were standing in line for approximately thirty minutes, and the line was not moving; then I excused myself and entered the restaurant in the backdoor. I located the maîtrede and gave him a decent amount of tip. I returned to the line to get Jean to enter the restaurant in the same way; by then, a table for two was waiting for us.

After dinner, we took a walk on the beach in a full moonlight. At midnight, we gave each other a toast with a glass of champagne for a happier New Year of 1983. It was twenty-six years ago almost to the minute when I crossed the Hungarian border to freedom, and now I was walking on the beach in Nassau in moonlight with the most beautiful girl in the world.

The festive and happy time came to the end; as soon as we returned to Miami, Jean, with the children, were headed home; and everyone was back to the old routine.

My next visit to see Jean and the children was in February; this time, I stayed longer than a long weekend. During my visit, we went downtown to the Smithsonian Air and Space Museum; Owen likes airplanes. It was very cold that day; the wind was piercing through your clothes. It was felt the most when we stopped on the mall to take a picture. In two days, we had one of the biggest snowfalls in the area. We tried to clear the driveway and the sidewalks, but the snowfall was so big Owen could dig a tunnel and crawl through it. On the roof, the snow was several feet high. Starting in the mid afternoon, all four of us sled in the backyard into the late evening with the outdoor light on. After several days when the airport reopened, the fun time was over, and I had to leave and go home.

My next visit was in March for Jean's thirty-ninth birthday. Jeanette and Owen prepared breakfast for their mother and served it in bed. I prepared the birthday dinner and baked walnut-chocolate cake.

In the summer, as a family, we took vacations to the Shenandoah National Park; the drive took us to the Skyline Drive. We spent a couple days at Big Meadows and then in Skyland Resorts where Owen sprained his ankle. Overall, everyone enjoyed the vacation. At other times, we took different trips as a family to different places.

On Jean's fortieth birthday, we went to a restaurant close to the White House; the dinner consisted of six courses and two kinds of wine.

My trips became a routine now; I visited every five to seven weeks. During my visits, everyone was very playful; we had lots of fun. We continued to have long telephone conversations almost every day between trips.

Many years later, I find out from Jeanette how much she looked forward and appreciated my visits because during my stay, she could be her age, and she didn't have to watch over and take care of her mother. Then she could be herself for a short time. During my visits, everyone was very playful; we had lots of fun.

During my three-month suspension from the construction sites, one of my coworkers had the "honor" to be my ears and eyes. He took photographs of his observations. One day, he brought in a large chunk of concrete from the University of Miami Station and put it on my desk, with photographs where he found it and where it came from. It appears the concrete was a corner piece from the station. After a short investigation, it was concluded that some of the reinforcing steel was missing from the reinforced concrete. The absence of the expansion joint was the reason for the concrete to fall. In the final investigation by an independent outside structural engineer and thorough x-raying the station, it was concluded that about 50 percent of the reinforcing steels were missing. That was one of the reasons for the missing expansion joint. The work stopped immediately; the station was shored up. Dade County did not want to demolish the station; it would be too embarrassing for them. They asked the joint venture to prepare a remedial design. With some small amount of demolition, adding more columns—by doing so, reducing the spaces between columns—it solved the problem. The investigation and the x-ray of the station to locate the reinforcing steel in the structure cost the county access of one hundred thousand dollars. The general contractor of the University of Miami Station was fired, and the bonding company's contractor completed the construction. They also had construction problems on other areas of the project, with unexplained extras and by not using specified materials, substituting it with non approved, lesser-grade materials.

On some days, at end of the day when there were no people on the construction site, the office manager and I got access to the construction site; we walked through and inspected the construction. I pointed out to him the construction discrepancies compared to the contract documents. He made notes of our findings. When he returned to the office, he prepared the report, and after typing, by midmorning it was on the owner's desk.

Getting this report almost every day, the owner was overwhelmed with problems, got upset and annoyed with his staff. The construction problems reached all the way to Washington. The federal government organized a crime task force from the Justice Department as undercover investigators to infiltrate the construction project in different work assignments. They exposed the corruptions during their undercover investigation and arrested several people who were related to the project.

Dade County was required to audit with an independent auditor, the county's transportation administration who oversaw the construction and the entire general and subcontractors who were working on the project. They had to review all payment requests from the contractors and all payments to them and all additional work requests by the contractor and all payments for that effort to the contractors. The investigations and the extra work to remedy all the problems took a year and the cost of millions of dollars. In the meantime, the Harry Weese & Associates office manager left and opened his office in Miami. I became deputy office manager and manager of the production.

The first segment of the Metro system opened in May of 1984. The same year, I was published in the Marquis *Who's Who* in the South and Southwest, nineteenth edition.

The work on the Miami Metro was coming to an end; The joint venture staff was decreasing to a handful of people, closing up the individual offices. I put my house up for sale in April of 1984. Stan Allan was transferring me to the Washington office of Harry Weese & Associates (HWA). As we agreed six years ago, the company will pay for my moving expenses. He notified one of the vice presidents in the Washington office of my pending arrival. Stan asked me to work out the details with the people there. He left to the Orient early May for a three-week vacation.

I made arrangements with the movers and started packing and set the moving date to July 2. When I called the Washington office and talked to one of the vice presidents, he was very cold, negative to the idea that I was coming to the Washington office to work. I found out later it was Ilona's influence that created this atmosphere. She worked in the office.

After Stan Allan returned from his vacation and visited us in Miami, I informed him of my conversation with the Washington office. He suggested—after my move to Maryland and when I was ready to start working—that I just go in the office, take my drafting equipment with me, find an empty desk, take my seat, don't say anything to anyone, and he will see me on his next visit there.

The plan was to have Bill visit me during the move, who was now fifteen years old, and will accompany me on the drive to Maryland. Since my Miami home was not yet sold, one of my former coworkers moved his family in to house-sit for me. Since he was unemployed, he could save on the rent and utilities. Muki, my dog, stayed in the house with them till I found a place, a kennel for him, once I was settled.

In the past several months when I was visiting Jean, I had engaged a real estate agent to help me to look for a house. I found one that was under construction; it will be completed in ninety days. I signed a contract and put down a deposit, but it was contingent on my selling the Miami house. The house was located in Silver Spring at a close proximity to the neighborhood where I lived before I moved to Miami.

The moving day arrived; a large moving truck was filled up with my furniture. The furniture was going to storage. The houseplants were dropped off in my friend Abraham's home in McLean, Virginia, and some of my personal items and clothing were going to Jean's home.

After living in Miami for over six years, Bill and I started driving on the afternoon of July 2; we spent two nights on the road in motels, arriving at Jean's in Gaithersburg in the early afternoon on July 4, 1984. The plan was that Bill and I will stay with Edna Sanders, who lives in the Leisure World in Silver Spring. Edna lives alone. Alan, her husband, passed away on March 19, 1981; he was seventy-three years old. Edna's mother, Gladys Schwenk, ninety-one years old, only lived with her for a part of the year. At other times, she stayed with her other children. (Gladys passed away in April of

1986 at the age of ninety-three.) Bill returned to Atlanta within several days after our arrival. I paid rent and bought the food that we needed for both of us during my stay. We enjoyed each other's company. Edna and I talked a lot; she told me stories of her siblings, of her family, and her children. She expressed her appreciation for the help and encouragement I had given to Jean in the last years during the darkest time in her life. She showed me the investments her husband, Alan, did for them and the records he kept with his own handwriting and how their hard work provided the means for their autumn years. After that time, she periodically called me for investments advice.

The house market in Miami was slow; I could not sell my house in a timely manner. My time was running out on my contract on the new house in Silver Spring. The contractor could not wait any longer and canceled the contract and returned my deposit.

Finally in November, I sold my house in Miami, but I had to take back a second mortgage, which I sold six months later on a discount. Before the settlement, Muki traveled here by airplane; when I picked him up in the airport, he was so happy to see me. We did not see each other for four months. After his arrival, I took him to a kennel; he stayed there till I moved into the house.

I found a house in Olney in the Williamsburg Village subdivision; the house was empty. The previous owner was transferred by his company. The real estate company purchased the house from them and made the mortgage payments. The house had been on the market since June; the mortgage interest on the house payment was 12.5 percent. That gave me a good opportunity to negotiate a better price for the house and for them to paint all the rooms and replace the carpet in the family and the recreation rooms. I stayed with Edna for five months before I moved in to my present home on December 19, 1984. This is the house where I live now. The house is on a plus half-acre lot with many mature pine and cherry trees, including several locust trees, in a narrow grove at the west side of the property. It reminded me of my home in Hungary where the street in front of the house where we were living was lined with locust trees. The house had four bedrooms, two full and two half baths, a large entry, and kitchen with eating space. The family room is over a two-car garage, good-sized living and dining rooms, and a recreation room with a pair of french doors that opens to the outside terrace. I bought this house, for five hundred dollars more than I sold the house in Florida.

I notified Stan Allan that my first day in the Harry Weese office in Washington will be July 15, 1984. When I arrived at the office at L'Enfant Plaza, everything went smoothly. I followed what Stan suggested and found a desk for myself. I knew all the vice presidents and the senior staff in the office. I had no idea what my assignment will be until Stan Allan visited the office in a couple of days later. Then I found out he wanted me to manage the production and the coordination with the engineers of the office's latest project, the restoration and renovation of the Union Station in Washington DC. One of the vice presidents in the office was the project manager. The selection of the preservation/restoration architect was through the public selection process. It was advertised in the local and national newspapers, such as the *Wall Street Journal* and the *New York Times*. One hundred four (104) qualification letters from architect/engineering firms were submitted, and from there, Harry Weese was selected for this project. The signing of the contract was pending on the completion of the successful fee negotiation.

During this time, I studied the original drawings and spent three weeks eight hours a day in the Union Station, crawling around to get familiar with the building, using a crowbar to dismantle areas to see how the building was constructed. I found a stairway leading down to the Turkish bath, but no baths were built. I looked for it and found cavities in the building where we could hide the future electrical conduits or the pipes for the mechanical system. I wanted to get the feel of the building and the thoughts of the architect, Mr. Daniel H. Burnham, on what he had in mind when he designed this complex. I wanted to be a part of the building and the building to be part of me. Later, I encouraged the staff to visit the building and get very familiar with it.

The original design of the Union Station was completed in 1904, and it was dedicated in 1908. The Union Station came about when planning for the centennial celebration of the establishment of the nation's capital in the District of Columbia, the aesthetic distaste created by the railroad with clutter and twenty-eight grade crossings at the public thoroughfares on the mall prompted Senator James McMillan, chairman of the Senate Committee on the District, to appoint a commission especially to devise a program for the city's park system. The commission was chaired by the most notable "city planner" of the day: Daniel H. Burnham of Chicago, fresh from his success as director of the 1893 World's Columbian Exposition in Chicago. He was also the architect of many of the Pennsylvania railroad stations. He was joined in the commission by landscape architect Frederick Law Olmsted, architect Charles F. McKim, and sculptor Augustus Saint-Gaudens. Upon reviewing the original plans for the city as created by the French engineer Major Pierre Charles L'Enfant, they came up with the recommendation for the location of the new railroad station. In 1903, President Theodore Roosevelt signed into law the Union Station Act, providing for the creation of a Union Station in Washington DC and authorizing the four railroads on the mall to join in a joint venture to be called the Washington Passenger Terminal Company and to build the station.

The station was designed in the tradition of the École des Beaux Arts of Paris, the most famous architectural school of the nineteenth century, modeled after the Roman baths of Diocletian and Caracalla. In keeping with the Beaux Art's emphasis on appearance, the significant exterior features of the station were designed to create an immediate visual impact massed in gleaming four-story white granite. An arcade loggia or portico wraps around the entire building, and a central pavilion on the south marks the main entrance. This pavilion is composed of three Roman arches and six massive ionic columns. Flanking the central pavilion, lower-arcaded wings had ionic pilasters rising between seven arches. The end pavilions are single-arched with ionic columns on either side. The east end pavilion houses the state entrance to the presidential suite. The building has a main hall, distinguished by a coffered ceiling and two flanking sky-lit halls, the west wing and the east wing. The presidential suite was used for receiving distinguished visitors from foreign countries and as a place where the president and his party could wait in privacy for their trains. A very large open concourse area, with a coffered and sky-lit arched roof, provides train boarding and baggage handling areas. The upper floors of the complex provides office space for the railroads; the basement levels were servicing and utility areas with no public access. Union Station had its heyday during World Was II, when as many as 175,000 military passengers a day passed through its portals going to port cities on their way to Europe. It embodied the era of grand train stations as well as the adventure and romance of railroad travel. The decline of rail travel in the 1950s also brought the decline of Union Station. The once magnificent station soon fell into disrepair thorough neglect. The Union Station was closed to the public; it cannot be occupied. The roof was leaking, and the plaster ceiling was falling. The building became unsafe. To house the Amtrak ticketing office, a hastily built temporary facility, the "replacement station," was built behind the historic station.

The first thing in the HWA office we had to do was hire the staff for the project. We hired over twenty architects and a secretary. During the interviews, I looked for people who were smarter than I, had a good education, and good experience. I am a good organizer and planner. I learned in the past that if you surround yourself with people smarter than you, that made your job easier, and also as an added bonus was you can learn a lot. You win in life with people, and you can move mountains when you work as a team.

In projects like this, with so many facets, you had to work as a team. To be successful, let other people have their input during the progress of the work. We ended up with an excellent hardworking team. The staff on this project moved to a separate office space in the same building from the rest of the office. We began the restoration process with exhaustive research into the history of Union Station. Old photos and paintings were painstakingly examined so that architectural and decorative elements could be authentically reproduced. During our field research, we found twenty-two layers of paint on the wall of the main hall. Paint was analyzed and duplicated with modern formulations. Interior plaster moldings and exterior stone work were to be repaired and replaced, including the floors, ceilings, wall coverings, decorative paintings, stenciling, and gold leafing. The lighting had to be duplicated as authentically as possible, and new mechanical systems had to be installed. IIWA was the overall manager of an extensive team of architects, historic preservationist, mechanical, electrical and structural engineers, lighting experts, paint consultants, material conservationist, masonry, and mortar and plaster analysts, and other specialist. First, we prepared a historic structures report, which detailed the history and condition of the building. We located the original Burnham drawings; they were used to determine the original intent and was used as the base drawing for the restoration work. Surveying the building room by room and quantifying the type of repairs and restorations were needed. Then we prepared a conceptual drawing for the new improvements and conceptual cost estimate with quantities. Using this approach, the restoration cost and how much other improvements we could do in our budget was established.

This was the first project when the federal government and a private company joined resources to develop a project; it was referred to as the public/private partnership. It was President Reagan's initiative to remove some financial burden from the federal treasury. The Union Station was privately owned but leased to the federal government for three and a half million dollars a year, for twenty-seven years. The building in 1964 was designated as a national historic landmark and to be preserved. The Congress recognized the historic importance of Union Station, and in 1981, passed the Union Station Act, providing funding for restoration of the station as a railroad terminal and authorizing private development for the new commercial spaces.

In 1983, Congress created the Union Station Redevelopment Corporation (USRC) as a not-for-profit private independent organization to oversee the restoration of the station. They also set aside funds; the budget was $70 million to restore the station to its original grandeur, appearance, and to bring the complex into the late twentieth century. The funding was part of the Amtrak appropriation. The guiding objective of the USRC was to bring Union Station back to life as a functioning railroad terminal, augmented financially with new commercial development. The Congress also establishes the directors and officers of the USRC. The board of directors were the secretary of the U.S. Department of Transportation, who served as chairman; the president of Amtrak; the mayor of the District of Columbia; the president of the Federal City Council; and the Federal Railroad Administration, U.S. Department of Transportation. Each served on the corporation board of directors during his or her respective term of office.

Our task was to prepare contract documents for the restoration and renovation of the building. The plan was for the federal government to lease the restored building to a developer and use that income to compensate the federal government for the amount it was paying for rent each year to the owners of the building, the Washington Terminal Company.

The upper floors of the Union Station had a 100,000-square-foot office space; it will be used as the Amtrak corporate headquarters. The remaining 250,000-gross-square-foot and an additional new 200,000-square-foot space will be added, and all will be converted into a shopping center with stores, restaurants; and for Amtrak station operation office spaces, ticketing and waiting areas. The areas in the building that was to be used for the shops and restaurants. The developer was to prepare the space for the specific tenants and sublease it to them. For the retail fit-out, the developer had to invest forty million dollars, and they will be responsible to manage and maintain the building after the completion of the construction.

We prepared a schedule for the time needed to do our work and the time for construction. Illustration of the schedule was over three feet long. Stan arranged a luncheon meeting with Mr. Keith Kelly, the president of the USRC, to show it to him and to discuss the schedule. When Stan returned the schedule, it was in three pieces. He gave me the first and the last piece of paper with the schedule; the combined time on it was my tentative time to produce the documents for the project. The work had to be accelerated because the constriction had to be completed and the building occupied before President Reagan's term of office ended. To determine the correct time to produce the contract documents for that, we had to establish the duration of the construction. We analyzed what could be the maximum number of workers in the site at any given time by not interfering with one another's work. Using this information, we could establish the time needed for the duration of the construction. The remaining time was for us to prepare the documents for the restoration of the Union Station. We worked six days sixty hours a week. The overtime duration was three months, then we went back to work on regular hours for three months, and we rotated back and forth for the duration of the project. When we worked overtime, we ordered dinner into the office several times a week, and the office paid for it. The design direction for the project was from Chicago. I organized the staff that one person coordinated the design and one senior architect oversaw the technical part of the project. During the day, I attended meetings with our client, the architect of the capitol or the developer and the Amtrak architects or coordinating the project with all the consulting engineers. In the evening, I reviewed the daily progress of the work in the office and briefed the senior staff with the results of my daily meetings. Every other Friday on the last two hours of the day, we had an office meeting to update the staff of the progress and happenings of the project. The staff briefed me on their findings in the building during their site visits.

I was appointed to the position of the project manager of the Union Station project in early summer of 1986, after the vice president who was the project manager left Harry Weese & Associates. In less than two years, we completed the preparation of the contract documents for the restoration and renovation of the Union Station. The groundbreaking ceremony for the construction was on August 13, 1986. The master of ceremony was Mr. Keith Kelly, president of USRC, and the remarks was made by Ms. Elizabeth Hanford Dole, Secretary of Transportation.

Early spring of 1986, my sister was operated with breast cancer; she had a mastectomy. She stayed in the hospital for three months, again because of the "efficient" hospital staff and the socialized medicine. The doctor saw her once a week when he replaces the bandage. During this time, I was in contact by telephone with Öcsi to find out her condition and her needs. I covered all the associated expenses for the operation and for her aftercare. To this day, she has no sign of the recurrence of her illness.

April 13, 1986, was Jeanette's sixteenth birthday. My present to her, in addition to the balloons, I placed 101 dollar silver coins on the floor from the outside of her bedroom door through the corridor down the stairs to the breakfast table. When she woke up and came down for breakfast, she was very surprised.

My Mother's sister, Aunt Zsuzsa, passed away on May 1, 1986, in Budapest; she was eighty years old. She was buried in the Farkasréti Cemetery in Budapest. With her passing, I only had her husband, Uncle Nándor, as the only surviving relative in their generation. He passed away on June 6, 1991; he was eighty-six years old. He is resting next to his wife. Now our generation will start to follow. I was not ready; I had to accomplish several more tasks in my remaining journey in this earth.

In the summer of 1986, Jean and I took a vacation and drove to the Catskills in New York for a week. We had our own cabin. This gave Jean some time to herself without the children. Edna was nice to take care of the family at home. We took long walks in the woods; we went canoeing on the lake and horseback riding in the woods. An accession, Jean's horse was not up to his daily routine. When we were ready to start our ride, the horse decided to return to the barn with Jean on it. With a new horse, we completed our ride. We tried to take and go somewhere for vacations each year. In July 1987, we spent several days in Williamsburg and in Virginia Beach.

For the celebration of Bill's eighteenth birthday on October 23, 1986, I took a trip to Atlanta. The past two years was a difficult time for Jo to raise

Bill. He skipped school so much that he was not allowed to graduate junior high. In the mornings, Bill missed the school bus; he could not get up in the mornings because he stayed up too late the night before. When Jo took him to school, Bill goes in the front door and walks out the back and walks home. Sometimes, they don't see each other during the day except in the morning. The school policy was to notify the parent only when the child reached the maximum unexcused absences allowed for the school year. I received a call from Jo before Christmas in one year; she wanted to know what to do with Bill. She found out where Bill was working selling Christmas trees; he stole one from them. After a lengthy conversation, the conclusion was for Bill to return the tree and let the owner decide the punishment.

When he was sixteen years old, I asked him to spend the Christmas with me; his response was that *he is spending the Holidays with his family, and I am not his family!* I asked him if he knows what he is saying; his response was *"Yes. I don't consider you as my family."* I will never forget his statement as long as I will live. I don't care how old he is; he cannot say this to his father. Similar behavior continues today. Before his last year of high school in the summer, he did some vandalism to his school. Jo had to hire an attorney to defend Bill. The punishment was he had to attend a special high school for unruly students.

When he started college, he received some scholarship and several different grants; one of them was for several hundred dollars a month for living expenses. He had to maintain a B average. At the end of the first semester, he loses everything; his grades were below the requirements. From that time on, I paid his tuition and related expenses. Sometimes, he requests me to send him the tuition earlier. This way, he can register for his classes before it is filled up, according to him. One time, he requested the tuition again for the same semester. I found out my earlier check, which was made out to his name—he spent it by giving a big party for his friends. This time on, I sent the tuition direct to the school. When he was suspended from college for a year because he failed several subjects, he did not tell me. The school felt he was taking up space from students who were serious and wanted to learn and to get an education. He requested the tuition I send to the school be returned to him. Bill used it to pay his credit card bills. Because I am a stupid parent, I paid his tuition for ten years till he graduated. During this time, he was changing to different majors and failing many subjects; in the end, he received a degree in BFA majoring in printing.

My cousin Öcsi did so much in the past decades to my parents and to my sister; he was there to help them any way he can. He was there when my Father was sick; he was there helping my Mother to make the funeral arrangements for him. He was there when my Mother was sick and she was in the hospital, and after her passing, he was there to handle her funeral arrangement. He was there when my sister had a surgery for cancer, and he is there now to watch over her. I wanted to show my appreciation and thank him for all of his good deeds. I invited him, his wife, and their daughter Cicka to visit me. I paid all the expenses, including the airline tickets for all of them. They arrived on April 26, 1986. Öcsi and his wife, Hajnalka (morning glory), stayed for three weeks and Cicka, two more weeks. I felt good that for the first time, I can do something for him and his family. This trip, financially, was not feasible for him. (Hungary at this time was under Communist government.) During their stay, I took them to see different shopping centers. When we went food shopping, they were surprised of the big selection and the overabundance. Everything was so plentiful here for them. He was a gourmet cook; he can be a chef in any good restaurant. He did all the cooking during their stay; he enjoyed it because everything was available, what he needed for the meal. We went sightseeing, visiting all the museums, went to Mount Vernon, and gave them a tour of Union Station, which was under construction; and I tried to explain to them how it will look when the restoration was completed. Since then, I sent them pictures of the restored building. Hajnalka and Cicka liked the malls and the department stores and Öcsi, the food stores like Giant and the Safeway. It was a big surprise for them to see things here after growing up under Communism. They had a visit, which none of us will ever forget. Years later, they were still talking about their experiences here.

He was the director of the laboratory for the National Food Investigation Institute in Hungary and the chief veterinarian. Later, he became the president of the institute. Hajnalka, his wife, was a research scientist and a department head for one of the research departments in the same institution. She was also a veterinarian by education.

It was a year since the nuclear explosion in Chernobyl took place. The contaminated clouds were moving over Hungary. The fallout from the clouds concerned him and called his office almost daily, directing his staff in the office where to take the samples for testing—for example, check the contamination on the grass where the cows were grazing. It impacts the contents of the milk then the population—and to what kind of tests they to perform.

The dedication of the restored Union Station in Washington DC took place on September 29, 1988, almost the last day of the government's fiscal year. The ceremony was on the Columbus Plaza in front of the Union Station; an estimated one hundred thousand people attended. The master of ceremony was Willard Scott, a radio and television personality. The keynote speaker was Ms. Elizabeth Hanford Dole, the then president of the Red Cross.

They restored station houses, about one hundred specialty retail stores, five restaurants and more than twenty-five international food shops, and a nine-screen cinema complex. Amtrak headquarters was on the third and fourth floors. The main floor of the station concourse was where Amtrak had the passenger services and information office, ticketing and baggage check-in, and baggage pickup. On the train's concourse, they had the waiting areas and the restrooms. The train's concourse and the shaping area can be accessed direct from the Washington Metro system. One of the biggest challenges during the restoration of the Union Station was to provide heating and cooling to all the major rooms, particularly to the main hall, to keep the historic integrity of the surfaces and not use the visible diffusers. We solved the problem by providing the supply air from the ceiling ninety-five feet up, and the return air intake was in the floor in four non-noticeable locations. To provide the proper temperature five feet above the floor, we had to pressurize the air and force it down. We were not allowed to use typical air registers because it conflicted with the historic ceiling. It was decided to use several thousands 3/8-inch diameter holes on the ceiling coffers where the air was pushed through, but the holes cannot be seen from the floor when you look up. To be sure that our idea was working, we hired a contractor to build a full-sized mock-up of the ceiling panels to see that everything was working in order and the calculated air pressure coming through the small holes didn't make a whistling sound. Everything worked out fine and met the requirements. The developer's engineer objected; he insisted it would not work. It was sent to the MIT Engineering Department, and they concurred with our design. In the end, everyone was satisfied with the solution.

The project was completed on budget and in time because it was a team effort; everyone showed dedication and commitment to the project. If you have this attitude, then managing the design team makes it that much easier.

A day before the public dedication on the evening of September 28, 1988, was a black-tie *Union Station Opening Gala* dinner with a live orchestra. Attending the event were Vice President and Mrs. George Bush and many dignitaries and invited guests, including myself, Stan Allan, and the senior people from Harry Weese's home office in Chicago and Washington office. The gala dinner was sponsored by the National Trust for Historic Presentation.

The president of the American Institute of Architects (AIA) who attended the gala dinner reported it in the *AIA Magazine* in its September 1988 edition that the *"Union Station's restoration sets an outstanding example of how historic preservation can be achieved through a public/private partnership."*

In the following weeks and months after the opening of Union Station, every major city newspaper headlined the opening of the station with headlines like *"The Rebirth of Union Station Combining the Old and New," "Union Station Chugs Back, and in First Class," "Union Station a Landmark Reborn,"* or *"Washington's Union Station Has Been Restored to Its Former Glory . . . and then Some."* Every major magazine from *Time, Newsweek, Historic Preservation, Commercial Renovation, Engineering News Record, Trains,* and many more, including all the architecture-related magazines; it is too many to list all of them. Several publications interviewed me. One of the magazines was the *Building Design & Construction* for their article. The fold-out front cover of the magazine showed the pictures of the team leaders of the project including my picture. Ted Landphair also interviewed me for his book called the *Union Station, A Decorative History of Washington's Grant Terminal.* In the last chapter, he made several references to me and to our interview.

The Washington Post newspaper reported on the September 22, 1989, edition that the *"Union Station stores gross income for the first year is 70 million dollars, and more than 40,000 visitors pass through the station daily, providing the 130 businesses average sales of $500 per square foot per year, $125 more than its operators had anticipated."*

The Union Station received eighteen international, national, and local awards, including in 1992 when three major awards were given to Harry

Weese & Associates (HWA) for Union Station: the *National Endowment for the Arts,* the *Federal Design Achievement Award,* and the *Presidential Award for Design Excellence.* The presidential award was the first for Harry Weese & Associates. The presentation of the award took place on January 28, 1992, in the Union Station. Several people from Harry Weese's Chicago and Washington offices attended in a black-tie dinner. I was accepting the award for the office.

In 1994, the office received the *Brunel International Design Award* for the category of Renovated Large Railroad Stations. The award was given every four years by a foundation located in Great Britain. They reviewed and selected projects from every country in the world. The award was given in the reception, held in the Union Station. All major architectural and engineering offices were represented from Europe, Asia, Africa, Australia, and the Americas. It was a big international reception, and it was an honor to receive this award.

In March 1989 on Jean's forty-fifth birthday celebration, in addition to the immediate family, Sandy Horan and Randy Barnes were with us. Edna did an excellent dinner with everyone's help. A month later was Jeanette's nineteenth birthday. We celebrated with a dinner on a cruise ship sailing on the Potomac. In September of the same year, we celebrated Edna's eightieth birthday in my home. Both of her daughters, Jean and Dell, and their families were present with Edna's siblings and their families and some of Edna's friends.

Sometimes Jean and I took day trips; both of us like nature. On one occasion, the whole family went for a drive to locate covered bridges in northern Maryland and Pennsylvania; we found several, one at Owen's creek; we had a picnic there before returning home. One late summer, we saw the annual air show of the renowned Thunderbirds in Andrews

Air Force Base open house. On one of my birthdays, Jean took me to Wolf Trap; we sat on the lawn, had a picnic, and listened to Kenny G. performing.

When Owen got older, he learned how to manipulate his mother. He had asthma, and he used it for his benefit, particularly when he had to help around the house like cleaning his room providing any helping hand to his mother. He played his mother the way Itzhak Perlman plays the violin. The person who did the majority of the work, in addition to school and homework, was Jeanette. She was mowing the lawn and cleaning the house, including the bathrooms. She did it because she felt her mother needed help. Even when she was not working, and she was home all day.

Because of the award-winning restoration of the Union Station in Washington DC and the overwhelming success of the new retail area. New York City Metro North Commuter Railroad Company advertised for the services for a restoration architectural and engineering firms with experience on large-scale restoration projects for the restoration/rehabilitation of the Grand Central Terminal in Manhattan.

The selection was through the public selection process similar to the Union Station.

It was advertised in the local and national newspapers. Over sixty qualification letters from firms responded. Harry Weese & Associates (HWA) responded to the request as a joint venture with Beyer Blinder Belle (BBB) Architects located in New York City. Beyer Blinder Belle's office just completed the restoration of the Statue of Liberty and the immigration building on Ellis Island. In the end of the selection process, the joint venture of HWA and BBB was selected for the restoration of Grand Central Terminal in New York City.

The terminal restoration and adaptive-reuse project was a multidisciplinary, multiphase project to extensively modernize this seventy-five-year-old train terminal, yet preserve its fundamental architectural excellence, similar to the work performed on the Union Station in Washington DC. The scope of work for this project included restoration and adaptive reuse of over 1,600,000 square feet of space—including two levels of train tracks and platforms, approximately ten acres at each level, and several levels of office, retail, and terminal support facilities. Restoration, repair, and replacement of the extensive stonework, carved ornamental, and other decorative features were a major component of the work. Retrofitting modern mechanical, electrical, and communication services behind and within historic finishes and substitution of modern materials where the original was no longer available was a significant challenge. The type of construction and details were similar to Union Station construction. During our research, we found out that some of the subcontractors—when the buildings was built—like the steel manufacturer and supplier were the same for both buildings.

I was the project manager for Harry Weese & Associates. My assignment was to manage the BBB project staff in New York and incorporate to the project my newly acquired experience from the Union Station. My responsibility included overseeing the preparation and production of the work description report, conceptual cost estimates, working drawings, and specifications and phasing plan for the project. Also to coordinate the work of engineering and specialty consultants and the quality control.

I started commuting to New York City at the beginning of December of 1989. I leave home Monday morning and return Friday evening for the next four and a half years, followed by part-time commuting for two more years. My travel time from home to the office in New York took me approximately two and a half hours. During my commute to New York with Delta Air Lines, I had the opportunity to meet and travel with Katie Couric, Connie Chung, Sam Donaldson, Mrs. Martin Luther King Jr., Ms. Arianna Huffington, Johnny Cash, and the secretary of state, Dr. Henry Kissinger, and other known celebrities. On the first six months, I stayed in different hotels and then I found a one-bedroom rent-controlled apartment through friends in Stuyvesant Town apartment complex at First Avenue and east Fourteenth Street. I walked to the office, which was located six blocks from my apartment, at Tenth Street between Fourth and Fifth Avenues.

For the restoration of the Grand Central Terminal, I received the second presidential award for the outstanding achievement in design. The president and Mrs. Clinton hosted the award presentation ceremony for *"Celebrating the Arts and Humanities in our National Life"* on December 20, 2000, in a reception held at the Constitution Hall in Washington DC. *The Award for Design Excellence* was given to me by President Clinton at the same time when the *National Medal of Arts* and the *National Humanities Medals* were presented. Some of the recipients were Maya Angelou, Eddy Arnold, Mikhail Baryshnikov, Horton Foote, Itzhak Perlman, Barbara Streisand, and Quincy Jones. This experience is to be remembered forever. President Clinton was the fifth president I had the opportunity and the pleasure to meet.

The beginning of the fall of the Communism was when in Poland, on August 30, 1980, the workers and the leaders of the newly formed Solidarity union in the Gdansk shipyard won concessions from the Polish Communist government after a seventeen-day strike. The government recognized the right to form independent unions and to strike. This concession was unheard-of before under Communism.

Happenings[18] before the collapse of Communism in the world and in Hungary are the following:

- *March 13, 1985:* Mr. Konstantin Chernenko, the seventy-three-year-old Soviet Union leader died. This was the third funeral in two and a half years of a Soviet leader. Succeeding him was the fifty-four-year-old Mikhail Gorbachev. He is the youngest man to take charge in the Soviet Union since Joseph Stalin. He advocated "détente" and called for a "real and major reduction in arm stockpiles."
- *November 21, 1985:* President Ronald Reagan met with Chairman Mikhail Gorbachev in Geneva. Mr. Gorbachev was scheduled to visit the United States in the following year.
- *December 8, 1987:* History was made in Washington. Soviet leader Mikhail Gorbachev and President Reagan in the White House signed the first treaty to reduce the size of their countries' nuclear arsenal.
- *January 1, 1988:* Legislation initiated by Soviet leader Mikhail Gorbachev under his plan for *prestroika,* or restructuring, will transfer a major part of economic responsibility from the government to individual enterprises.
- *May 31, 1988:* President Reagan visited the Soviet Union, met with Soviet leader Mikhail Gorbachev, and appeared before an audience at the Moscow State University.
- *March 26, 1989:* The first free election in the Soviet Union (USSR); maverick politician Boris Yeltsin won an outstanding vote of confidence.
- *June 4, 1989:* Polish voters gave Solidarity candidates a huge victory in Poland's first competitive election in four decades. Mr. L. Walesa was elected to be Poland's president.
- *September 10, 1989:* Hungary opened its borders to the West—the end of the Communist government after more than forty-four years.
- *November 9, 1989:* The Berlin wall has been the most visible symbol of Communist oppression since its creation twenty-eight years ago. At the stroke of midnight, the East German government opened is

---

[18] Information from the book *Millennium Year by Year.*

borders, and the wall that sliced through Berlin was transformed in to a relic of a Cold War that has passed into history.

- *December 24, 1989;* The Rumanian Communist dictator Nicolae Ceausescu and his wife, Elena, were executed in Bucharest.
- *May 29, 1990:* Boris Yeltsin emerged in triumph as the president of the Russian Republic in the third round of balloting. The other member nations of the Soviet Union (USSR) became independent countries, and they elected their own government.

In the summer of 1989, I decided to visit Hungary and take Bill with me. This time, he was older—twenty years old. Hopefully, he will remember and enjoy it more than our last trip when he was only twelve years old. This was his second trip and my seventh. We left on August 8, 1989, from Dulles International airport at six fifty-five in the evening with Pan American Airlines. We traveled through Frankfurt, Germany, and arrived in Budapest the next day at two in the afternoon. We were staying with Öcsi and his family in Budapest. We visited all my cousins and their families from both sides of my family. We took trips to see several medieval castles and historic sites. As in the past, every time I visit Hungary, it included a trip to the cemetery to visit my parents and other members of the family there. In this occasion, for my parents' grave, I ordered a head and gravestone from a stonemason and had it installed during our visit. From now on, no upkeep and maintenance was required for the grave. We had several long visits with Uncle Nándor; he was eighty-four years old. I didn't think that I would see him again after this trip. Ever since his wife, Aunt Zsuzsa, passed away four yeas ago, I helped my uncle financially every month. He had to give up his part-time job collecting rent in the building for the government. His retirement was meager, similar reason as was for my Father's—the years he worked before 1947 was not counted to be part of his retirement years. The time for our stay went by very fast; we left Budapest on August 30 at eight fifteen in the morning, changed planes in Frankfurt, Germany, and arrived in Washington DC at four fifteen in the afternoon. This time the "atmosphere," the "air" was different in Hungary than any of my past visits; there were no armed police or military standing on the street corners, no guards with machine guns in the airport surrounding the airplanes when we arrived and when we departed. The public transportation and all government employees were unusually nice. It was a big celebration with fireworks on August 20, commemorating the harvest. This holiday is similar to Thanksgiving in the States. This action by the government was the prelude to September 10, 1989, when the Communist dictatorship ended in Hungary.

This was the decade when I reached the zenith of my career. I had the opportunity to work on two major historical restoration projects, the Union Station in Washington DC and the Grand Central Terminal in New York City. Both received the presidential design awards from two different presidents of the United States.

Several other major happenings took place in my life during this decade; my Mother became seriously ill and passed away. I met a person and her family whom I became fond of. The Communism ended in the world and in Hungary—as we know it, as I lived it, and I experienced it in Hungary. I am disappointed and sad that my parents cannot experience this historic event, of the rebirth of Europe! The rebirth of a country, the nation of Hungary.

Bill's summer visit.

Miami, Florida, 1980.

My Mother, with her sister Zsuzsa and her husband Nándor.

/Dunakeszi, HU. 1981/

Last picture of my mother.

She is seventy-eight years old.
Dunakeszi, Hungary, June 30, 1982.

Jean, Jeanette, and Owen in Miami.

Christmas 1982.

Jeanette.

In her *"railroad uniform."*
It was a gift from her father.
Their last outing to the Baltimore
Railroad Museum. February 1983,
Silver Spring, Maryland.

Bill's eighteenth birthday.
Atlanta, Georgia, October 23, 1986.

My cousin Öcsi and his family during they visit.
April, May 1987, Olney, MD

Union Station, Washington DC, September 1988.

> To
> Karl J. Landesz
> in sincere appreciation for his
> outstanding leadership and contributions
> to the education and enlightenment
> of his fellow team members
> in the successful restoration
> of
> Union Station
> Washington, D.C.
> 1988
>
> "The Trailer People"
> Jose Silva   Tom Bronson   Susan McGlohn   Tim Wenbeskin
>   Bundy Brockington

Gift from the staff.

Grand Central Terminal.

New York City, New York.

Jeanette's nineteenth birthday with Randy.

April 1989, Silver Spring.

Öcsi and his family with Bill.

/Budapest, HU. August 1989/

Bill with my sister Marika.

/Dunakeszi, HU. August 1989/

X

The '90s through June of 2000

The year 1990 was a quiet year for me, doing the same routine that I was doing in the last years by commuting to New York—leaving on Monday morning and returning home Friday evening—to work on the restoration and renovation of the Grand Central Terminal. This routine was interrupted for a short time with Bill's visit from Atlanta. I took a time off from work, and we spent two weeks together. Bill returned the following year with his girlfriend, and they stayed with me for one week.

1991 was the year I visited my sister in Hungary to see how she was doing, check on her well-being. This was my eighth trip. I departed on June 22 and returned in July 10, 1991. During my visit, I bought her a TV and some window curtains. Her TV was old and had no sound; it was not worth to be repaired. She was very happy to have a new TV, particularly for the coming winter days when she could not be outside. I also purchased split wood (4,500 lb.), and I stacked the wood in the woodshed for her. In the winter, she would use the wood in the stove to heat her home and to cook with.

Before I left to visit Hungary, I met a person in the Aspen Hill Shopping Center at McDonald's, who owned the Amway franchise in Hungary. I found out when and where he will have the meeting in Budapest, and I took Cicka to one of the meetings. During my visit, Öcsi and Hajnal, his wife, took off some time from their work; and we took several days' trip by car. The trip took us north and the northeast of Hungary. We visited several small cities, six old forts, and medieval castles from the twelfth and thirteenth centuries. Some of the buildings were restored, and some were in ruins. Seeing the old buildings and walking on the sites gave me goose bumps by knowing its history.

The following are some of the places we visited:

Visegrád (Vee-shay-grad): The town is located by the shores of the Duna River in the northern part of Hungary. The town's history goes back to Roman time when the empire was in its heyday. The fort with a castle was built between the years 1245 and 1263. King *Károly Robert* built the royal palace in 1330. The building was the most impressive building at the time. For a short time, it was the capital city of Hungary. During King Mátyás's rule in 1543-1686, it was the cultural center of Europe. The building was restored in 1970.

Sárvár (Shar-war): The town with a fort, it was settled in the twelfth century. During the sixteenth to seventeenth century, it was the center of the Hungarian culture. Here was where the first book was printed in Hungarian language in the year 1541. The castle in the town is a museum now.

Hollókö (Ho-lo-ku): The town has less than a thousand residents. UNESCO registered the old town with its fifty-eight buildings for its architecture, and it became protected in 1962, and it was added to the world historic sites in 1987. The majority of the buildings are occupied. Besides as a residence, the buildings are also used for daycare, doctor's office, police station, post office, restaurants, stores, museums, hotels, and as a city hall. In principle, it is similar to Williamsburg in Virginia, only the buildings are several hundred years older. The town with the fort was established and built in the second half of the thirteenth century. The fort was built on the highest area of the surrounding landscape (elevation of 1,100 feet). During our visit, the fort was under restoration. Öcsi and I climbed all over the scaffolding, and we had a closer look of how the over-five-hundred-year-old building was constructed, and how it survived the times.

Köszeg (Kers-egg): The first settlement for the town can be traced back to the Stone Age. The town's first permanent building and the fort were constructed in the first half of the thirteenth century. Again as usual, during my stay, I was very busy, accomplished a lot, and learned a lot. The time went fast. I am very grateful and thankful to my cousin Öcsi to have this opportunity to see all these historic places.

In the year 1992 on May 19, Jeanette graduated from Maryland University, College Park Campus, from the College of Business Management and Marketing. The commencement exercises was held at two thirty in the afternoon at the campus in the Cole Student Activities Building. After graduation, she received a full-time employment from the company where she was working part-time during her college years. She had been working part-time since she was sixteen years old.

In June of 1993, the office sent me to Miami Beach, Florida, to attend the annual transportation convention. One day, I rented a car and went to see what damage the recent hurricane did to my old house there. The damage was extensive: part of the roof was missing; the screen above the pool area was gone. The three fruit trees, the royal palms in the backyard, and the palm tree and the shrubs in the front yard were not there. It was sad to see the destruction, but they were working on it, and it looked like the house will be rebuilt.

On my return trip, I stopped for several days in Atlanta to visit Bill. We went and visited different places, and we had a good time. One of the places we went to was the President Carter Liberty, and not far from there was the building housing the cyclorama painting about the civil war, illustrating General Sherman marching on to the South.

I took a trip to Hungary; it took place between July 6 to 21, 1993. This was my ninth trip. I visited my sister several times a week. I spent lots of time in the Castle District with Cicka. It became tradition for us that, during my visits, we have a pastry lunch in the pastry-ice cream shop there.

The city was digging up the road there to replace and repair old pipes. It was interesting to see the different layers below the surface representing different centuries of road surfaces, back to the Romans' time.

Öcsi and Hajnal had a property close to Lake Balaton in the town of *Révefülop* (Rape-Phillip). It is a small vineyard; they bought the property to be their future retirement place. Up to now, they only built the basement part of the house and use it as a wine cellar. The cellar has a large table, several barrels of wine, and also it is used for wine-tasting with his friends. On the site, they also had a small wooden building with bunk bed, using it when they spend the night there.

In another occasion, we took a long weekend trip by car to *Tiszakecske* (Tee-sa-catch-ka) where their best friend *Károly Szabó* spends his summers. He is retired. He is a widower; his wife passed away several years ago. We stayed there for several days. Both of them liked to cook. The cooking took place outside in a big kettle, which hung over an open fire—the way they used to cook in the old West. We picked and had fresh fruits; he had lots of different fruit trees on the property, and he grew his own vegetables. In the return trip, we stopped in the city of *Kecskemét* (Catch-ca-mate) to visit his friend's daughter's family. She was the vice president of a company, distributing American cigarettes in Hungary. Her husband owned and managed a Greek restaurant. We had a nice Greek meal there. We also took a short trip just outside Budapest to a small town named *Ocsa* (Ocha) to visit a Presbyterian church. When the church was built in the thirteenth century, it was a Roman Catholic church. Around 1560, it became a Presbyterian church. Then an addition was made to it in the seventeenth century.

Öcsi liked to go and spend time in different farmers' market, and I went with him; it helped me to observe and to learn the prices of food and fresh vegetables. It gave me a better understanding of what amount of support I shall give to my sister.

This trip turned out to be a quiet and relaxing trip compared to previous trips.

In 1995, January 18, Nagymama, Helen "Sally" Horan, passed away in Ardenvoir-Entiat, Washington. She was ninety years old, born in 1904 on February 25 in Joliet, Illinois. I attended the funeral service; it was held on January 21 in Wenatchee, Washington. All of her families were there with their descendants. They came from all over different states, including from Alaska. During the short stay, I had breakfast, lunch, or dinner with different family members. It was the last time I saw everyone in the family. It was not an easy trip for me. Generally, I don't attend funcrals. She was the last person who passed who molded and guided me during one of my most difficult times of my life's journey. What I learned from her left an imprint on me. She will be with me for the rest of my life. To her funeral, I traveled by plane from Washington DC to Seattle, and from there to Wenatchee. Leaving Seattle and flying over the mountains, it was interesting to see the ocean side of the mountain had no snow on it, but once we flew over the peak of the mountain, heavy snow appeared on the other side. The west side of the mountain receives the warmer air form the ocean; the clouds only provide rain. But when the clouds rise up and go over the mountain in to the cold air, it turns to snow. After the service, my return trip was by car; Harold offered me a ride as they were driving back to Seattle. On our way, we stopped in Roslyn, Washington, where they were filming the CBS weekly television show the *Northern Exposure*. We visited the set and took pictures and had lunch in the "Roslyn's Café an Oasis" restaurant. When we were driving on the Interstate 90 and getting close to the Snoqualmie Pass, the snow on both sides of the highway was a vertical wall over two stories high. I never saw snow that high before. We arrived safely in Seattle; we spent a night there. In the morning, they flew back to Florida. I was flying to Houston, Texas, for a three-day visit with my sister Gisela and my nephew Andrew (Campbell) and his family. He was my sister's youngest son. He is a doctor with his own medical clinic. One evening after dinner in his home, he autographed and gave me his latest book he wrote with other doctors. The book was titled *Health Effects of Toxic Chemicals, Silicone, Asbestos, and Man-Made Fibers.* We talked a lot; I did not see him for several years. We had a good time. It was nice to see and spend time with him and his family. I returned home on January 25, 1995.

My next trip to Hungary took place in September 5 to 20, 1995, and this was my tenth trip. I spent lots of time with my sister and visited all my cousins on both sides of the family. During my visit, I stayed with my cousin Öcsi at his home in Budapest. This time, we took one-day trips to historic places. One of the trips took us to *Ópusztaszer* (O-pus-ta-ser). It is a national historic park and is known for the first parliamentary meeting held by Árpad, the chief of the Magyars, and seven tribal leaders who settled in the Carpathian Basin, the territory where their descendants live today, known as Hungary. The settlement took place between the years 895-900. To commemorate the parliamentary meeting, the Hungarian government built one large and seven smaller *tepee*-shaped buildings, representing Árpad and the seven tribes. Also part of the complex was a large round building housing the *Feszty-Cyclorama,* the painting that was painted to celebrate the one thousandth anniversary of the Magyar's conquest of Hungary. The artist is Mr. Árpad Feszty (b. 1856 and d. 1914) painted the cyclorama between the years of 1892 and 1894, with two of his artist friends, Mr. Laszlo Meanyanszky and Mr. Pále Vago (the cyclorama is 400 feet long and

50 feet high). All three are well-known artists. Also in the park are the ruins of a monastery dating back to the year one thousand.

Again, it was an active and very educational trip; I was ready to go home to rest.

After dating for eight years, Jeanette (Alayne Chambers) and Randy's (Randall Scott Barnes) day arrived; they got married on October 28, 1995. The service was five-thirty in the afternoon at the Gaithersburg Presbyterian Church, Gaithersburg, Maryland. The Reverend Harold S. Horan, Jeanette's uncle, conducted the ceremony. (He is from Baton Rouge, Louisiana.) All their families from both sides and all their friends attended. Unfortunately, Randy's mother, Linda, cannot be there as she passed away in 1988. The reception immediately followed the ceremony with a sit-down dinner for 125 invited guests in the Ceresville Mansion in Frederick, Maryland. Jeanette paid for all the wedding-related expenses, except her wedding dress and the necessary accessories for it, which was my gift to her. I never saw Jeanette so radiant, so glowing, and so happy. The wedding and the followed reception were very nice. All the invited guests received special attention; for dinner, everyone had an assigned table with name cards.

Mike Horan unexpectedly passed away on November 18, 1996, in Ardenvoir, Washington, during a fire in his home. He was only sixty-five years old. The house was constructed a long time ago; for insulation in the walls, sawdust was used. The electric wiring started the fire there. When the fire started, he was in a different part of the house and went outside to look for his wife, hoping she already escaped from the burning house. When he did not locate her, he returned to the burning building to look for her. Meantime, she escaped in the back of the house by jumping from the second-story window.

In July 24, 1997, in midmorning, I received a call from Jean that on the previous night (July 23, 1997, at 11:30 p.m.), Jeanette had a car accident on Route 108, close to the Howard County line. The road was wet and slippery from a short, recent rain. She was taken by helicopter to the Washington Hospital Center in the intensive care unit where she stayed for about ten days. Her injures were severe. After the internal bleeding stopped, she had to learn to walk, to read, and write; her memory and her everyday skills had to be rebuilt. Randy was by her bedside practically twenty-four hours a day every day during her hospital stay. His devotion to her help saved her life and gave her a reason to live. God felt it was too early to call her to his side; He had other plans for her and let her live to be reborn. She was in the hospital for four weeks, followed by out-patient therapy for three months.

Seven years later in 2004, for Randy's and Jeanette's birthdays, I wrote each a short note and included it in their birthday cards. I enclosed those notes, first on Randy's, his birthday is in February, and then Jeanette's, hers is in April.

February 21, 2004

Dear Randy.

Happy Birthday!!!

Some time you refer to Jeanette as my daughter. I feel that way too, she is the daughter I never had.

I like to take this opportunity to thank you when several years back during the stormy times of your lives, when your mate jumped ship and almost lost her life in the process. You stood by her after the accident with your caring, with your love and with your devotion to her. During her re-birth you helped her to re-gain her senses, her will. I thank you for that.

With newfound devotion to each other and with God's help, today you have a remarkable, beautiful little person. He is running around in your home and enjoying his young life, and giving joy to his parents and every one around him.

I appreciate all your patience, caring, devotion and love you have for them.

Thank you again, *and thank you* **for You to be You.**

Happy birthday Randy! I wish you for many more to fallow in the coming decades.

With love and appreciation:

Karcsi

April 13, 2004

Dear Jeanette.

Happy birthday.

Ever since you give life to that presses little person, I started looking back, reviewing, and going over one by one the years, the happenings in your life, for the past twenty plus years since I know you.

During the reflection I fined my self on the day when your life and life of people around you are changed. It happened in the late evening in a rainy day on July 23, 1997. The day was, when you where re-born, when you regained the direction and purpose of your life. God ended one chapter of your life, but he was not ready to give up on you, God saw the potential in you and let you live, let you embark on a new journey. You started a new life, a new beginning with a "Knight on a white hors" by your side to help you, watch over you and sometimes guide you.

Since that rainy day you made dozens of people very happy by being there for them, you find time in your busy life to help them in they needs.

Thank you for all the joy and happiness you provided to all those people.

Thank you for You to being You.

You will have everything in your life what you want and dream for, but some times it takes time to reach the dreams and wishes in ones life. You know it from experience God has its own way, when and why things are happening and in the way it happens.

You are an excellent Mother, a loving wife and a great person. Every one is very proud of you. I wish you all the happiness and for many more birthdays to fallow.

Happy birthday Jeanette! With all my love to my newly found Daughter.

Karcsi

In November 4, 1997, after a long illness of lung cancer, William Scot Horan passed away in Buena Park, California. He was sixty-five years old. He was the third *brother* I lost, the second in the past two years. He helped me a lot in my early days, taking me to school every morning. I am very appreciative for that. I visited him and Joan, his wife, for several days in his home in California during his illness. Both of their children were married and had several grandchildren. By then, he only could sleep sitting in his favorite armchair. He took me to see the *Crystal Cathedral* in Garden Grove, California, where he was an usher. Shortly after my visit, he passed away. He was laid to rest next to his daughter in the memorial gardens by the Crystal Cathedral.

In the 1997 spring, Bill and his girlfriend Monika (Weiss) came for a several days' visit. Monika was from Poland. The Georgia State University's (GSU) school of art and design invited her to give lectures in the university for three months. She was an established young painter, an artist in Europe. Bill was in his last year of the GSU school of art and design, planning to graduate the coming December. The purpose of the trip was to introduce

Monika and ask for my help; they would like to get married. Several times, we had long conversations, including their future, what he plans to do after graduation, what are their plans for their future. I offered to pay for the wedding, the reception, and for Bill's suit and for her dress and the accessories. I asked them to establish a budget and provide a detailed estimate.

On December 3, I traveled to Atlanta for Bill's wedding. Harold and Del came up from Baton Rouge where they live, as he will officiate the ceremony. The day before the wedding, dinner was held in Bill's aunt Jenny's home. All the participants in the wedding were present. The service was on December 6, 1997, at two in the afternoon in *the Little Chapel* of the *Glenn Memorial Church* at the Emery University Campus, Atlanta, Georgia. The reception was held in one of their friends' house. It was very nice, and I was tactfully donned. Their wedding present from me was that I paid off Bill's credit card debts, which came to be several thousand dollars and bought them a two-year-old Honda. Bill had no debt for his education; it was paid by me. This way, they can start a new life together debt-free. When the time came for me to return home, Bill and Monika took me in their new car to the airport. In one of the shops, they bought me one of the stuffed dwarfs from the children's story of the *Snow White and the Seven Dwarfs*. The dwarf's name is Happy as it symbolized how they feel.

A week later, I return to Atlanta for Bill's graduation; it was on December 14 at one in the afternoon. He received the degree of bachelor of fine arts. It took him ten years to graduate; he was changing majors several times. Many of his classes were not completed, which he did not receive credit for. After the graduation ceremony, we walked next door to the senior's exhibit where the graduates' theses were exhibited. He had no prospects for employment, and he did not look actively for work. In the evening, we went out to a nice restaurant to celebrate this occasion. On the next day, I returned home.

On June 5 of 1998, I reached a milestone in my life's journey, the big six and the zero. But I felt like I was forty-five. To celebrate this occasion, a big dinner was held at Jean's home. All the children where there: Bill, Monika, Jeanette, and Owen. Bill and Monika came up from Atlanta for this occasion, and they spent several days with me. They prepared a homemade card for me, referencing some of my expressions in one side. On the other side, they expressed their personal good advices. Jean prepared the dinner with the children's help in the end. In the past years when we had dinners together, I liked to know what was for dessert. I like sweets. I would like to start my meal with the dessert. But in the past, that never happened. This time, my wishes were granted, and my first course was a dessert, and Jeanette served it to me. I appreciated everything that everyone did for me that day. The dinner was excellent. Thank you to all of you.

I decided that on my way to Hungary, I would visit Monika's parents in Warsaw, Poland. I started my trip at three ten in the afternoon on Tuesday, July 28, 1998, from the national airport to New York JFK, then to Warsaw, Poland. I arrived next day at eight fifty in the morning. Monika's mother, Gabriela, was waiting for me in the airport; from there, we went to her home. Monika's father, Janusz, stayed home. Several years back, he was in a car accident; it left its mark on him. He retired; he was a reporter for the *Polis Catholic* newspaper. She teaches piano now in the Warsaw Conservatory; she used to be a well-known concert pianist in Europe. Our communication was a little bit bumpy; we used sign language and different dictionaries. He knew some words in Hungarian as he was born there. His family left Hungary when he was a young boy. She knows some English from her concert days. On the first day, I had lunch in their home. In the evening, I took them out to eat close to my hotel. I was staying in the Hotel Forum International in downtown Warsaw. They lived in the outskirts of the city. We met every day at midmorning in my hotel. They showed me the city of Warsaw, the old downtown, the school where Monika studied art, and the conservatory where she studied music. Monika also plays the piano and several other instruments. We were walking everywhere. We stopped several times to rest. We also visited the Wilanowie Pales; now it is a public park and museum. My visit lasted three and a half days. We had a good time and a nice visit; it was very educational for me. This was my first trip to this country. I left on July 31 at eight thirty in the evening, and seventy minutes later, I arrived in Budapest, Hungary. The approximate distance between the two cities is like the distance between Washington DC to New York City.

During my visit, I stayed again with my cousin Öcsi in Budapest. I took a time out and visited all my cousins. I also spent time with my sister. Cicka and I had our lunch in the Castle District pastry shop. We also took a trip again to *Tiszakecske* (Tee-sa-catch-ka) to visit their friend Szabo, Károly. We spent a night there.

The *Holy Crown of Hungary* recently was returned to Hungary from the United States where it was kept for safekeeping since the Second World War. During my visit, it was exhibited in the main hall of the parliament building with honor guards standing by it. The exhibit was open to the public, and I went to see it. The *Holy Crown of Hungary* was a gift from the pope Sylvester II in the year 1000 for the crowning the first Hungarian king, Steven. The coronation took place on Christmas Day of the same year. With the coronation, Steven became Roman Catholic and the whole nation with him. Later, Steven became a saint in the church. Till then, the Magyars were pagans. Steven's father, *Géza* (Ga-sa), allowed the pope's representative to live in his court. Steven received some of his education from them. It was breathtaking to stand so close to something so old in that magnificent hall.

This visit was again quiet, but educational. My return from Budapest took me through Zurich to Washington Dulles International Airport. I left on August 12 at nine thirty in the morning and arrived at three nineteen in the afternoon. It was nice to be home again.

Since Bill's graduation over six months ago, he was still unemployed. During different telephone conversations, I suggested maybe he would have a better opportunity here. They can stay with me until both of them can find employment. After some time went by, they agreed, and they would move. They arrived on August 12, 1998. Again, he had several thousand dollars worth of debt that I paid. According to Bill, Monika will look for employment, and she will work. He wanted to attend American University's master's degree program in fine arts. He applied, and he was accepted; he enrolled part-time. The program required a second language; he took Spanish at Montgomery College. I paid for his tuition and for his books, but he had to pass all the courses he took. At the end of the first semester, he was out of the school and was looking for employment, but not very hard. During his school days, I gave him, based on his estimate, a generous amount of money every month to cover his expenses like extra food, gas, insurance, and telephone. A separate telephone line was installed in the house for them on my expense for their privacy. After Monika learned to drive, she used their car, and I lent Bill my small car to use. In the beginning, he found some short-term, temporary employment. He talked about going back to school. I told him I was not paying for it anymore. If his heart was set to go back to school, he should work and save money and attend evening classes. He was almost thirty years old, and until now, he was a "professional" student. After this, he started behaving strangely. Stayed up all night and slept in the day. He did not have time to look for employment. He decided and made the change in all bathrooms, including mine, that the toilet paper rolls should roll down facing the wall. He felt it made more sense that way. When I wanted to change it back in my bathroom, he became very upset. During their stay, they did not help around the house. When they ate, only sometimes they put the dishes in the sink, but not the dishwasher. All the time I had to straighten out the house in the evening after returning home from work. They parked their cars on the driveway so that when I came home from work, I had to park on the street. Then I had to move their cars for me to park in the garage. He threw all his clothes I gave to him on the floor after using it, leaving it there for days and walking all over it. After several days passed, I asked him several times to put his clothes away. After, there was no response from him. One evening, I collected all clothes from the floor, put it into a plastic bag, and placed it in the guest bedroom closet. I told Monika that in the morning, I would donate the clothing to people who would appreciate it more. When he returned late that night, Monika told him what I did and what I planned to do with his clothes. He ransacked the house, throwing things around, damaging several things in the process when he was looking for his clothes. I could not sleep all night; I barricaded my bedroom door. I was afraid of him. I was afraid of his temper. To date, I have not received an apology from him. When several days later I asked Bill to mend himself, to change his attitude, I received no response. After this behavior, I asked them to leave. They moved out on April 20, 1999. He took my car and kept it over a year. After all of this, I offered to give him and transfer the car to his name. I waited over eight weeks for a response when we can go to the DMV. When I received no answer, I asked him to return the car. I gave him a clean car with good working condition and with no damage to it. He returned the car several weeks later and the car was damaged, dirty, and was not maintained at all. I had to give the car away as junk. Shortly after, they separated; Monika moved to Jersey City, New Jersey, just outside New York City. They got divorced on April of 2001.

The happy times between Jean and I slowly faded away; we were having some bumpy times and some rough patches in our relationship. She was not as compassionate as she was in the past. She did things, which differed from what I believe in. I am energetic; I like to do things, keep myself occupied, be busy, learn, travel, go and see things. I am like a galloping horse. Unfortunately, she is a turtle; many times, she retreats into her shell. The time will come before long when you have to stay home because of the late autumn years. We had several conversations; those conversations did not go anywhere. After several months went by, then on September 15, 1998, we met for the last time in my home for a last conversation. Our relationship ended, and it lasted almost sixteen years. During those years, I asked her to marry me several times, but she was looking for a knight in shining armor, and I was not that knight. Shortly after our relationship ended, she found her *knight in shining armor,* and she married him. Looking back now, if we were married then, probably we would be divorced by now. It was not meant to be. I am glad which way it turned out. God's guiding hand was on my shoulder and watching out for me.

I traveled to New York City on October 1, 1998, for the dedication of the restored Grand Central Terminal. It was nice to see the results of the past ten years of work. On the dedication, there were the past and the present leading politicians from the local and the federal governments. The honorary guest was Carolina Kennedy, representing her late mother, Jacqueline Kennedy-Onassis, who saved the station from the wrecking ball. Then the owners of the Grand Central Station wanted to demolish the station the same way as they did with the Pennsylvania Railroad Station. She and other dignitaries like Philip Johnson, the architect who established the *Committee to Save Grand Central Station.* The fight ended up in the U.S. supreme court, and they won. That victory also was celebrated on that day.

Edna Sanders, after a short illness in her eighty-ninth year, passed away at her home in Silver Spring on April 27, 1999, at one in the morning. Her children, grandchildren, and great-grandchildren were with her. (She was born on September 10, 1909, in Johnstown, Pennsylvania.) The service was held in the Gaithersburg Presbyterian Church on April 29 at eleven in the morning. Her husband, Alan, passed away in 1981. In later years in my life, I felt she was my substitute mother; we got on very well. Many times, we had long conversations either in person or by telephone. I visited her periodically in her home, and we had dinner together. In the winter, she stayed with Del in Miami or in Baton Rouge; I watered her plants, sorted her mail, and looked after her house. I appreciated the help she and her husband did for me after my arrival at this country and the years that followed. I turned to Alan in the early years several times for his advice. They were caring and generous people, and they lived a quiet life, but their hearts were made of gold. Thank you again for everything you did for me.

After the service, Del and I had a long conversation about her mother and about her parents. Upon returning home, she sent me a nice note as a response to our conversation.

I invited Cicka (Kovacs, Hajnalka) to visit me; this was her second trip. She arrived on May 17, 1999, and she stayed till June 18. During her visit, I took her to the Shenandoah National Park; we stayed in the Skyland Hotel. During our drive in the Skyline Drive, we saw lots of deer. In the morning, the deer were grazing outside the hotel room window. This kind of things you cannot see in Hungary. In our return trip, we stopped and visited the Luray Caverns, which left a big impression on her. We also took a trip to Colonial Williamsburg and stayed for several days, and then from there, we drove to Virginia Beach. She likes water and also for her to see the Atlantic Ocean. We stayed in a hotel on the beach for four days. At daytime, we were on the beach; at night visited different seafood restaurants. She enjoyed the *surf and turf* dinners. When we were back home, we went shopping and sightseeing in Washington DC. I took her to my office and to see the restored Union Station; last time when she was here, she saw it when the station was under construction. We also had dinners with Jeanette and Randy.

She also spent some time with Bill in his home. He became an estranged person; he and I are not communicating anymore. He has a chip on his shoulder. It is more of his loss than mine; he just has to grow up and to come to his senses.

During Cicka's stay, we had a good time. We saw a lot, and she enjoyed it a lot. Every time I see her, she still talks about this trip of hers.

January 23, 2000, was a big day in my life; it was my last day of smoking after smoking for over thirty-nine years. It took me over two years to slowly reduce may daily intake to five cigarettes a day. I tried to stop several times before, but I did not make it. I started smoking in April of 1960 when I was in the army and stationed in Texas. The cigarettes in the army were given to us for free. We had lots of time on our hands between classes. This was the time I started smoking. My heydays of my smoking were the years of 1989 and 1990 when I lost my son and going through my divorce. That was the time when my daily consumption was three packs a day. Both of my parents were smokers. When I was about sixteen years old, my father offered me a cigarette. I smoked it, and I got sick from it; I did not smoke after that till I was in the army in this country many years later.

That same year on March 4 to 10, I took a trip to Baton Rouge, Louisiana, to visit Harold and Del Horan. He was the minister for the University Presbyterian Church there. During my stay, we went to several times to New Orleans to see the sites, including during Mardi Gras. It was interesting to watch the different floats, with people in different costumes. We listened to jazz played in the street corners. The life and the lifestyles were different in New Orleans than any other part of this country. Harold retired from the church on April 30 of 2000. They moved to Charlottesville, Virginia, to be closer to their daughter Sandy and her family and the grandchildren. (Harold was ordained on July 15, 1965, in the Chevy Chase Presbyterian Church, Washington DC.)

On my return trip from Baton Rouge, I stopped over for two days in Atlanta, Georgia, to attend Elizabeth Campbell's, my grandniece, wedding. She was the daughter of Rolland my sister Gisela's oldest son.

In June 30, 2000, it is my last day after twenty-three years working in the office of Harry Weese & Associates, Architects as an associate and as a project manager. I had a happy and successful career there. I am very thankful and grateful for all the help and opportunities I received there. The opportunity to work and manage prestigious projects, like Union Station in Washington DC or the Grand Central Terminal in New York City, which both received presidential awards; the Mormon temple in Bethesda; National Gallery of Art in Washington DC; and to work on the Miami and Washington Metro to name a few. Also, I am very thankful for the opportunity to work with all those smart, hardworking, conscientious individuals. Thank you for your help; it made my life so easy.

This also will be the end of my forty-four years of working career.

This decade was a slow decade, with not too much excitement. But it had some exceptions, like breaking up with Jean after almost sixteen years of friendship. I told myself, *That's life!*

The other was when my life's journey came to a new juncture when my working career came to the end, the time when I retired. My life from this time on would be drastically different. I had to start a new lifestyle, which I never thought would ever happen to me. This new lifestyle I called the *pasture years.* The years ahead of me hopefully will have new opportunities with new challenges for the remainder of this journey.

Ruins of the fort in Visegrád with Cicka, 1991. **The town of Hollókö, way to the fort,** 1991.

Révefülöp, **Öcsi's vine cellar,** 1993.

Tiszakecske. Outdoor cooking by Öcsi. /1993/

Roslyn, Washington, Jan. 24, 1995.

Jeanette and Randy, Oct. 28, 1995.

Monika and Bill's wedding, with Jo and me,
Atlanta, December 6, 1997.

Monika and Bill with my wedding gift.

Bill's graduation.
/Atlanta, Ga. December 14 1997/

My 60th birthday.
/Gaithersburg, MD June 1998/

The Wilanowie Pales.
With Monika's parents Gabriela and Janusz Weiss. /Warsaw, Poland. July 29, 1998/

Cicka at my desk in my office.
/Washington DC. June 1999/

XI

The "Pasture" Years

(July 2000 through 2004)

The architect's office of Harry Weese & Associates where I worked for over the past twenty-two years closed its doors on June 30, 2000. I decided not to look for other employment. The first day of my retirement, July 1, was the first day and the beginning I called the "pasture" years of my life.

In the beginning, I was very restless; it was very strange for me to be home all day. In the past forty-three years, every morning I got up and went to work, and now I didn't have to do it anywhere. Never have I imagined that some day like this would have come. I always believed I would work in an office till I die. I am the type of person that cannot be idle; I have to do something all the time.

I read it in the comics called *Pickles* by Brian Crane, *"There are three things needed in this life to be happy for, something to do, something to love, and something to hope for."* I have no shortage for things to do. I have my family to love. I hope I can accomplish things that I want to do before my sunset arrives.

In a few days, I came up with a list of things to-do around a house, which was neglected in the past and needed some attention. Then another to-do list, like organize the collection of photographs, work on my stamp

251

and coin collections or the items I collected on projects I worked on, like the Union Station in Washington DC, the Grand Central Terminal in New York City, and the Baltimore, Miami, Washington Metro projects. Then to research and organize my parents' family tree and do same traveling. To write my memoir, my life's journey, was on the bottom of the list.

The first thing I did was to organize some of the major projects I worked on. I started with the Union Station restoration project. I went over and reviewed the information that was collected during the research and the preparation phase of the project. It included correspondences, reports, photographs, copies of original plans, newspaper articles dating back to the beginning of the century when the station was built, and current newspapers and magazines on the project. All these materials I then cataloged and organized and put in to six four-inch binders. It represents the history of the Union Station. I am very proud of this project, and I am very grateful that I had the opportunity to manage the restoration of this magnificent station. May 1, 1957, was the gateway to my arrival at Washington DC to my new family and to my new home. I am most proud of the Union Station project than any other projects I had the opportunity to work on. Following this, I assembled my collection of materials on the restoration of the Grand Central Terminal in New York and the different metro transit projects I worked on.

To break up the routine between assembling the different projects, I worked on my paper money and coin collection. Some of which I inherited from my parents, the rest I collected during my travels in different countries.

Next item on the list was to organize over sixty years of photographs, slides, and old family documents stored in several boxes—put the photographs and the documents into albums and prepare an index for it.

When I finished, I had close to thirty volumes. The collection included pictures from my childhood days in Tehran and in Hungary and old family pictures, some dating back to 1912. My grandfather's collection of old documents like birth, death, and marriage certificates dated back to 1833. The papers included my Father's and his brother's work permit in Turkey when they worked there between 1925 and 1931 and their old passports and also my old report cards from first grade to my last graduation, including my diploma. I have my homework booklets from third and fourth grades. I also received similar information on different members of my Father's family.

I have my Father's diploma, dated June 20, 1913, and different awards given to him for his work during the past fifteen years. One was the award he received at the time of the Elizabeth Bridge (Erzsébet híd) dedication in Budapest in 1964 on November 21. The award was for his contribution to the design of the bridge. The bridge spans over the Duna River. During one of my visits, my Mother gave me all the letters my sister and I sent to Santa. Some of the letters were scribbling; we were too young to write. Added to the scribbling was my Mother's handwriting for clarity and the interpretation of our requests. She also gave me some of the Christmas presents, like my first stamp album, which was requested in one of Santa's letters. My parents tried to comply with one of the requests from the Christmas letters. I received several of the small religious books. My early religious education came from these books. My Mother taught us at home. Teaching religion by anyone was illegal. If the authorities knew about it, then you and your family disappeared indefinitely.

All these documents and information were given to me during my different visits to Hungary.

With this collection of documents and pictures of my Father and his nine siblings, I assembled a book containing 195 pages, with individual family trees on each sibling. Then I made several copies of it. During my visit to Argentina and Hungary in 2002, I gave a copy to each of my cousins or their descendants.

Before I completed the assembling of the book on my Father's siblings, I took a short time out and took a trip to Hungary (September 5-26, 2000). It was my twelfth trip. The main reason of my frequent trips—every two years—to Hungary was to see my sister; her physical and mental health was not in the best at times. The other times, I kept in touch with her by calling my cousin Ocsi; he visits her once or twice a month. He gives her help and looks after her in my absence. She doesn't have a telephone; when there was an opportunity to have it installed several years ago, she rejected the idea.

Now for installation, it required several years of waiting.

During my stay, I unexpectedly ran into Andrea Landesz; she was visiting from Argentina. It was the first time I saw her since she and her husband, my cousin Egon, visited me in Florida twenty years ago. We met several times, and we tried to catch up on the happenings in our lives for the past twenty years. At each trip, I learned things, and something different and new things happened that I enjoyed. In the end of the trip, it was always nice to return home to the States.

On December 12, 2000, Helen Grindle Fuchs passed away in Silver Spring, Maryland. She was eighty-seven years old. She was the person who met me in the Union Station on May 1, 1957, when I arrived in Washington DC from Camp Kilmer Refugee Center in New Jersey. She worked in Dad's office on the Capitol Hill as his office manager and personal secretary. The past forty-three years, we kept in touch; she watched over and helped to navigate particularly the early years of my life in this country. In the last years of her life, I visited her several times a month, shopped for her, and ran errands for her. Once a month, I balanced her checkbook and wrote her checks, prepared it for her signature, then put it in envelopes and mailed it for her. Helen's husband passed away several years ago, and they had no children.

During my regular Christmas (in year 2000) phone calls were made to my family in Hungary. I invited Cicka (Öcsi's daughter) for a visit with her fiancé, István (Steven) Solti, for the following spring. They arrived on April 3, 2001, and stayed for a month. This was Cicka's third visit, István's first. We went and saw the cherry blossoms in downtown DC, visited several museums and shopping centers. They helped me in the garden with the spring planting and its preparation. They liked my barbecue-steak dinners with corn on the cob and with American salad. We had a good time. I was glad they came. The time went fast, and in no time, they had to leave to go home.

I was very interested and wanted to update and expand the Landesz family tree that my grandfather started in the 1890s and completed in 1933. He only included male and Catholic descendants except his immediate family.

First, my research was on the Internet. I found Landesz descendants in three continents and several cities in United States, Canada, Argentina, Belgium, and Holland. The Landesz who lived in Belgium was my first cousin Beatrix; the family lost contact with her over forty years ago. Everyone in the family, including her father and my uncle Lajos, thought she was dead. The International Red Cross tried to locate her in the late sixties for her father's request, but they could not find her. It turned out she was living in India and then in Nepal for twenty-plus years. That was the reason she could not be reached and located. She did not leave a forwarding address. I called each one of the newly discovered Landeszes to be sure that they were part of the overall family. When I talked to

Beatrix for the first time, she found out from me that her father and brother passed away several years ago.

Second, I contacted the Salt Lake City, Utah, Mormon Genealogical Society's office. They have photocopies of the original books and documents from all over the world where the births, marriages, and deaths were recorded by the churches and synagogues. I found old records dating between 1722 and 1895 in different towns and cities in Hungary where Landeszes lived in the past two-hundred-and-so years. I reviewed the microfilm copies of the record books in the Bethesda office and made copies of some of the pages from the books for my record. I spent several months going to the office three times a week.

At the same time, with Öcsi's daughter, Cicka's, help in Hungary, she went through the different telephone books there and provided me with the list of names and addresses of the Landeszes living in Hungary. I wrote to each one and requested information on their family. To my surprise, everyone responded. With all these information and based on my grandfather's family tree, I assembled a new family tree. My research goes back to approximately the year 1720 when a György (George) Landes was born and, in 1745, settled with his wife, Teréz (Teresa) Oberling, in a farm called Vaspuszta, located in the county of Komárom in Austria-Hungary. The closest town to the farm is Ăcs. His occupation was a wheelwright; he had eight children. When his last child was born in 1767, the *z* was added to the *Landesz* name to get the proper Hungarian pronunciation. From that time on, the records showed all descendents having the *z* after their surname. We are all his descendants.

I also researched the history of the *Landes* name. According to the ancient chronicles of Scotland, the early records revealed that the name *Landes* was a Norman surname, which is ranked as one of the oldest names. The Normans are of Viking origin and landed on Northern Scotland about the year AD 870 under their king, Stirgud the Stout. By 1070, the Norman nobles in the north of England where in rebellion. King Malcolm Canmore of Scotland invited many of the displaced nobles to his court and gave them grants of land. In about 1130, the earl of Huntington, heir to the Scottish throne, later to become King David of Scotland, also offered land to his Norman friends in England, particularly in Lincolnshire, Norfolk, and Suffolk. The surname *Landes* emerged as a notable Scottish family name in the county of Lincolnshire. These Norman noble Landeses became lord of the manor of Lincolnshire.

As I mentioned before, during my research I located Beatrix Landesz, my cousin. I never met her before. I decided to organize a small family reunion and invite her from Belgium. I invited Andrea from Argentina; the last time she saw Beatrix was forty-five years ago when Beatrix was living in Argentina with her father and her brother. I also invited my sister Gisela from Atlanta to spend several weeks together and to get acquainted. Andrea arrived on May 14, 2001, and stayed till June 26. Beatrix arrived on May 15 and left on July 2. My sister got here on May 17 and stayed till June 7. I asked everyone to bring old family documents, pictures, and the story of their life in words or in writing. The information they provided was a big help and addition to my research and to the updating of the family tree. We spent lots of time in the nation's capital visiting museums and landmarks. We visited Great Falls, the Arlington National Cemetery, and the Basilica of the National Shrine of the Immaculate Conception. We had lunch in the Union Station. We visited Annapolis and the Navy Academy. We had barbecue dinners at home. We took a trip to Charlottesville to visit Harold and Del; Gisela was Harold's aunt by marriage. During our stay, we visited the University of Virginia and Monticello; Harold was our guide. One night, the Horan's invited us for dinner in their home. My sister spent a night with them; we stayed in a hotel. We had a nice visit. In another occasion, we took a day trip to Skyline Drive in the Shenandoah National Park, where we had a picnic. It was a clear day, and we enjoyed the nice view. From there, we took a side trip to Luray Caverns. For farewell dinner, we went out to *Normandie Farm,* a French restaurant in Potomac, Maryland. I am glad I had this time and opportunity to visit with them and learn more about them and the Landesz families.

It was planned that I was going to take a trip to Charlottesville, Virginia, on September 11, 2001, to visit Harold and Del and spend some time with them. That morning after I had my breakfast, I was sitting in my favorite chair and reading *The Washington Post* and listening to the television broadcast when the *Good Morning America* program was interrupted with a news bulletin, showing one of the towers in the World Trade Center in New York City on fire. The speculation for the cause was ramped. Several minutes later, we could see an airplane fly into the second tower. Shortly after when the second plane crashed into the South Tower, I left and started driving with the radio on and listening to the broadcast. All planes in the air were requested to check in with the closest airport tower and to land immediately. The reporter was concerned that two airplanes were not responding and were not counted for and were missing. About the same time, an airplane flew very low over my head in the easterly direction. Several minutes later, the broadcast announced a plane crashed in to the Pentagon in Arlington, Virginia. The time was 9:39 a.m.; it was flight AA 77. The fourth airline, UA 93, crashed at Stony Creek Township near Somerset, Pennsylvania. When I arrived at Charlottesville, I saw in the television a rebroadcast of the collapse of the towers, the panic on the surrounding streets. It turned out radical Islamic terrorists hijacked four airlines. Two flew into the World Trade Center. Building 1, the North Tower, was hit by flight AA 11 at 8:45 a.m. and collapsed at 9:51. Building 2, the South Tower, was hit by flight UA 175 at 9:05 a.m. and collapsed at 10:28 a.m. Thousands were dead.

To take our minds off the happenings of the past hours, we took a trip to Lexington, Virginia, and visited VMI. When we returned to Charlottesville in the late afternoon, we attended a special memorial church service. I returned home from Charlottesville on September 13. When I arrived home, I found twenty telephone and thirty e-mail massages from all over the word regarding the happenings of the last days.

On October 6, 2001, in the morning, I received a surprise, but not unexpected, call from Randy that Jeanette gave birth in the Shady Grove Hospital to a healthy boy at 6:56 a.m; he weighed 8 lb. and was 20 in. long. His name is Corey Peyton Barnes. The *Peyton* name is his great-grandfather's name in his father's side. In a short time, I was in the hospital to see my "grandson." He is a beautiful healthy boy, and Jeanette and Randy were beaming with joy, and they were very proud parents.

On October 7, 2001, the joint forces of the United States and Great Britain attacked Afghanistan because of the happenings on September 11 by the radical Islamic terrorists on the World Trade Center. It was retaliation for the Afghan Taliban government for harboring, adding, and supporting the al-Qaida Islamic terrorist organization, led by Osama bin Laden in their country. The September 11 attacks were connected to the Osama bin Laden organization.

In the spring of 2002, I traveled to Argentina (April 6-30) to visit two of my late uncles', Gyula (Julio) and Lajós (Louis) Landesz, families. Both of them left Hungary with their families in 1948 and 1950, respectively. I stayed in Andrea's home; she lived alone. Her children, Patrik and Florencia, and her husband, Egon, passed away several years ago. Her son, Partrik, passed away on June 20, 1993, her daughter, Florencia, on August 17, 1995, of breast cancer, and Egon on December 19, 1995, from stroke. Andrea lived in the town of Palomar, a twenty-minute train ride, ten miles northwest of Buenos Aires, the capital city of Argentina.

The other family was my late uncle Lajós's family. He was my godfather; I don't recall we ever met. This was the first time I met my uncle's wife, Aunt Nani, and her son Luis (Lali) Szalontay and his family. Lali was from her first marriage. During my visit, I collected documents and pictures from both of the families. We had long conversations about their lives in Argentina and their past in general. I gave each of the families a copy of the 195-page book on my Father and his nine siblings.

We celebrated Andrea's seventy-fifth birthday on April 14. At that occasion, I met her grandson Alvaro and his fiancée, Ines. Alvaro was her daughter's son. The celebrations took place at Lali's home with a big barbecue party, Argentine style. My gift to Andrea and to all adults at the party was a silver coin minted in Hungary in 1927, the year Andrea was born. On the night before the party, I gave Andrea a laptop and a printer. The laptop was Jeanette's old computer; she gave it to me to give it to Andrea when she found out I was looking for a used computer for her.

Buenos Aires is one of the largest cities in the world. It is located by the river *Plate*, the widest river in the world, discovered by the European conquistadors at the beginning of the sixteenth century. The city was first founded in 1536; it was a humble settlement of adobe houses in the next two centuries. Now, Buenos Aires is considered the "city of Paris" in the Americas.

We spent lots of time in Buenos Aires sightseeing, visiting the old part of the city. We visited antique shops at the *Plaza Derrego* and the *Design Center*. One of our weekend visits was to the *Plaza Derrego*; it had a fair where I purchased two paintings from an established artist, Ms. Patricia Aballay. The paintings illustrated natives from the northwest regents of Argentina. Also, I bought several eight-inch-high metal sculptures from another artist. The sculptures show different individual musicians with their instruments. We visited old churches like the *San Telmo Church* and the *Church of the Pillar* and the *Recolete* Cemetery where Eva Perón is buried. We also visited the *Plaza de Mayo* where at one end is the *Cathedral of Buenos Aires* and at the opposite end, the *Pink House,* the home of the president, like our White House. She showed me the exclusive shopping area on *Florida Street.* You can see there living statues on the street as a street art. We visited the *Galerias Pacifico*—it is a shopping mall that has a café with pastry—and looked at the great frescos on the ceiling by Argentine painters. We walked the city's beautifully landscaped wide avenues. During this time, some unrest had taken place in Argentina. In the last six months, they had four presidents. The public security was questionable. Unemployment was very high. I saw children begging in the street; it reminded me of my early days in Germany.

Every day, a policeman got killed, even when they were wearing bulletproof vests all the time. Sometimes after dusk, driving in the street was dangerous. Cars didn't stop at stop signs or streetlights because there was a good possibility your car will be hijacked and the occupants kidnapped and held for ransom. During Tuesdays through Thursdays, hired people marched with signs and chanted antigovernment slogans in front of different government buildings. The opposition parties paid these people. For a day's march and unrest, they received breakfast, lunch, and twenty pesos.

Andrea, Lali, and I took a car trip two hundred miles south to Villa Gesell, a resort town by the ocean. Lali drove. During our drive, for miles as far as the eye could see, were grazing cattle. Sprinkled between the cattle were ostriches. I never saw a sight like this before, the large amount of open land and all those cattle. In Villa Gesell, Andrea pointed out the buildings Egon, her husband and my cousin, built—several single—and multifamily homes, including their old vacation home where they spent a lot of their summers. She showed me the restaurant they owned where she was the chef and her husband greeted the guests upon their arrival.

My uncle Gyula died on May 19, 1969; he was buried there in a new cemetery. That area, before it became a cemetery, was where he used to hunt for pheasant. During our stay in Villa Gesel, when we were out one day, someone broke in to the house where we were staying and took everything—all our clothes, including the toothbrush, toothpaste, soap, deodorant, electric shaver—I mean everything. Next day, I went shopping to replace all the stolen items. On our return trip, we stopped at the city of Mar del Plata, located by the ocean. We visited the fish market and had a great Argentine lunch in a close-by seafood restaurant on the wharf. When we walked on the wharf, we saw a large sea lion eating a fish; upon completing its meal, it returned to the sea. After several days by the seashore, we returned to Andrea's home.

The following week, Andrea and I took a several days' trip to the northeast region of the country. The *Misiones* area was by the Argentina and the Brazil border. We were to visit the largest waterfalls in the world located in the *Iguaçu National Park*. During our walk in the park, I had the opportunity to see a *toucan* bird. It is a colorful bird with a large beak. I've never seen a bird like that before. We took a side trip to Brazil to visit *Itaipu,* the largest hydroelectric power plant in the world, located on the *Paraná River* between Brazil and Paraguay. The capacity of the plant is twice of the *Grand Coulee Power Plant* in the United States. It provides electric power to Brazil and Paraguay. We also visited a semiprecious-stone mine, where I bought some stones. On my next trip to Hungary, I had it made into a ring, pendant, and brooch. I gave the ring to Jeanette on her next birthday. The pendant was for Owen's future wife when he gets engaged; Owen selected the stone for the pendant. For the brooch, I don't know yet who will receive it.

After returning from Argentina, I completed the updated and expanded family tree, and I made twenty copies.

At the fall of the same year, I traveled to Hungary (August 11 to September 23, 2002); this was my thirteenth visit, and then to Holland (September 23-26). I visited and met all the Landeszes who contributed information to the new updated family tree; I gave a copy of the new family tree to each of the families. Some of these families did not know how they were related to one another. During my visit, I took pictures of them. I also visited the old cemeteries and took pictures of the old graves in the town of Ăcs and other places where Landeszes lived in Hungary in the past centuries, based on my research and information provided by the families. I also visited different cities where monuments commemorated Landesze's from different wars. I took pictures of the monuments. The local families helped to locate the graves in the different cemeteries and the monuments in the towns.

I visited all my cousins and gave them each a copy of the book I prepared on my Father and his nine siblings. They were surprised of the book's content; they saw many of the documents and pictures for the first time. At this occasion, I met for the first time after all these years Andras. He is the son of my father's sister Isabella. He is older than I. He is retired now. Before his retirement, he was the president of the Hungarian Motion Pictures Production Company. We had several nice visits; he also gave me more family information, pictures, and documents on my aunt and on his family. He passed away a year later.

On my return trip from Hungary, I stopped over in Holland for three days to meet and visit my namesake Karl (Karel) Landesz and his wife, Györgyi. Before they escaped from Hungary in the early 1960s, he and his wife visited my Father to meet his older namesake. They met me in Amsterdam airport. From there, we drove to their home, about twenty miles south, the town called Wassenaar. It is located between Amsterdam and The Hague. During my visit, we went to see the New Church (Nieuwe Kerk) built in 1351 in the city of Delft, where the lineage of the House of Orange-Nassau, the Holland Royal House, family's last resting place were. We had a cup of coffee on the plaza in front of the church. This church was built as a Roman Catholic church, but when the Reform movement took over Europe, the church was stripped from all interior finishes and left abundant.

We returned to Amsterdam for a visit, and we spent a day there. In the city, at the back of every building was a canal, almost like we were in Venice, Italy. We also visited Rotterdam, the largest seaport in Europe. We had lunch in the *Euromast Tower;* the restaurant was top of the Tower, 350 feet up. We had a window seat with a beautiful view of the city below us. From the tower, my host, the other Karl, pointed out several oil refineries where he was a project manager and under his direction was constructed. He was a chemical engineer. When he attended the university in Budapest, Hungary, he spent the weekends with my uncle Gyula and his family; and he had home-cooked meals with them. Karl's parents lived several hundred kilometers from Budapest. He also gave me information on his family and on the other Landesz family's members he knew of. The time, went by fast, but I saw a lot in a few days. We are keeping in touch by telephone or by e-mail.

Collecting all this additional information during my visit to Argentina, Hungary, and Holland, I updated the *new updated family tree,* adding more information and photographs next to each names; it was a long and time-consuming process.

In the end, I had twenty-four pullout pages; some of the pages were over three feet long, with documentations of ten generations of descendants and their families.

Andrea didn't want to spend the Christmas alone; she asked me if she could spend it with me. She arrived on November 25, 2002, and stayed till January 3, 2003. This was her second visit. This visit was different because it was the winter season. She hoped it would snow. She had not seen snow in the Christmas season since she left Hungary in 1948. In Argentina, December was the summer season. We went Christmas shopping. I showed her the decoration in several malls. Jeanette and Randy took us to the Seneca Park to see the holiday decorations there. One evening, Jeanette, Randy, and Corey came over for a Hungarian dinner prepared by Andrea. After we finished eating, we retired into the family room. They sat on the floor about six feet apart from one another. Corey stood supported by one of them when he decides to walk independently toward the other parent. That repeated itself several times. It was Corey's first independent steps. Andrea got her video camera and documented the big occasion. Upon returning to Argentina, she made a short film of her visit here, editing it with short stories and with music. She gave each of us a copy. During her stay, her wish came true; it snowed. She played in the snow like a kid. We made small snowmen in the yard and put on a hat and a scarf. She also took a trip to Buffalo, New York, to visit her grandson and his family. He was getting his master's degree from the New York University. Before she left, we decided that she would make a return visit in the spring to see the cherry blossoms.

I received a call on January 7, 2003, from my office manager when I was working in the Harry Weese office in Miami. It has been over twenty years since the last time I talked to him. He located me by making several calls to different acquaintances of his till someone had my telephone number. He recently returned from over twenty years of overseas assignment. He worked in Athens, Greece, and Seoul, South Korea's metro systems. His employer now, the Washington Group International Inc. (WGII), was negotiating with Virginia to design and build the Washington Metro extension through Dulles airport to Loudon County. The extension was approximately twenty-five miles long, had eleven stations, and a maintenance yard. He was asked to set up an architectural office for this project. He wanted to know if I would come out of my retirement and be part of this new office. During our conversation, he indicated that it will take some time to finalize the negotiations. I accepted the offer; let's see what the future will bring. I helped him to locate other ex-Harry Weese employees to see if they were interested to join us and to work on the project.

On February 14, 2003, after a long consideration and encouragement from my family, I began to write my life's journey, *the journey of a refugee*. At the time, I did not know the emotions it would cause when I revisit the early years of my journey. Nothing in life is easy.

The winter of 2003 turned out to be the coldest winter in the past twenty-five years. In three days, from the fifteenth to seventeenth of February, we had twenty-four-inch snowfall. State of the emergency was declared. Businesses were closed.

President Bush, in his television address to the nation and to Hussein—Iraq's strongman—announced to Hussein to leave Iraq in forty-eight hours or face war. It was broadcast at 8:00 p.m. (EST) on March 17, 2003. Two days later, the invasion of Iraq started at 9:33 p.m. (EST) and was announced by the president at 10:15 p.m. The major allied forces consisted of the USA, British, Australian forces, and thirty-plus countries provided minor support. By May 1, the allied forces completed the occupation of Iraq. Hussein and his family were hiding. Later during the search, his sons were killed, and Hussein was captured. The new Iraqi government put him on trial for crimes and atrocities he committed against the Iraqi people.

To celebrate my sixty-fifth birthday, Jeanette and Randy took me to the Ruth's Chris Steak House in Bethesda for dinner. It was very nice of them to do this. The food was excellent. I enjoyed it very much. We had a good time.

Hurricane Isabel's rain and wind battered the region on September 19, 2003; thirty-four people died because of it. Power was out for over two million customers in the region. I didn't have power for twenty-five hours. Business, federal, and local governments were closed. Metro shut down, the first time in Metro's history that it stopped running.

On Christmas eve, I had dinner with Jeanette, Randy, and Corey in their home. It was very nice of them to invite me. On Christmas day, I was home alone. I looked back and reminisced about the past Christmases I had when I was growing up with my parents. Then, there were four of us; now it is one. Then, we had some conversation, some sounds, some movements, and some activity in the room; now everything was silent. The pasts are pasts and are no more, only in memories. The present is painful to be all alone. That's life.

But I am thankful to be alive, and I am very grateful for that.

On my 2002 visit to Hungary, I collected more information of my grandfather's writings, specifically his poems that he wrote to his future wife when they were dating. He wrote forty poems during that time between 1882 and 1888. They got married on October 28, 1888. They had ten children. The paper where the poems were written on was turning yellow, and it was very brittle. I made a copy of the poems and read it; I enjoyed it. I found it very warm, very interesting, very compassionate. His poems described the time they lived in and his feelings, the devotion he had for her. Also the same time, I located several of his short essays on smoking, young people's behavior—a total of eleven; he wrote late in his life in the early 1940s. Some of the essays were very appropriate even today. I wanted that his descendants, especially the young generation, to enjoy his writings. I contacted a friend Magyar Agnes in Hungary in early 2004 and requested her to help me to publish my grandfather's poems and his writings. I organized the poems that on one side of the page was the type-written poem and the opposite page was the copy of the same hand-written poem. I wrote the first chapter, a brief essay about my grandfather's life and the story of the poems. I titled it from one of his poems *"Was Not Born in a Pales"* in Hungarian, "Nem Szuletem Palotaban." It was issued as a private publication, and twenty-six copies were printed.

On my 2004 visit to Hungary, I gave a copy to my grandfather's children's descendants and other Landesz family descendants who knew him late in his life. A copy of the book was also sent to the town library in Ăcs where he was born in 1860 and attended school.

President Ronald Wilson Reagan, our fortieth president of the United States passed away at the age of ninety-three on June 5, 2004, on my sixty-sixth birthday. He had Alzheimer's disease. He was born on February 12, 1911, in Tampico, Illinois. He was a radio announcer, actor and, in 1966, was elected governor of California for two terms. In 1980, he was elected, and in 1984, reelected as a Republican president of the United States. During his presidency, he was the architect, with Pope John Paul II, of the fall of the Communism in the world.

My first day as a full-time employee with WGII to extend the Washington Metro was on September 2, 2004. The office was located in Vienna, Virginia, close to the Tysons Corner Shopping Center. I was the manager of architectural production. I had a low-six-figure salary, the highest in my career. In the past twelve months, I worked for them part-time, as-needed basis, as a consultant on different assignments.

The pasture years gave me the opportunity to slow down, look back, review, organize, and assemble the events and the happenings of my life. It was interesting to see and relive the good and happy times and try to forget the bad and sad times, reflect and see what I learned from the past, how it altered, changed my life, what I would do differently if I had the same opportunity and another chance. I have the time now to sit back and reminisce and look forward and plan the remaining years of this journey.

The Royal Pales in the Castle district. The Duna River is in foreground.
/Budapest, Hungary September 2000/

Cicka, Steve, Bill, and I.
Olney, Maryland April 2001/

The reunion.
Left to right: Beatrix Landesz from Belgium; Meitia Kuo, my son Bill' girlfriend; Bill; Gisela Campbell, my sister from Georgia, USA; Andrea Landesz, my cousin's widow from Argentina; Owen; Randy; and Jeanette with Corey.
Olney, Maryland, June 2001.

Randy, Jeanette, and Corey. He is about two hours old.
Corey Peyton Barnes, born at 6:56 a.m., 8 lb., 20 in.
Gaithersburg, Maryland, October 6, 2001.

Andrea, me, and Nani, my aunt.
Mrs. Lajós Landesz. Trip to Argentina,
April 6-30, 2002.

The *Pink House* in Buenos Aires, it is the same as the *White House* in the US.

Iguacu National Park

Located at the border of Argentina and Brazil.

Itaipu Hydroelectric Power Plant.

Located on the Parana River between Brazil and Paraguay.

Pointing to a name of an ancestor on the monument.

Trip to Ăcs, Hungary, September 2002.

Györgyi, wife of Karel; Károly Landesz; and I, Károly Landesz, with Karel.

He is my older namesake.

Wassenaar, Holland. My visit on September 23-26, 2002.

Grandpa Karcsi with Corey.

Gaithersburg, Maryland, December 2002 and 2004.

Celebrating Andrea's (77) and Jeanette's (34) birthday. They were born on the same day.

Olney, Maryland, April 13, 2004.

XII

Observation

You read my journey; you can see I am a survivor. Before I close this chapter of my life and before I complete this writing, I would like to express my observations and reflect on what I saw and learned in the past forty-plus years living in this great country of ours. I will write it in a refugee's point of view that cares a lot for this country and the people in it.

I grew up in Europe during the war years, the first half of the last century. During that time, the world's politics influenced and shaped millions of lives, including mine. More people were killed, and more lives were disrupted then than in any other time in history. I lived under Fascism and Communism. I developed an interest in politics during the early years in my life. I wanted to understand why people, politicians behaved the way they behaved, why people wanted to hurt other people. I observed firsthand how politics shaped people's mind and their lives, how dictators had their ways, how they controlled the population of a nation.

I also wanted to know how the rest of the world lived; for that, the only thing I could do was to listen with my Father to the "forbidden" radio broadcast, which provided the opposite view I was living in. By listening to this "forbidden" broadcast, we could pay with our lives if anyone found out and reported it to the government, the secret police. The informer, in exchange, received favors. Reporting people was a common practice.

The "forbidden" broadcasts we listened to were *Radio Free Europe, Voice of America, BBC* (British Broadcasting Corporation) *and the Radio Vatican.*

After my arrival at the States, living with the Horan's, I learned the history and the functions of the American government from them and books they provided me. I had a personal experience with leading politicians in our time during my lifetime.

It was exciting and educational to live in this time in the world, to be part of its history, closely observing, and to live in different political lifestyles. This experience provided me with firsthand knowledge. It is rare for a person to have this experience, survive it, and then to talk about it. This experience and knowledge gave me the advantage, and now, the opportunity to write about it and express my observation on the following subjects: *the politicians and their politics, segregation, the presidents and the presidency, the war, First Amendment, unions, immigration, business,* and *the people.*

The politicians and their politics. Today is not the same democracy we had when I came to this country. The politicians then were compassionate and caring. When I arrived, and during the following decade, with all political campaigns for local and national office, the candidates campaigned as an individual on their merit, his and her experiences, their beliefs, and the best way they can represent the people. It was not emphasized then which party the candidate belonged to. During the 1960 presidential and congressional campaign, I was in Washington State, campaigning for Mr. Horan (Dad). It was a common practice during the campaign to only speak in positive ways and not to mention political affiliation of any other candidates. When you voted, you voted for the individual, how he or she can best represent you, and not because the candidate was affiliated with a specific party. The party affiliation was not an issue.

Now the people are voting for the party, not the individual candidate. Because of it, a handful of senior politicians are deciding for us by using their opinions, their beliefs for what is good for us. In other words, they are forcing their beliefs and their agenda on you; it doesn't make any difference if you agree with it or not. Periodically, the electorate got tired of this type of leadership, dictatorship, and then they cleaned "house" and got rid of this type of politicians. Unfortunately, when they throw out the "bathwater," sometimes they throw out the "baby" too, the "good guy" with it. This type of candidates whose emphasis was party affiliation and not their capabilities, were misleading the people with their intention. Their only reason for running for office was for their own and their backer's personal gains, not because they wanted to represent and to work for the constituents. They don't care about the people they represent. This is one of the reasons the politician's honesty, integrity, trustworthiness—based on survey—is in the bottom, below the reputation of the used car's salesman.

Unfortunately, our modern-day politicians are very corrupt, and if some drastic changes are not taken in the near future, we will lose our prestige in the world like the Roman Empire did. It collapsed in corruption and in their greediness, and consequently, they lost their leadership and their prestige in the world. Look where is the Roman Empire now? It is in ruins. I make a bet majority of the young generation don't know what I'm talking about. It was the foundation of the world's modern-day governments before the politicians and leading citizens' abuse, corruption brought it to its destruction. Other nations have corrupt politicians and corrupt, greedy businessmen too, but we are the ones who are preaching, truth, fairness, and morality to others. I received an earful from several cabdrivers in Poland during my visit there in the time when President Clinton had his escapades in the White House with the intern.

We are entrusted to lead and protect the world, but we have abused that trust. We are behaving as big bullies. We want to influence the world based on our two-hundred-year history. The rest of the world has several thousands years of history on us. At the same time, we don't want to learn anything about the rest of the world, but we want to influence and rule them. How many hours of world history are taught in our schools? How many schools teach different European languages? How many schools teach European, Eastern, or Asian cultures? How many schools are teaching the basics of different religions in the world for the better understanding of others? All this would go a long way for a better understanding of mankind and to earn respect for us from the rest of the world's population. At the least in return, they will understand and respect us for our effort.

We are so self-centered that we believe they should learn our language, they should learn our culture, they should learn our history, and they should follow our principles and beliefs. We disregard the people of the world, their history, their culture, their principles, and their beliefs. Don't you think we are a little arrogant about it?

The politicians think because they go overseas for fact-finding trips they become an "expert" of the country they visited. How? By staying in a hotel bar, drinking and playing golf on exotic golf courses! If politicians don't have even the minimum background education, knowledge on the countries of the world, and they don't know the basics about it, then how can they advise and be experts in their fields, and how can the politicians can make the proper decision? Sometimes, they don't even know some of the country's leading politicians' name or properly pronounce their names or the country's name.

Many times, our ambassadors do more harm than good in their posts. I experienced it firsthand that an ambassador and his wife showed no respect with his actions in public to the country's culture and religion where they were assigned. This is not an isolated incident. Our government did not do anything about it even when that government filed the protest with the State Department.

It is common practice for an ambassador to be named because of his or her deep "pockets," but at the same time, they also should be examined as how to capable the person is and their family are to represent our country with dignity and respect. Many ambassador positions are given to supporters who donated large amount of money to the successful presidential candidate. Then the newly elected president appoints the ambassadors. In other words, they bought the post, not earned it; and they are not necessarily qualified for it.

To reduce corruption in the U.S. Congress and the sponsorship of "pork projects," which is wasting taxpayers' hard-earned money by the members for their own gain, it should establish the following rules and guidelines:

(1) Any spending projects and their sponsors, including the lobbyist, should be disclosed, with the information of how the public will benefit from the project and why it is needed. The discloser should take place in major newspapers and prime-time TV public announcement every day for thirty days, then to have a public hearing before they are considered by the U.S. Congress. On the public hearing, the member(s), sponsor(s), the lobbyist are to explain the benefits of their project and how it will help or impact mankind. If the project is voted down, recalled, or withdrawn, it cannot be reinstated for not less than five years. No projects are to be named after a member minimum of ten years after the project is completed and are in use. Each earmarked "pork project" has to be independent, cannot be attached to any other bill or bills. Each "pork project" shall be voted on separately. Every "pork project" has to have transparency and have to have specific assignments.

(2) Since the late 1950s, we have term limit for the president of the United States (two consecutive terms, maximum of eight years). Every state has a term limit for the governor. It is time now to have a term limit for the members of the U.S. Congress. It is not a new idea, but it is more necessary now than ever. Members of the U.S. Senate have two consecutive six-year terms, a total of twelve years. The U.S. House of Representatives to have six consecutive two-year terms, a total of twelve years. No member of either House is to hold

chairmanship positions on committees and subcommittees more than two years in their term in Congress. The Speaker of the House and the Portent of the Senate term is limited to the member's term who is the Speaker and the Portent at the time. This new procedure will bring in new, fresh members, hopefully with common sense. Yes, we will have more turnover, but with new ideas, and it will be better in representing and better for serving the people. Now we have members in the Congress who are too old to function properly. Their staff makes the decision for them; therefore, they cannot represent the people who voted for them. Sometimes, it appears the U.S. Congress is the geriatric home for the members. At other fields, career seniority means experience and knowledge; in politics, it means more corruption.

(3) To have opportunity for all people to run for Congress or any elected office, not just the rich and already-corrupt individuals. It would be a big improvement if we established a limit how much money a candidate can spend from outside supporters and his and her and their families' money (prevent money laundering) for the primary and the final campaign till the election. They should publicly report all donations at the end of each month; if not, they personally have to pay for it and return all donations. It is up to each candidate how to budget his or her expenses. It would be a good practice for the public office they are running for. This concept also would be used for the presidential election. This would help to eliminate some if not all corruption.

(4) To eliminate corruption and graft, each member of a public office are to report any money or gift received to all the major media for publication with names, who provided the gifts and why, and what for, then turn the money and items over to the U.S. Treasury in forty-eight hours after they received it or after returning from their foreign travel. In the event of failing to do so, they should be automatically expelled from his or her elected office. Blaming the staff is not an excuse for not complying with these requirements.

Any candidate who doesn't like these guidelines should not run for office.

In Europe and in Asia, the politicians are more corrupt than in this country, but we are catching up very fast. But we are the only one to preach integrity, fairness, and humenright to the whole world.

Segregation. When I was in the U.S. Army in the spring of 1960, when I learned about the segregation and the discrimination in this country, more specifically when I was returning from boot camp in Kentucky and was going to my new assignment, I was planning to drive from Washington DC to Fort Sam Houston, Texas, with an African American friend who lived in Washington DC. I befriended him in boot camp. I found out very fast it was impossible because of the segregated restaurants, hotels, toilets, even the water fountains. I ended up driving alone. I saw the same things and more during my assignment in Texas. One thing was clear to me—the Southern whites didn't want to be in the same room with, as they refer to them, the "black people, the Negro's." I was surprised to see the dark side of this country. With one fundamental exception, I supported the laws that were passed by Congress in the mid sixties against segregation. The Congress meant well, maybe a little too well. The part of the law where providing financial support to people who did not work. I recognized why this part of the law was so important to President Johnson and the Southern and liberal Democrats, because they heard the same thing that I heard when I was stationed in Texas and driving through the South. The Southern whites didn't want to work with the "black people." That part of the law destroyed the African Americans' family life when no support was provided to families if a male member lived in the same household. But provided more support if the family grew with more children. If they truly meant to help, then they can look for examples from President Roosevelt's presidency by providing employment in exchange for financial support. In my opinion, because of lack of this opportunity for the American Africans, they had to endure for several decades a different type of slavery by not being part of and contributing members to our society, which they are otherwise, would be entitled to. On the other hand, President Johnson and the Democratic U.S. Congress knew what they were doing. It gave them the opportunity for decades to establish guaranteed voting base. The Democratic Congress provided financial support for nothing in return; they bought hundreds of thousands of votes for generations to come. This way, circumventing the law agents buying votes on the African Americans' expense. I am a moralist; I find their action despicable, and it was not moral and dignified. It is very sad, but this is how the liberal politics work.

The Democratic Party made the African American's cause year after year their central piece of their agenda. They held the presidency and the majority of Congress for many years; they did nothing or very little. The past forty-plus years, the Democratic Party held the States Assembly and the governors' office in Southern states where they needed the most help, and they also did nothing or very little. If the Democratic Party truly wanted to help and to "solve the problem"—they can do it—to make the African Americans independent and not depend financially on the politicians, but then they will lose the vote; therefore, they don't want to totally and completely solve the problem. They wanted to hold out the "hope," the "carrot," as long as possible.

Only one person helped the African Americans' cause without any hesitation, without any personal gain; it was Martin Luther King Jr. He believed in the "cause." He believed to help other people without "color." He was a minister who preached nonviolent protests against injustice. He won the 1964 Nobel Peace Prize. He wrote several books. Anyone after him were the "pretenders." They were only looking out for him or herself, which is one of the reasons the progress is slowed. They also were playing the "carrot" game. As long as the "cause" dragged out, the longer they were in the limelight and the longer they profited from it. When some established, successful African American suggested that they help themselves—study hard, work hard, and don't look for handouts, those individuals are ridiculed for it; they are called "Uncle Toms" by the Liberal establishment.

After when the slaves were freed by President Lincoln, in the following state election, many educated ex slaves were elected as Republicans to the Sate Houses in different Southern States. When the time came to take their seats as newly elected legislators, the fellow democratic colleagues locked them out. They never took their seats. I had a privilege to meet and work with one of the descendants of the locked-out legislator. It was also interesting to see several documentary programs not too long ago on the Public Television on the same subject. In the sixties and seventies, many African American individuals and families left South and moved to the North East to find work to better their own and their families' life. They did not see their future and their children's future with the handout that the government provided to them with strings attached to it. They worked hard, encouraged their children to study. One of the participants in the documentary stated what her father told her when she was starting her schooling: *"Study hard and stop asking for a piece of the pie, make your own pie."* Now, those children are well-to-do and respected members of our society. To be a success in life, you have to make your own opportunities. Always remember when one door shuts, another opens.

If you want to work in this country, you can; maybe you have to move to another city. Some people move thousands of miles or even from a different country to have a better life. Let's not forget this country of ours is made up of immigrants.

The presidents and the presidency. During my lifetime, we have had twelve presidents, ten since I have lived in this country. I have met four of them. Looking back, there were two kinds of individuals running for president.

Those who were sincere and who were strong in character and in courage had his agenda, his vision, long before he became the president and could relay his vision to the people. With his vision, he does great things for the nation and for all people in the world. He would not let special-interest groups sidetrack that vision. With his determination, with his policies, and with his vision, the Communism collapsed in the world. He was President Ronald Reagan, our fortieth president (1981-1989). We had individuals, candidates who had as many "visions" as states in the Union. Then when they became president, they "leaked" their "vision" one by one to see the "public's"—the vocal extremist—reaction before making it their own vision. Some individuals became president in a "vacuum." Some presidents catered to a special group of people with extreme thinking, and their advice then influenced the president.

We have had presidents who did not want to be a president, but the circumstance made them president. They were called upon in different times and different circumstances, and they accepted the challenge. One was called upon by both parties in 1948 to run for president, but he refused. He did not believe a professional military man should be president. The people kept after him and, in 1952, agreed to run on the Republican ticket. He was commander of all the Allied forces in Europe during the Second World War. He had seen enough war, he said, now he would fight for peace. Everyone liked him because he was a totally honest person. It was President Dwight D. Eisenhower, our thirty-fourth president (1953-1961).

We had a president—sometimes people refer to him as an accidental president—that never ran for that office; he did not want to be president. He was asked to be the vice president in 1973 when Vice President Spiro Agnew resigned in disgrace. Then fate made him president when President Nixon resigned in August 1974. That time was when the nation was in turmoil and needed a strong, honest leader. He faced the task of ending a war—a war not of his own making. In the short three years during his presidency, he made unpopular decisions, which in time united this country, but then prevented him to continue his presidency. He sacrificed his future for the good of the nation. He was President Gerald Ford, our thirty-eighth president (1974-1977).

In the past fifty years, we had one president with great potential, great leadership, and great future. He was the youngest president to take office. He was forty-three years old. The election was one of the closest in history. Because the political upheaval of the time, his presidency was short-lived. He was assassinated on November 22, 1963, in Dallas, Texas. If he lived, he probably would have been one of our greatest presidents of our times.

He prepared himself for the presidency. When he was a senator, he wrote a book called *Profiles in Courage* about United States senators who had risked their careers to fight for things they believed in. It won a prize for the best American history book of the year. In his 1961 inaugural speech, he urged Americans to "*ask not what your country can do for you, but what you can do for your country.*" He was President John F. Kennedy, the thirty-fifth president (1961-1963). I had the privilege to meet President Kennedy and the First Lady in a White House reception dinner party.

There was one other president in my lifetime, which made a big impact not just in the United States, but also in the world. He protected the world population from a tyrant dictator and guided this country and the world in one of the hardest and difficult times in its history. He became the president at a time when this nation was in despair over the Great Depression. He rallied Americans with, "*The only things we have to fear is fear itself.*" The world would look different today without his leadership and without his presidency. He was President Franklin D. Roosevelt, the thirty-second president (1933-1945).

In my opinion, there are only two presidents in the past sixty-plus years who knew the world history and understood the people in it, their customs, the world's politicians, and their politics; they were President Roosevelt and President Eisenhower.

President Jimmy Carter, the thirty-ninth president (1977-1981), did more good for the nation and for his reputation after he retired from the presidency.

About the other presidents, I learned long time ago that if you cannot say positive things, then don't say anything.

The war. I have firsthand experience on the war. I lived in it, and I survived it. I was a recipient of the bombings by the Allied forces in the Second World War. I saw it firsthand what destruction war can do. I lived in a camp in Germany for several years during Second World War. The war is hell, and you are living in hell, and you don't ever forget it. The German army located their military in the cities, using the civilians as a human shield. But the Allied forces did not hesitate to bomb the cities with civilians in it. It was not uncommon after the bombings to find several thousands of dead civilians in the ruins of buildings. There is no morality in war! But you have to do it if you want to survive and you want to be free.

From our nation's past history, we can see that when the public is united behind the president during wartimes—putting their politics to the side—then the nation wins that war, and at the same time, lives are saved, and the duration of the war is shortened (First and Second World Wars). Once the politicians start bickering, so-called "airing of their opinions" or providing "free expression" of their "opinions" come to surface, then we lose the war. If this bickering were positive and constructive to see how to improve and support our troops, then maybe it would be acceptable. But when the bickering is to embarrass the opposition or because some individuals are looking for personal gain, I call their action criminal. Their actions kill our soldiers and kill people. In some countries, for this kind of behavior, they are executed as traitors. Some politicians, hard-liners who are representing a handful of people, but because they have longevity in the U.S. Congress, they act like they are the president of the United States (conveniently forgetting the U.S. Constitution, more specifically Articles II and I). Sometimes, people don't understand or don't know that in our Constitution, we have only one commander in chief, which is the president of the United States. We don't have 535 (100 plus 435) presidents or co-presidents'. The hard-liners are deepening the social divide by "*imposing their minority views on a more moderate majority*" (by President Carter in *Our Endangered Values).* In the case of war, once the president and the Congress have established the nation's direction and its goals jointly, and afterward some descendant politicians or descendant group of individuals try to tell the world what to do, how to run the war, questioning decisions, then we lose the war (Korean, Vietnam, and Iraq). When a nation is not united, then the enemy takes advantage of it. They don't understand our freedom of expression, they only see our weakness in it. The more we disagree, the more it increases the enemy's morale and the morale of their troops. In any army, the troop's morale is more than half to win each battle and for winning the overall war. Our bickering helps the enemy in war and at the same time demoralizes our military. People who disagree on this subject are incompetent and not very bright. I don't care who these persons are. It is proven in thousands of years of history that the troop's morality is a big factor toward winning a war, any war.

Democracy is not free. You have to fight for it! You have to sacrifice for it! People forget those everyday people who win the wars. They are the members of the military, not the politicians. But in the end, politicians are the ones who take credit for it when the war is won. If the war is lost, then the fighting men and women and their families suffer for it when they return home (Vietnam).

First Amendment. It is part of the Bill of Rights. The Bill of Rights was added to the Constitution in 1791, and it has ten amendments. The First Amendment has five parts: the freedom of religion, freedom of speech, freedom of the press, freedom of assembly, and freedom of petition. I only want to talk about two: the freedom of speech and the freedom of the press.

Freedom of speech, wording in brief, *"means that you are free to speak out and give your side of things, others are free to listen."* It sounded good, and it was great until a handful of extremists or liberal individuals and their organization arrived and started questioning, analyzing, and censoring every word we are saying and writing today. They are setting up new standards for our freedom of speech based on their extreme point of view. They are establishing what is right and what is wrong based on their belief. If we don't comply with their demands, then they threaten to sue us, and in the end, we are silenced. It is a type of McCarthyism from the early fifties; you are accused, and you have to defend yourself. Hitler started this way in Germany, but many people have forgotten it by now. Not the government, but the hard-line extremists and their liberal organizations are censoring us; they are pushing their agenda because they cannot take criticism and want to dictate us. If you don't call this action as a censorship, then what is it? Oh, it is called "their type of free speech." It reminds me of when I was living under Communism, where we had to consider, review, analyze everything we were saying. We are not far from that kind of living conditions, that kind of lifestyle—the dictatorship.

Freedom of press, wording in brief, *"means that members of the press do not have to get what they are planning to print or say approved by the government beforehand. They are free to print what they wish as long as it is not a deliberate lie."* The news media many times make deliberate misleading statements for the sake of attention or for the sake of profit. Later, they apologize; but for the accused, it is too late—the damage is done. They make some excuses referencing the First Amendment. Sometimes, they create news in slow-news days. I am naïve; I was under the impression that the *news* means "report actual happenings." I don't call it when the reporter is editorializing or expressing their opinion, and they distorted reporting as news. I call it commentary. The news media are very distorted, very prejudiced, and very liberal. They are not balanced in their reporting. They prefer sensationalism compere to reporting the facts. They like to report negative news to boost their ratings. They don't see the good things in people or in happenings. You don't have to look hard to find a lot of good, caring people, and happenings in this country or in the world. By reporting good things, the people will learn from it. By helping one person at a time, this country will improve and will be better. It would be nice to have some media reporting with only positive news. Unfortunately today, their reporting are nothing more than a collection of misrepresentation of facts to manipulate the public to their agenda.

Unions. In principle, it is a good organization with a good mission and good cause, as long as the management is realistic with their demands and with their cause. When they get greedy and lose their mission, then they do more harm than good with their unrealistic demands. Several large corporations are forced to close or to drastically reduce their production at the workers' expense. Just to name some, these are Pan Am, Air Florida, and Eastern Airways. They are no more. Because of cheaper foreign labor costs, U.S. and Bethlehem Steel closed or reduced its production, and the workers lost their livelihood. The companies cannot afford the high expenses to stay in business and to be competitive. In some cases, union members lost their pension and even their medical benefits. At the same time, the union management survived and prospered. Now, the American auto industry is in jeopardy. Not too long ago, they negotiated for medical benefits and high wages; it can force the American auto industry to extinction. The unions demanded for large salary increases and unrealistic benefits from companies, which also helped the inflation to grow. Many retired union members are finding out in their old age that when they need the help most, they don't have the income and benefit that was promised. Many, if not all, of the union leaders don't look out for the workers. Sometimes, they are collaborating with the underworld, or the underworld is running the unions. The workers are finding it out it is better for them in the long run to stay out from the unions. Some forty years ago, over 60 percent of the labor force were in unions; now it is only about 20 percent. The unions have to learn to work for the people for a long and steady duration, not just for a "day."

Immigration. I was an immigrant who arrived close to fifty years ago. Then and the following years, to enter legally to this country, you had to wait for your turn. You had to have a sponsor. The sponsor can be an individual, a family, an organization, an employer, or a church. The sponsors are responsible for you. I was sponsored by Hon. and Mrs. Horan. I waited in different refugee camps in Austria for several months for my turn for entry to the States. Shortly after my arrival, I attended day and night language classes. In the class, the student were from different countries of the world. We studied hard, did more work than what was required. We all were very eager to learn—to learn the language, the new customs, and the new culture. We wanted desperately to fit in. This is our new home now. The procedure for emigrants to have a sponsor was a practiced for a long time, and it would by nice for this practice to continue today. Unfortunately, with some leading politicians', including our president, help and their encouragement, the government is ignoring the sponsorship requirement and encouraging aliens not to wait—just immigrate illegally. It gives the politicians new rallying case to "solve" the illegal-emigration problem. At the same time, for individuals from European countries who want to visit our country as tourist or visit relatives or friends, their visa request are denied, particularly if they are females. Including the citizens of countries whose military are our allies in Iraq. We have approximately twelve million illegal immigrants from south of the border in this country now, and it grows to an estimated one million a year. Personally, I don't know what to "solve," what is the problem. It is simple, they illegally entered this country; they are fugitive from the law. They should be deported. They broke the law of this country, and they are not political refugees. If we are lenient in this case, then we should be forgiving to people who rob a bank, break into your home, rape your family members and molest your children. They also should go free or any other criminals who committed any crime.

Why do we have double standards? What is the difference? The law is the law. Why are the illegal immigrants different from other people who are breaking the law?

Any business hiring an employee, the employer have to complete a form provided by the federal government (Customs Enforcement Division). It is called the *Employee Eligibility Verification Form.* The form is filled out by the prospective employee in front of the employer representative. The form requires three different identification documents from the list of five provided in the form; the prospective employee has to provide the original documents. The documents are as follows: driver's license, social security card, U.S. birth certificate, green card or a passport. The foreign person's passport will show the type of visa, indicating the person is eligible to work if any. For example, the student visa is good for part-time work with maximum twenty hours a week. The form also states penalties for the employer if it does not comply with the requirements. This form should be forwarded to the agency then the immigration office to make unannounced visits to employers for spot check of compliance. If the employer does not comply with the law, then they are to receive a large fine, maybe as high as two hundred fifty thousand dollars for each illegal immigrant they employ. The government is to close the plant/companies till the fine is paid in full. After several companies have to close their business because they cannot pay the fine, so be it. It will send a massage; then the other businesses will be more careful, and they will stay in compliance with the law. They have to learn to conduct a lawful business, sponsor the workers, and take responsibility for them, provide permanent job for them for a long time, and not to be greedy. The illegal immigrants should not receive any support or help, which is comes from the taxpayer's money, including but not limited to any signs and informational pamphlets written in Spanish. We are already paying too much tax. Private companies who print anything in Spanish, it's cost should not be used as a business expense for tax purpose. Tax-exempt organizations and churches that are, in any way, supporting illegal immigrants are breaking this country's law by harboring individuals who are breaking the law. These organizations should lose the tax-exempt status. The illegal immigrants from the south of the border, if they are sincere about their intention to live permanently in this country, should learn to speak and read the English language as I did. If you live in this country, then you should speak the language of this country, not the other way around that several hundred million citizens of this country have to learn their language. The money is now spent on supporting the illegal immigrants; it should be spent on our citizens who are living in poverty. It is not our responsibility as taxpayers to support and provide welfare to the countries south of our border. The money from the fines should be used to subsidize the enforcement office. All illegal immigrants should be deported with no questions asked, with one exception. The immigrant farm workers—they are doing the same work year after year for the same people—should be treated as "permanent" resident during the years they lived and worked as immigrant farm workers. Their children should receive schooling and other limited benefits paid by the farmers they are working for. For the farmers, it is part of the cost of doing business; otherwise, no one will harvest their crop, and then they'll go out of business.

Business and the business leaders. Unfortunately in the recent decades, they have become very greedy with our politicians. They have become corrupt, altering the company's books to benefit themselves with outrageous compensation to the expense of the public and to the stockholders. No person in the world tidal to receive tens of million dollars and sometimes several hundred million dollars worth of compensation a year. This outrageous benefits compensations have to stop. At the best, the maximum compensation in any individual in a company—including salary, bonuses, stock options, and any other benefits—they receive should not to exceed forty times the average salary of all the company employees, excluding the top twenty executives and managers' compensation. Only one executive in the company should receive this large amount of compensation. All other executives' compensation should be less. The bonuses and stock options to all executives should be based on pre-establish performance. The salary cannot exceed 50 percent of the yearly compensation. When any executive retires or resigns, the maximum amount of compensation to receive if employed in that executive position in the last ten years should be three times the past ten years' average yearly salary. If the individual service in that position is less than ten years, then the compensation should be prorated accordingly. If the individual is fired or asked to resign, then the individual is not entitled to any lump sum retirement or departing compensation. In the long run, this policy will restore some confidence and respect to the business industry and help to some extent reduce and control prices of their products.

Any company who makes more than twenty billion dollars profits a year than the average should be put in a trust. The money is to be used to develop and manufacture alternative energy. The money is put in to the trust, and it is not tax deductible. Trust is to be managed by a certified public accountant, with scientists and with private individuals. Under no conditions should politicians and lawyers be part of the trust. The management of the trust and the board of the trust are to be accountable with how they allocate and spend the funds in the trust. The results are to be made public every year. No one can serve more than three years.

The people. I find people in this country very private, not communicative, and introverted. Living in apartment buildings for many years, beside greetings, you don't have any other conversation or contact with your neighbor. It was very similar when I moved to my house. You don't know anything about them; everyone is occupied with their work, their family. They don't have time for anything else. In addition to their busy lives, they are confronted with restrictive new regulations, laws passed by the politicians, that they have to comply with. Like what food we eat and where to eat it, the air can we breathe at home in our cars or in the street, how to rear our children, and how we can express "properly" our selves. A California legislator even wants to legislate what type of light bulb we are allowed to use in our homes. Every segment of our lives is regulated by different segment of our political society. They feel the citizens of this country are incompetent and stupid, except them. They think they are superior over us and they have to rule over us, control us, and dictate to us how to live, with some of this nuisance laws and regulations. Let the people be responsible to themselves. Educate them, not rule them. If after, people fail, then they should learn from their mistakes.

This creates an atmosphere in peoples life—with all these rules and regulations—that people don't want to be responsible for anything; their approach is that the responsibility belongs to someone else. They don't care. They don't look life in the balanced-perspective way. They feel they will be taken cared of by the taxpayers, particularly young people. They do not consider, don't care for others, don't have respect to others and to the authorities; they want everything for nothing. They are greedy. They don't want to work and learn from it; they want to be leaders instantly with high pay and without any education and without experience.

The judiciary system and our laws need drastic overhaul. The present laws overwhelmingly protects the accused; we need more protection for the victims. In many cases, it appears to me the victims have no rights at all, particularly if they have a dishonest, greedy lawyer who twists the law to fit the case even if it needs to be at the victim's expense.

Unfortunately, this nation is a down spiral, and I hope it is not too late to stop it.

Five decades ago, the nation was united. Look at it today! Then it was right after when the Second World War ended. Everyone was ready to help one another to build a better future for themselves and for others. People were caring, courteous, conscientious, and helpful to one another. Then we are all were Americans, and we called ourselves Americans. Then came the extreme politicians, the hard-liners, with their "helping" agenda. They started dividing the country by ethnicity, by people's origin. Then we were called Polish Americans, African Americans, Asian Americans, Japanese Americans, and so on. Then followed by corrupt, dishonest, and greedy politicians and the business establishment. Then the time came when no politicians, union leaders, and business executives cared for the everyday people, except to themselves, which is continuing today. This attitude reflected in their campaigns, the laws they pass, the lifestyles they live. Now, we have no individuals for the young people to look up to. We need a new political model that rejects the narrow and sectarian for a broader nation of national interest, a politics of reason rather than one that appeals to people's fears.

The stench of partisanship is so strong in Washington these days that it is difficult to remember that it was not always the case that Republicans and Democrats where at each other's throats. But in truth, there was a time when friendship and simple human compassion were far more powerful than any political differences.

I am writing this not for criticism or to complain but to make people think and reflect. We live in an honorable, decent country, but if the politicians the unions and the businessman continue behaving this way, the nation will lose its prestige, its greatness, and its leadership in the world. Therefore, the people, the citizens of this great country of ours will lose and suffer. I love this country; this is my home. I am a realist with a little optimism thrown in.

XIII

The Conclusion

I am slowly approaching the end of my life's journey on this earth. I had a wonderful, happy, successful, and meaningful life with some bumps along the way; but that is what life is all about. During my journey, I was not alone; my guardian angel sat on my shoulder and watched over me, and God directed traffic to make my life a smoother journey. My upbringing, my parents' guidance, and their example influenced my life during my travels on life's highways. I grew up with love and caring for one another, caring for others and to mankind. Sometimes, we did not have food to eat, but we had one another. The values I received from my parents are my inheritance from them.

I came a long way starting out in the Middle East, and then my journey took me through several countries in Europe before I arrived here to the "promised land." I have lived under Fascism, Communism, and now Capitalism. Sometimes, it can be referred to as Idealism. I experienced firsthand the three ways of life in the twentieth century, the behavior of mankind, and the way of life in each type of lifestyle. Very few individuals can say that and live to talk about it. As a young person, I survived the bombings in World War II, the long train ride to Germany, and the life in the camp there, begging in the street in Germany for food so that we can have another day to live. I survived the 1956 Hungarian uprising and the escape it followed. All these experiences made me stronger, more understanding, more tolerant, and a better person in life.

I was extremely lucky throughout my life's journey because I was in the right place at the right time. I know God guided me all the way because without his help and his protection, I would not be here today.

I lived my life based on what I saw and learned from my parents when I was growing up and from my adoptive parents and my Father's last words to me on December 28, 1956, the day I left home and started my journey to the unknown. Those words of his are etched into my mind forever.

Life is short!
Do well to others!
Respect others!
Be polite and considerate to others!
Be a conscientious hard worker!
Consider all opportunities because the same opportunity seldom repeats itself.

On the last days when I was visiting my parents on my second trip to Hungary in 1967—by then my Father was terminally ill with cancer—we had our last conversation as Father and son. He was talking and I was listening. He was looking back and sharing his life's experiences and his life's journey of seventy-two years with me. He was also telling me that human life on this earth is brief compared to the universe and what is happening around us. He expressed it this way, "*Time we spend on this earth is the time it takes to blink an eye.*" He also told me to "*enjoy life and appreciate every minute of it. Because some day I will wake up and discover it, it went by."*

My Father was right; my life on this earth was short. It went by so fast that the time it took is like the *"blink of an eye."* The happenings in my life moved so fast that sometimes I just wish time could stop so I could have some time to think, look back, and reflect on things.

My upbringing and my Father's words, his wisdom, guided me throughout my life in this unforgettable journey. Sometimes, being *"nice to others"* was hard to follow because in this world not everyone is nice to you.

I learned it from my parents when I was growing up to help others. Throughout my journey, I have been trying to follow their advice. Sometimes, I provided financial help as a gift or as a loan; and sometimes, I helped with deeds, doing things to others to make their life a little bit easier or enjoyable. Other times, I gave comfort just by listening and by being there. I like to help people. By helping people in any way, it can give me happiness and joy. Helping others is like having a birthday; it is a joyful occasion for me. On my birthdays or on any holidays, if I can help someone, that is the greatest present for me. I enjoy it more than if I receive a present in a box wrapped in paper tied with a ribbon. I'd rather give than receive. It is very hard for me to receive.

I read that we are tested every day in our life. Life is a school; learn its lessons of forgiveness, understanding, and compassion.

As a young refugee in this country, I had an opportunity to be a guest at a black-tie reception at the White House given by the president and Mrs. Kennedy. Furthermore, in different times in my journey, I had the pleasure to meet and to have conversation with two other presidents and two vice presidents who later became presidents.

When I arrived at Washington DC, I did not know one word of English, and I had twenty dollars in my pocket, courtesy of the Red Cross. In the later years, with hard work and great deal of luck, I ended up reaching in the old-fashioned way the American dream. If you work hard, there is no limit to what you can accomplish. This can only happen here in this country, that anyone can reach the American dream.

In my work, I accomplished things that many people who were born in this country are envious of. Some of the projects I worked on are three major metro transit systems. I was a manager on two major historical-building restoration projects, one in Washington DC and the other in New York City. Then receiving the presidential design award for each of these projects, from two different presidents of the United States.

I have one regret. In my personal life, most of the time, it was a lonely journey. I missed a family life that I had when I was growing up in my parents' home. I missed having a family of my own. I missed out on love, to have a life companion, a friend, and a partner in life, a loving wife, and to be a caring husband. I missed out to share on family happiness and sadness, to share the family life's unpredictable turns and twists, its ups and downs, and now in the end of my life's journey, to share the memories.

In the autumn years of my life, my adoptive family—Jeanette; her loving and devoted husband, her partner in life, Randy; Corey, their beautiful son, their pride and joy; and her brother, Owen, give me happiness and joy in my life now; it makes up for the losses I missed out in the past.

Because of my adoptive family's urging and their encouragement, I put my journey on paper for their generation and for the future generations to come to see that sometimes there is more to life than meets the eye and to take the opportunity when it presents itself and to take responsibilities for their action.

If fate would let me, then on May 1, 2007, on the fiftieth anniversary of my arrival at this city where the first phase of my journey to the unknown came to the end, I plan to celebrate the occasion by retracing the last miles of that long journey from Union Station to my late adoptive family's home in Chevy Chase, where I started my new beginning, my new life, in a new world.

The story of my life's journey in this book ends the year two thousand-four in the year when we are celebrating my Mother's hundredth and my Father's hundred tenth birthday. Happy birthday to both of you! Thank you for our life, thank you for your sacrifice for us, thank you for you being you. Thank you for everything!

Even if I reach the sunset of my life's journey tomorrow and my time ends here now, then the time I spent on this earth ends extremely well. It was an incredible journey. I have accomplished things in my life that I cannot accomplish anywhere else in the world.

I am very grateful and thankful to everyone who has given me guidance, direction, advice, encouragement, opportunities, and a helping hand.

A very special thanks and my deep devotion to God and to my guardian angel for watching over me and protecting me throughout my journey in this earth and letting me become the person who I am today.

Thank you!
Thank you!
Thank you!

The End

★　★　★　★　★

Thank you for taking the time
to read
this refugee's journey.

Get Published, Inc!
Thorofare, NJ 08086
09 March, 2010
BA2010068